MW00909264

FREE BLACKS IN
ANTEBELLUM TEXAS

FREE BLACKS IN ANTEBELLUM TEXAS

EDITED BY

Bruce A. Glasrud
and
Milton S. Jordan

Denton, Texas

Printed in the United States of America.

10 9 8 7 6 5 4 3 2 1

Permissions:
University of North Texas Press
1155 Union Circle #311336
Denton, TX 76203-5017

The paper used in this book meets the minimum requirements of the
American National Standard for Permanence of Paper for Printed Library
Materials, z39.48.1984. Binding materials have been chosen for durability.

Library of Congress Cataloging-in-Publication Data

Free blacks in antebellum Texas / edited by Bruce
A. Glasrud and Milton S. Jordan. -- Edition: First.

pages cm

Includes bibliographical references and index.

ISBN 978-1-57441-614-5 (cloth : alk. paper)

1. Free African Americans--Texas. 2. Texas--History--Republic,
1836-1846. 3. Texas--History--Revolution, 1835-1836. I. Glasrud,
Bruce A., editor. II. Jordan, Milton S., editor. III. Schoen, Harold,
1904-2000, author. IV. Muir, Andrew Forest, 1916-1969, author.

E185.93.T4F74 2015

305.896'073076409034--dc23

2015016624

TABLE OF CONTENTS

PREFACE

One of the surprising gaps in the published studies of African Americans in Texas history is the coverage on free blacks in the antebellum period. The primary purpose for this book, *Free Blacks in Antebellum Texas,* is to fill that gap, at least in part. In the late 1930s and early 1940s two students at the University of Texas at Austin conducted extensive research on and wrote about the pre-Civil War free black community in Texas. Although their work was never published in book form, Harold Robert Schoen and Andrew Forest Muir each managed to publish significant parts of their projects as journal articles. In the intervening years their works have remained the standard. Even though some research and publication on the topic has since been done, their work commands our attention.

The reasons for the lack of major attention to the study of free blacks are important to consider. First, of course, slavery was the cornerstone of Texas society and economy in the years before and during the Civil War, and it is on that issue that most scholars have focused their studies. Furthermore, the number of free blacks in Texas at any one time was likely less than one thousand. Such a small number of individuals perhaps also meant that few resources are available for their study. And, sometimes it is just a matter of interest, or of thinking that since Schoen and Muir have written about the topic, quite well in fact, why should someone else tackle such a task? In fact, the solid work they have done encourages us, and hopefully others, to further investigation of history from the bottom up.

We then bring to students, scholars, Texas history aficionados, and those interested in black history this compendium of the research and writings of Harold Robert Schoen and Andrew Forest Muir who cover the role and status of free blacks in the Republic of Texas and statehood Texas respectively, Schoen in six chapters, Muir in four.

We have, as editors, made one important editorial change in the manuscripts of both Schoen and Muir. We do this with permission. That is, since their studies were produced in a different time and era, and with different nomenclature than that of today, where the authors have used the word "Negro" we have changed that to read either "black" or "African American," depending on what seems to fit at that place in the story.

Like any authors or editors, we have incurred a number of debts. The editor and staff at the *Southwestern Historical Quarterly* were particularly helpful; from them we received permission to use seven articles. Of the three additional articles, two derived from the *Journal of Negro History*, and the third from its companion, the *Negro History Bulletin*. We thank the Association for the Study of African American Life and History as well as the editor and publisher of those journals for permission also. Two readers, Alwyn Barr and Randolph B. Campbell, read and commented favorably on the manuscript proposal as well as offering first-rate suggestions for additions and changes. Beginning with our initial inquiry, University of North Texas Press director and editor, Ron Chrisman, provided encouragement. Managing editor Karen DeVinney of UNT Press carefully edited our manuscript and transformed it into a book. We received help from a number of additional colleagues such as Light Cummins, Cary Wintz, Dan Utley, Cecilia Gutierrez Venable, Scott Sosebee, Deborah Liles, and Merline Pitre. Pearlene Vestal Glasrud and Anne Elton Jordan supported and polished and stuck with us. Unfortunately neither Harold Schoen nor Andrew Muir lived to see their work in a book, but the book would not have been possible without their work. Thanks Harold and Andrew.

Bruce A. Glasrud, San Antonio, Texas
Milton S. Jordan, Georgetown, Texas

FREE BLACKS IN ANTEBELLUM TEXAS

INTRODUCTION

FREE BLACKS IN ANTEBELLUM TEXAS

Bruce A. Glasrud and Milton S. Jordan

In October 1835, Emily D. West, a free black woman from Connecticut, signed an agreement to come to Texas to work a year for Colonel James Morgan; she arrived in what would become the Lone Star State in December. Four months later, as the Texas Revolution progressed, Mexican troops captured her along with other black servants and white residents. Later erroneously referred to as Emily Morgan, a slave, she became the subject of a widespread myth perpetuated mostly in the mid-to-late twentieth century claiming she was the object of affection in the song, "The Yellow Rose of Texas" and that she remained in the tent with General Santa Anna at the battle of San Jacinto, thus distracting him at this crucial military engagement. Even a hotel in San Antonio is named for her—the Emily Morgan. Emily D. West, not Morgan, lost her papers at the Battle but with help from friends this free black woman was able to secure a passport to return to the east coast in early 1837 (since free blacks were not wanted in the new Republic). The real Emily West probably was not the "Yellow Rose of Texas"; though she may have been with Santa Anna at San Jacinto, likely it was not willingly. Perhaps, as historian Trudier Harris put it, she was raped by Santa Anna.[1]

Nearly thirty years later (1864), Britton "Britt" Johnson, a slave of Moses Johnson in Young County, asked for and received his freedom in order to search for his wife and two daughters who had been captured during a grisly Comanche attack known as the Elm Creek Raid. He searched widely in West Texas and Oklahoma among various bands of Comanche and Kiowa. Finally in June 1865 Comanche chief Asa-Havey, desiring better relations with the U.S. government, paid a ransom to another chieftain, and returned Johnson's family to an Indian agent and then to Johnson. Fortunately, about the same time that Johnson's family returned, they and all other blacks in Texas were declared legally free when U.S. General Gordon Granger read the Emancipation Proclamation at Galveston on June 19, 1865, "Juneteenth." Johnson and his family moved to Parker County where he became a freighter. Unfortunately, on a freighting trip in 1871, Johnson and two black teamsters were attacked by about twenty-five Kiowa under war chief Quitan near Salt Creek; Johnson and the two teamsters fought mightily but were killed and their bodies mutilated.[2]

What the West and Johnson stories illustrate is that free blacks and slaves experienced the dangers and risks of life on the frontier in Texas. Those risks required of all of them the strength and fortitude displayed by West and Johnson.[3] Those experiences, and many others, point to the spirit and abilities of free blacks in antebellum Texas. Sometimes with support from a few whites, as well as their own efforts, they struggled, worked, and survived. Naturally many more such stories could be told if they had been recorded; fortunately, some records do exist for free blacks. (It is much more difficult to locate records about individual black slaves.)

The stories of Emily West and Britt Johnson illustrate that scattered information about free blacks can and will be located.

Although the first blacks to enter Texas were slaves, such as the intrepid Esteban with Cabeza de Vaca in 1528 and those who traveled with Coronado in 1691, free blacks also became part of Texas society during the Spanish and Mexican periods. Juan de la Concepcion arrived with Ramon in 1716, and both de Alarcon and de Aquayo included Afro-Mexicans in their expeditions. By 1792 there were at least 450 (non-military) free blacks in Tejas as well as 155 in Laredo. As Jesus F. de la Teja noted, free blacks "were well represented in Spanish Texas from the beginning."[4] That situation was true economically as well; free blacks could be found in numerous property-holding and occupational categories. One such man, Pedro Guizar, was a sculptor who designed and constructed the Rose Window and the façade of San Jose Mission.[5]

Both the Spanish and Mexican governments recognized and supported free people of color and as a result some left their homes in the United States and migrated to Texas. As Lance R. Blyth noted, by the end of the eighteenth century "Texas was a racial melting pot."[6] Soon after, Louisiana creole Felipe Elua purchased his and his wife's (Mary Otero) freedom and moved to Texas in 1807. They settled in San Antonio where they became landowners and farmers. Lewis B. and Sarah Jones immigrated to Texas from Mississippi in 1826; Samuel H. Hardin married Tamar Morgan in 1838. She came to Texas as a slave in 1832, but purchased her freedom; by 1840 she owned four town lots, 100 acres of land, and four slaves. Greenbury Logan arrived in Texas in 1831; a blacksmith, he earned enough to purchase his wife's freedom. Logan subsequently fought in and was wounded during the Texas Revolution. Afro-Mexican Pedro Ramirez worked on ranches near San Antonio prior to Texas independence. A white man, David Towns, moved from Louisiana with his slave wife; he soon freed her and their children.[7]

Some black men and women escaped from slavery in Louisiana and settled in Texas. Between 1803 and 1808, after the United States acquired

Louisiana from France, a number of black slaves left Louisiana for Spanish Texas and in particular for Nacogdoches on the eastern edge. In 1804 a party of Louisiana black runaways entered Texas in search of their freedom. The group included six males, a woman, and a young boy. However, despite the order of the governor of Texas, the commandant at Nacogdoches, under duress, gave the runaways back to the Americans. Later he was replaced for disobeying orders. In 1807, seven more runaways reached Nacogdoches; this time they were allowed to stay. Others followed including a few couples who wished to be married. The black runaways became Spanish citizens; they spoke Spanish and used Spanish names.[8]

Free blacks in Texas found varied conditions and experiences. Later a friend and interpreter for Sam Houston, William Goyens (sometimes spelled Goyans, sometimes Goings or Goines), migrated from North Carolina and settled near Nacogdoches in 1820. He married a white woman in 1832 and became a prominent blacksmith, freighter, and landowner. Harriet Newell Sands came to Texas from Michigan in 1834 with her white common-law husband. Celia Allen, emancipated with her four children in 1832 for "faithful service," nevertheless was claimed as a slave by a prominent white Texan and fought successfully in court for her freedom with the help of her attorney, William B. Travis.[9] As historian Alwyn Barr phrased it, "clearly sparse frontier population and greater acceptance by Mexicans created more freedom of movement and opportunity for free Negroes in Texas than in the United States."[10] By 1836, the year Texans achieved their independence from Mexico, the black slave population totaled 5,000 and the number of free blacks, 150. The latter number likely does not reflect Afro-Mexicans who became part of the general population. Nonetheless, the end of Mexican rule quickly resulted in severe reductions in the status and number of free blacks in the newly emerged Republic. As scholar Angela Boswell pointed out so well, "race had been a matter of social status that could change, rather than a biological determinant of social status" as emerged in the Republic of Texas.[11]

Scholars who investigated aspects of the lives of free blacks in Spanish and Mexican Texas included Jesus F. de la Teja whose general article for the *Handbook of Texas* was entitled "Blacks in Colonial Spanish Texas." Lance R. Blyth, "Fugitives from Servitude: American Deserters and Runaway Slaves in Spanish Nacogdoches, 1803–1808" and Elizabeth A. H. John, "A View from the Spanish Borderlands," also discussed issues connected to free blacks.[12] General book sections on free blacks during these and the succeeding years were David A. Williams, "Spanish Colonial Period to Statehood," in *Bricks without Straw: A Comprehensive History of African Americans in Texas* and Alwyn Barr, "Explorers and Settlers" in *Black Texans*. Ruthe Winegarten included material on free blacks—called "Free Women of Color"—in both her books titled *Black Texas Women*. Randolph B. Campbell, in *An Empire for Slavery*, considered free blacks in a few concise pages.[13] The most important and impressive study of Spanish and Mexican Texas and blacks is Douglas W. Richmond's journal article, "Africa's Initial Encounter with Texas: The Significance of Afro-Tejanos in Colonial Texas, 1528–1821." This valuable work covers what no one previously had studied carefully—that is people of African descent in Mexican and Spanish Texas. Richmond skillfully mined the original documents to create his research article. Francis Galan discusses free blacks along with slavery in his recent article, "Between Esteban and Joshua Houston: Women, Children, and Slavery in Texas Borderlands."[14]

The lives and status of free blacks in the Texas Republic and in statehood have been well explored by two Texas historians, Harold Robert Schoen and Andrew Forest Muir. Each prepared his respective topic as a student at the University of Texas. Each soon published articles in the *Southwestern Historical Quarterly*, and Muir in two other journals, the *Negro History Bulletin* and the *Journal of Negro History*. Harold Schoen's study of free blacks during the period of the Republic of Texas, originally a master's thesis followed by a Ph.D. dissertation on the topic, is a complete, well researched, and readable work. Schoen was born in New York and moved early to California. He later attended the University of Texas and became interested in free blacks in the antebellum South. Upon graduation, he taught at Amarillo College for a short time. One of his publications from before he left Texas was a coauthored study, *Monuments Erected by the State of Texas to Commemorate the Centenary of Texas Independence.* When Schoen returned to California he sought a university position at Santa Barbara State College (now the University of California, Santa Barbara). He was not hired; the provost thought him too "radical." Also, black history was not considered a serious academic area in the 1950s. For a number of years Schoen owned and operated a silver and coin store in Santa Barbara where he resided until the year 2000 when he died at the age of ninety-six.[15]

Harold Schoen divided his study into six segments and published them as separate articles, all of which we include here. He explored in his chapters the "Origin of the Free Negro in the Republic of Texas," "The Free Negro and the Texas Revolution," "Manumissions," "Legal Status," "The Law in Practice," and "The Extent of Discrimination and Its Effects."[16] Schoen's first chapter, a revision of his master's thesis, covered the legal basis for free blacks in the Texas Republic. He noted four avenues to that designation: purchase of freedom by a slave, manumission by an owner, escape from an owner, and immigration of already free blacks into the Republic. He also discussed Benjamin Lundy's unsuccessful effort to create in Texas a free black republic and in the second chapter the dutiful participation of free blacks on the Texas side during the Texas Revolution.[17]

What Dr. Schoen pointed out to us in chapter three is that even when white Texas slave owners wished to free or manumit their slaves, the Texas legislature allowed it in only two instances. Certain white citizens supported the right of particular free blacks to remain in the Republic even though the Texas legislature, acting on behalf of the Republic's white citizens, attempted to expel free blacks from Texas, as Schoen reported in his fourth chapter, "Legal Status." The primary statute governing free blacks in the Republic appeared in 1840; that law barred free black immigration and provided that resident free blacks were to leave Texas within two years or be sold into slavery. Free blacks did not want to leave their homes nor did they want to be sold into slavery. White friends and acquaintances helped those affected by the law to remain, so Schoen tells us in his instructive chapter five, entitled "The Law in Practice." The final chapter from Schoen, "The Extent of Discrimination and Its Effects," concluded that discrimination could sometimes be alleviated, and that "aid and protection based upon the whims and interests of white persons to particular Negroes in a class barred from equality was the solution offered by the Republic and bequeathed to the state."[18]

Andrew Forest Muir took a somewhat different approach to the study of free blacks during statehood; he focused on the period of Texas antebellum statehood and explored the lives of free blacks in articles covering selected Texas counties. Muir was born and raised in Texas, earned his bachelor's and master's degrees at Rice Institute (now Rice University) and his Ph.D. in history at the University of Texas. Muir ultimately became a professor of history at Rice Institute. In addition to his articles on free blacks he published three books and numerous articles. In 1957 Muir received a prestigious Guggenheim Fellowship that enabled him to edit and publish his book, *Texas in 1837: An Anonymous Contemporary Narrative.* Unfortunately for scholarship, Muir died at a young age in 1969.[19] The topics covered in Muir's four chapters included in our book are "The Free Negro in Harris County, Texas," "The Free Negro in Fort Bend County, Texas," "The Free Negro in Jefferson and Orange Counties, Texas," and "The Free Negro in Galveston County, Texas."[20] Muir's studies focused on the antebellum Texas counties with the largest free black populations. Muir was the first historian to mention the previously discussed Emily West in a scholarly article, his article titled "The Mystery of San Jacinto."[21]

Muir's study of free blacks in Harris County is the most complete analysis of Texas free blacks during statehood; he discussed state laws and how they affected and regulated free blacks. He likely exaggerated the use by free blacks of the chance to exchange freedom for slavery allowed by an 1858 law, but this is a very thoughtful and well-researched chapter. In Fort Bend County, Muir discovered that in a semi-legal manner free blacks remained in the county through a locally approved system of guardianship. He overlooked the fact that most blacks with Mexican names were indeed Afro-Mexicans. In one other well-done article, Muir discovered that in Jefferson and Orange Counties free blacks not only purchased and owned land, they held slaves. These counties also housed the influential and successful Ashworth family. That family managed to remain in the state due to a law, the Ashworth Act, which exempted the family and a few other free blacks from restrictive provisions that would have forced them to leave the state. In Galveston County at least thirty free blacks resided, but due to the harshness of Texas laws they remained quiet about their free status. A few free blacks, in order to remain in the state and city, indentured themselves. In his research, Muir acknowledged the difficulty of locating sources related to free blacks, but as he iterated, "the historian . . . must deal with what he can find, and his work, no matter how irksome and exacting, is its own reward."[22] Andrew Forest Muir and Harold Robert Schoen deserve our thanks and any rewards they received.

Although their studies remain the most thorough and complete investigations, Schoen and Muir are not the only authors who explored the free black experience in Texas. To this date, the one other author who closely examined Texas free blacks was Prairie View A&M University historian, George Ruble Woolfolk. Woolfolk, who became the first African American to be inducted as a Fellow of the Texas State Historical Association, compiled an impressive list of publications on blacks in the Lone Star State. Among his publications on free blacks was a book-length work, *The Free Negro in Texas, 1800–1860: A Study in Cultural Compromise* as well as two articles on the subject, "The Free Negro and Texas, 1836–1860" and "Turner's Safety Valve and Free Negro Migration." Among Woolfolk's notable contentions was that free blacks in Texas lived and worked in situations that were not "miserable," as a few scholars, including Muir, argued.[23] The editors of this book concur with Woolfolk; free blacks in

Texas developed their own survival skills and used networks of family and friends to offset legal and personal challenges or limitations.

Recently, John Garrison Marks published a convincing article in the *Southwestern Historical Quarterly*, "Community Bonds in the Bayou City: Free Blacks and Local Reputation in Early Houston." Marks takes Woolfolk's conclusions a step further although he unfortunately did not mention that venerable scholar. Marks noted that numerous records "reveal the significant interactions between free blacks and whites in Houston and the liberties Houston's free blacks secured for themselves." Marks discovered that free blacks successfully maintained untrammeled lives because on the local level they created positive reputations within black and white communities that enabled them to exist beyond the vagaries of white behavior. Reputations were significant; and Marks concluded that free blacks "certainly did not maintain desperate lives on the margin of society, subject to the capricious whims of white patrons, nor could they ever afford to do so."[24] Marks's thoughtful study illustrates that interest in free blacks in the Lone Star State continues into this century. Though disagreeing with a few of the ideas of Schoen and Muir, his study expands upon and is in reality complementary to their publications.

Other general studies of Texas' free blacks include an article by Douglas Hales, "Free Blacks," for the *Handbook of Texas* and two master's theses. Virginia C. Moorer produced "The Free Negro in Texas, 1845-1860," at Lamar State College of Technology (now Lamar University) in 1969. Alexander T. M. Pratt completed his thesis at Prairie View Agricultural and Mechanical College (now Prairie View A&M University), "Free Negroes in Texas to 1860," in 1963.[25] For insight into law and free blacks, a good read is John E. Fisher, "The Legal Status of Free Blacks in Texas, 1836-1861."[26] When it comes to the legal status and the state laws affecting slaves and free blacks, a very good book is available, edited by Randolph B. "Mike" Campbell, and compiled by William S. Pugsley and Marilyn P. Duncan, *The Laws of Slavery in Texas*. Chock full of information, this book includes two articles by Lester G. Bugbee, Campbell's "The Law of Slavery in Texas," A. E. Keir Nash, "The Texas Supreme Court and Trial Rights of Blacks, 1845–1860," Mark Davidson's "One Woman's Fight for Freedom: *Gess vs. Lubbock*," and one more by Campbell, "The End of Slavery in Texas: A Research Note." The book also includes Harold Schoen's work about discrimination and its effect on free blacks during the years of the Republic, which is also included here. The Campbell, Pugsley, and Duncan book is too often overlooked, or at least not mentioned.[27] But it is a first-rate compendium that also includes primary documents and statutes.

Some writers and researchers focused their efforts on individual free blacks in Texas. Particularly well-covered, in addition to the previously mentioned Emily West and Britt Johnson, are William Goyens and members of the large, successful, and prominent Ashworth family. Studies on Goyens include Linda Devereaux, "William Goyens: Black Leader in Early Texas"; Daniel James Kubiak, *Monument to a Black Man (William Goyens)*; Diane Elizabeth Prince's master's thesis in 1963, "William Goyens, Free Negro on the Texas Frontier"; and her article, "William Goyens, Free Black on the Texas Frontier." On Goyens see also Victor H. Treat's insightful chapter, "William Goyens: Free Negro Entrepreneur," in *Black Leaders: Texans for Their Times*, the book edited by Alwyn Barr and Robert A. Calvert.[28] Works that depict aspects of the famous and large Ashworth family of free blacks are varied but few in number. Start with the hard to locate, privately printed book by Vanda V. Ashworth, entitled *The Ashworth Family*. Patricia Clegg discusses the Ashworth family life and emergence during the Republic of Texas in her article, "The Free Negro in the Republic of Texas: The Experiences of the Ashworth Family of Southeast Texas and Others." In a short article for *The Handbook of Texas*, Nolan Thompson discussed "William Ashworth," the prominent early settler and leader of the family. Thompson also, for *The Handbook of Texas*, presents us with information on the remarkable Ashworth Act, a law enacted by the Texas legislature that allowed the Ashworths and a few other free blacks to remain in Texas despite state laws to the contrary.[29]

Although the vast majority of whites in Texas supported slavery, not all white Texans followed suit. Anti-slavery in Texas is covered quite thoroughly by Zoie Odom Newsome in her master's thesis "Antislavery Sentiment in Texas, 1821–1861" at Texas Tech University. One other student included anti-slavery sentiment in his thesis; see Eugene Barriffe, Jr., "Some Aspects of Slavery and Anti-Slavery Movements in Texas, 1730–1860."[30] A strong anti-slavery feeling emerged in the German community where perhaps one-half of the German settlers in Texas opposed slavery. Adolf Douai, editor of the German-language San Antonio *Zeitung*, regularly spoke against slavery and published his anti-slavery articles in both German and English. Northern abolitionist Benjamin Lundy visited Texas three times in the early 1830s and determined that Texas would be the ideal place for a free black community. Few supporters emerged, and the advent of the Texas Revolution ended his plans. Methodist minister Anthony Bewley, an ardent critic of slavery, was lynched by slavery proponents in September 1860 for his views.[31]

During the early 1840s, one other option for freedom was introduced by Stephen Pearl Andrews. Born in Massachusetts, Andrews worked as an attorney in Louisiana before coming to Texas in 1839. His option included having the British anti-slavery society and government provide money to pay Texas slave owners for their slaves, and then create Texas as a nation or state without slavery. But, too many individuals, in Texas as well as the southern United States, rejected any suggestion of making Texas an anti-slavery haven. Following a trip to England, where he was well received, Andrews returned to Texas in fall 1843 and a mob drove him out.[32]

One additional option for freedom for black slaves in Texas was escape; generally that meant running away from their homes, whether on a plantation, small farm, or urban area, and crossing the Rio Grande to Mexico. Slave owners zealously guarded against such permanent loss but some former slaves did manage to escape to freedom. Authors who researched and discussed this effort included Marjorie Brown Hawkins, whose master's thesis concerned "Runaway Slaves in Texas"; also with the same title was a short popular piece, J. Marvin Hunter's "Runaway Slaves in Texas."[33] Ronnie C. Tyler's interest in the topic was long-standing; his Texas Christian University master's thesis covered "Slave Owners and Runaway Slaves in Texas." He also focused on the next step with his first-rate article, "Fugitive Slaves in Mexico." The latter topic also fascinated Rosalie Schwartz; she wrote a master's thesis at San Diego State University on "Runaway Negroes: Mexico as an Alternative for United States Blacks, 1825-1860," and followed that up with a book, *Across the Rio to Freedom: United States Negroes in Mexico.*[34] Ultimately about 5,000 escaped Texas slaves resided in Mexico. That fact led to an effort on the part of slave owners, using the Texas Rangers, to attempt to recapture the former slaves by force and return them to Texas. The venture was not successful. It has been the subject of at least three studies: Ronnie C. Tyler, "The Callahan Expedition of 1855: Indians or Negroes?" Ernest C. Shearer, "The Callahan Expedition, 1855," and Michael L. Collins, "The Callahan Expedition."[35]

Free blacks in Texas of necessity acted carefully, since their lives were controlled by white law and white actions. Having a prominent white as a friend and sponsor came to be important, and laws and the courts upheld their rights, but only a few hundred free blacks were able to remain legally in the Lone Star State. Also, as historian Earl W. Fornell reminded us, free blacks were at the mercy of slave catchers. Individual free blacks did get captured and sold into slavery, particularly those who docked on board ship at Galveston.[36] The travails of Rachel Hamilton further reflect the precarious position of free blacks. Hamilton was brought by her owner, Andrew Jackson Hamilton, to Travis County, Texas, in 1847. She subsequently married Nathaniel Grumbles, also a slave in Travis County. Hamilton was freed by her owner, an anti-secessionist and later reconstruction governor of Texas. Although she was able to secure work as a hired servant in Austin, Texas law provided that newly freed blacks could not remain in the state without permission of the legislature. She was arrested and rather than leave her family in the state she chose to select a white guardian (essentially owner) in order to remain in Texas;

she became the caretaker of the daughter of her new "guardian," Aaron Burleson.[37] Rachel Hamilton's story tells us much about the resilient status of black Texas women whose lives were controlled either by white men or by white law, sometimes both.

Despite the fact that free blacks in Texas were greatly outnumbered by the white population as well as by black slaves, they lived their own lives amid these hazards. There is no doubt that they constituted an unwelcome anomaly in Texas. As Randolph Campbell phrased it, free blacks "posed in the eyes of the Texas legislature a threat to slavery and to the belief that Negroes were fit only to be slaves."[38] As a result harsh constitutional and other legal restrictions confronted the non-slave black population. But survive they did, and some quite well, whether as leaders of the community or as land owners or as wage earners. George Woolfolk stated this situation positively: free blacks "in Texas found in the crucial clash of the core values an opportunity for progress and dignity seldom afforded in the western hemisphere."[39] Interestingly, Texas historians have begun to pay attention to this numerically small group, and an increasing number of books and articles have been published. On the other hand, and the major reason for this book, since the late 1930s and early 1940s no author has written as fully as Harold Schoen and Andrew Forest Muir about the history of free blacks in antebellum Texas society. These two described the lives of free blacks in Republic and Early Statehood Texas; for that we can thank them. This book, *Free Blacks in Antebellum Texas*, not only represents the first time either author's works have been published as a monograph, but it places both sets of articles complementary to one another in one complete story.

NOTES

1. Trudier Harris, "The Yellow Rose of Texas: A Different Cultural View," in *Juneteenth Texas: Essays in African-American Folklore*, edited by Francis E. Abernethy, Patrick B. Mullen, and Alan B. Govenar (Denton: University of North Texas Press, 1996), 315–332. Additional realistic accounts include Francis E. Abernethy, "The Elusive Emily D. West, Folksong's Fabled 'Yellow Rose of Texas'," in *A Texas Folklore Odyssey*, edited by Francis E. Abernethy (Denton: University of North Texas Press, 2001), 319-329; Margaret Swett Henson, "West, Emily D," *The Handbook of Texas Online.* http://www.tshaonline.org/handbook/online; Margaret S. Henson, "She's the Real Thing," *Texas Highways* 33 (April 1986): 60-61; James Lutzweiler, "Emily D. West and the Yellow Prose of Texas: A Primer on Some Primary Documents and Their Doctoring," in *A Texas Folklore Odyssey*, edited by Francis E. Abernethy (Denton: University of North Texas Press, 2001), 294–316. For a lucid, convincing account of the life and historiography surrounding Emily D. West, read Jeffrey D. Dunn, "'To the *Devil* with your Glorious History!' Women and the Battle of San Jacinto," in *Women and the Texas Revolution*, edited by Mary L. Scheer (Denton: University of North Texas Press, 2014), 179–208, especially pages 191–200, 206–208.

2. Michael E. McClellan, "Britton Johnson," *The Handbook of Texas Online* (http://www.tshaonline.org/handbook/online); Bruce A. Glasrud and Paul H. Carlson, "Black Americans in West Texas," in *Slavery to Integration: Black Americans in West Texas* (Abilene, TX: State House Press, 2007), 13–16; Christy Claridy, "Britton Johnson," *Texas Ranger Dispatch Magazine* 33 (2011): 4–7. For a fictionalized biography, see Margaret Carol Moring, "Brave Nigger Brit" (Master's thesis, University of Texas at Austin, 1972).

3. For a broader perspective see Sue Clark Wortham, "The Role of the Negro on the Texas Frontier, 1821–1836" (Master's thesis, Southwest Texas State University, 1970).

4. Jesus de la Teja, "Blacks in Colonial Spanish Texas," *The Handbook of Texas Online* (http://www.tshaonline.org/handbook/online); Douglas W. Richmond, "Africa's Initial Encounter with Texas: The Significance of Afro-Tejanos in Colonial Texas, 1528–1821," *Bulletin of Latin American Research* 26.2 (2007): 200–221.

5. de la Teja, "Blacks in Colonial Spanish Texas."

6. Lance R. Blyth, "Fugitives from Servitude: American Deserters and Runaway Slaves in Spanish Nacogdoches, 1803-1808," *East Texas Historical Journal* 38.2 (2000): 3–14, quote on 3.

7. Ruthe Winegarten, "Free Women of Color," in *Black Texas Women: 150 Years of Trial and Triumph* (Austin: University of Texas Press, 1995), 1–13; Alwyn Barr, "Explorers and Settlers," in *Black Texans: A History of African Americans in Texas, 1528–1995*, 2nd ed. (Norman: University of Oklahoma Press, 1996), 1–12; William Loren Katz, "William Goings and Greenbury Logan—Patriots of the Lone Star Republic," in *Black People Who Made the Old West* (Trenton, NJ: Africa World Press, 1992), 45–48.

8. Blythe, "Fugitives from Servitude," 3–14; Elizabeth A. H. John, "A View from the Spanish Borderlands," *Proceedings of the American Antiquarian Society* 101 (1991): 86–87.

9. Victor H. Treat, "William Goyens: Free Negro Entrepreneur," in *Black Leaders: Texans for Their Times*, edited by Alwyn Barr and Robert A. Calvert (Austin: Texas State Historical Association, 1981), 19–47; Linda Devereaux, "William Goyens: Black Leader in Early Texas," *East Texas Historical Journal* 45.1 (2007): 52–57; Winegarten, "Free Women of Color," 1–13.

10. Barr, "Explorers and Settlers," 1–12, quote on 5.

11. Randolph B. Campbell, *An Empire for Slavery: The Peculiar Institution in Texas, 1821–1865* (Baton Rouge: Louisiana State University Press, 1989), 54–55; Angela Boswell, "Traveling the Wrong Way Down Freedom's Trail: Black Women and the Texas Revolution," in *Women and the Texas Revolution*, edited by Mary L. Scheer (Denton: University of North Texas Press, 2014), 99.

12. de la Teja, "Blacks in Colonial Spanish Texas"; Blyth, "Fugitives from Servitude: American Deserters and Runaway Slaves in Spanish Nacogdoches, 1803–1808"; John, "A View from the Spanish Borderlands."

13. David A. Williams, "Spanish Colonial Period to Statehood," in *Bricks Without Straw: A Comprehensive History of African Americans in Texas* (Austin, TX: Eakin Press, 1997), 1–35; Barr, "Explorers and Settlers," 1–12; Winegarten, "Free Women of Color," *Black Texas Women: 150 Years of Trial and Triumph*, 1–13; Ruthe Winegarten, "Free Women of Color," *Black Texas Women: A Sourcebook* (Austin: University of Texas Press, 1996), 1–13; Campbell, *An Empire for Slavery*, 54–55, 110–114.

14. Richmond, "Africa's Initial Encounter with Texas: The Significance of Afro-Tejanos in Colonial Texas," 200–221; Francis X. Galan, "Between Esteban and Joshua Houston: Women, Children, and Slavery in Texas Borderlands," *Journal of South Texas* 27.2 (Fall 2014): 22–36.

15. Harold R. Schoen, Walter Woodul, L. W. Kemp, and Pat Neff, *Monuments Erected by the State of Texas to Commemorate the Centenary of Texas Independence* (Austin, TX: The Steck Company, 1939). On Schoen's life, see Campbell, ed., *The Laws of Slavery*, 117.

16. Harold Schoen, "The Free Negro in the Republic of Texas: Origin of the Free Negro in the Republic of Texas," *Southwestern Historical Quarterly* 39 (April 1936): 292–308; Harold Schoen, "The Free Negro in the Republic of Texas: The Free Negro and the Texas Revolution," *Southwestern Historical Quarterly* 40 (July 1937): 26–34; Harold Schoen, "The Free Negro in the Republic of Texas: Manumissions," *Southwestern Historical Quarterly* 40 (October 1936): 85–113; Harold Schoen, "The Free Negro in the Republic of Texas: Legal Status," *Southwestern Historical Quarterly* 40 (January 1937): 169–199; Harold Schoen, "The Free Negro in the Republic of Texas: The Law in Practice," *Southwestern Historical Quarterly* 40 (April 1937): 267–289; Harold Schoen, "The Free Negro in the Republic of Texas: The Extent of Discrimination and Its Effects," *Southwestern Historical Quarterly* 41 (July 1937): 83–108.

17. Schoen, "The Free Negro in the Republic of Texas: Origin of the Free Negro in the Republic of Texas," 292–308; Schoen, "The Free Negro in the Republic of Texas: The Free Negro and the Texas Revolution," 26–34.

18. Schoen, "The Free Negro in the Republic of Texas: Manumissions," 85–113; Schoen, "The Free Negro in the Republic of Texas: Legal Status," 169–199; Schoen, "The Free Negro in the Republic of Texas: The Law in Practice," 267–289; Schoen, "The Free Negro in the Republic of Texas: The Extent of Discrimination and Its Effects," 83–108, quote on p. 108.

19. "Andrew Forest Muir," *The Handbook of Texas Online* (http://www.tshaonline.org/handbook/online/articles); Andrew Forest Muir, *William Marsh Rice and His Institute*, edited by Sylvia Stallings Morris (Houston: William Marsh Rice University, 1972); Andrew Forest Muir, *Thomas Jefferson Ewing: Ward Politician* (Houston: privately published, 1952); Andrew Forest Muir, ed., *Texas in 1837: An Anonymous Contemporary Narrative* (Austin: University of Texas Press, 1958). In a recent issue of *The Wright Collection*, Hugh and Chris Wright referred to Muir's *Texas in 1837* as "one of the best edited and the best annotated Texas books."

20. Andrew Forest Muir, "The Free Negro in Fort Bend County, Texas," *Journal of Negro History* 33.1 (January 1948): 79–86; Andrew Forest Muir, "The Free Negro in Galveston County, Texas," *Negro History Bulletin* 22 (1958): 68–70; Andrew Forest Muir, "The Free Negro in Harris County, Texas," *Southwestern Historical Quarterly* 46.3 (1943): 214–238; Andrew Forest Muir, "The Free Negro in Jefferson and Orange Counties, Texas," *Journal of Negro History* 33 (1950): 183–206.

21. Andrew Forest Muir, "The Mystery of San Jacinto," *Southwest Review* 36 (Spring 1951): 77–84.

22. Muir, "The Free Negro in Harris County, Texas," 214–238; Muir, "The Free Negro in Fort Bend County, Texas," 79–86; Muir, "The Free Negro in Jefferson and Orange Counties, Texas," 183–206; Muir, "The Free Negro in Galveston County, Texas," 68–70, quote on p. 70.

23. George Ruble Woolfolk, *The Free Negro in Texas, 1800–1860: A Study in Cultural Compromise* (Ann Arbor, MI: University Microfilms International, 1976); George Ruble Woolfolk, "The Free Negro and Texas, 1836–1860," *Journal of Mexican-American History* 3 (1973): 49–75; George Ruble Woolfolk, "Turner's Safety Valve and Free Negro Migration," *Pacific Northwest Quarterly* 56 (July 1965): 125–130. See also his articles, "Cotton Capitalism and Slave Labor in Texas," *Southwestern Social Science Quarterly* 37 (1956): 43–52; "Sources of the History of the Negro in Texas, With Special Reference to Their Implications for Research in Slavery," *Journal of Negro History* 42 (1957): 38–47; as well as his remarkable institutional study, *Prairie View: A Study in Public Conscience, 1878–1946* (New York: Pageant Press, 1962). For a biographical sketch of Woolfolk see Randolph B. Campbell, "George Ruble Woolfolk," *Handbook of Texas Online* (www.tshaonline.org/handbook/articles). For Muir's statement, see "The Free Negro in Harris County," 214.

24. John Garrison Marks, "Community Bonds in the Bayou City: Free Blacks and Local Reputation in Early Houston," *Southwestern Historical Quarterly* 117.3 (January 2014): 267–282, quotes on 269, 282.

25. Douglas Hales, "Free Blacks," *The Handbook of Texas Online.* http://www.tshaonline.org/handbook/online); Virginia C. Moorer, "The Free Negro in Texas, 1845-1860" (Master's thesis, Lamar State College of Technology, 1969); Alexander T. M. Pratt, "Free Negroes in Texas to 1860" (Master's thesis, Prairie View Agricultural and Mechanical College, 1963).

26. John E. Fisher, "The Legal Status of Free Blacks in Texas, 1836–1861," *Texas Southern Law Review* (1973): 342–362.

27. Randolph B. Campbell, ed., *The Laws of Slavery in Texas*, compiled by William S. Pugsley and Marilyn P. Duncan (Austin: University of Texas Press, 2010).

28. Daniel James Kubiak, *Monument to a Black Man (William Goyens)* (San Antonio: Naylor, 1972); Diane Elizabeth Prince, "William Goyens, Free Negro on the Texas Frontier" (Master's thesis, Stephen F. Austin State University, 1963); Diane Elizabeth Prince, "William Goyens, Free Black on the

Texas Frontier," in *The Bicentennial Commemorative History of Nacogdoches* (Nacogdoches, TX: Nacogdoches Jaycees, 1976), 73–76; Victor H. Treat, "William Goyens: Free Negro Entrepreneur," in *Black Leaders: Texans for Their Times*, edited by Alwyn Barr and Robert A. Calvert (Austin: Texas State Historical Association, 1981), 19–47; Linda Devereaux, "William Goyens: Black Leader in Early Texas," *East Texas Historical Journal* 45.1 (2007): 52–57.

29. Vanda V. Ashworth, *The Ashworth Family* (Lufkin, TX: privately printed, 1987); Patricia Clegg, "The Free Negro in the Republic of Texas: The Experiences of the Ashworth Family of Southeast Texas and Others," *Texas Gulf Historical and Biographic Record* 41 (2005): 35–54; Nolan Thompson, "William Ashworth," *The Handbook of Texas Online* (http://www.tshaonline.org/handbook/online); Nolan Thompson, "Ashworth Act," *The Handbook of Texas Online* (http://www.tshaonline.org/handbook/online).

30. Zoie Odom Newsome, "Antislavery Sentiment in Texas, 1821–1861" (Master's thesis, Texas Tech University, 1963); Eugene Barriffe, Jr., "Some Aspects of Slavery and Anti-Slavery Movements in Texas, 1730–1860" (Master's thesis, University of Southwestern Louisiana, 1968).

31. Jonathan Randel, "San Antonio Zeitung," *Handbook of Texas Online* (http://www.tshaonline.org/handbook/online/articles); Rudolph L. Biesele, "The Texas State Convention in 1854," *Southwestern Historical Quarterly* 33 (April 1930): 247–61; Merton L. Dillon, "Benjamin Lundy in Texas," *Southwestern Historical Quarterly* 63 (July 1959): 46–62; Donald E. Reynolds, "Reluctant Martyr: Anthony Bewley and the Texas Slave Insurrection Panic of 1860," *Southwestern Historical Quarterly* 96 (1993): 344–361; Donald E. Reynolds, "Anthony Bewley," *Handbook of Texas Online* (http://www.tshaonline.org/handbook/online/articles).

32. Charles Shively, "An Option for Freedom in Texas, 1840–1844," *Journal of Negro History* 50 (1965): 77–96.

33. Marjorie Brown Hawkins, "Runaway Slaves in Texas" (Master's thesis, Prairie View Agricultural and Mechanical College, 1952); J. Marvin Hunter, "Runaway Slaves in Texas," *Frontier Times* 26 (1948): 40–43.

34. Ronnie C. Tyler, "Slave Owners and Runaway Slaves in Texas" (Master's thesis, Texas Christian University, 1966); Ronnie C. Tyler, "Fugitive Slaves in Mexico," *Journal of Negro History* 57 (1972): 1–12; Rosalie Schwartz, "Runaway Negroes: Mexico as an Alternative for United States Blacks, 1825–1860" (Master's thesis, San Diego State University, 1974); Rosalie Schwartz, *Across the Rio to Freedom: United States Negroes in Mexico* (El Paso: Texas Western Press, 1975).

35. Ronnie C. Tyler, "The Callahan Expedition of 1855: Indians or Negroes?" *Southwestern Historical Quarterly* 70 (1967): 574–585; Ernest C. Shearer, "The Callahan Expedition, 1855," *Southwestern Historical Quarterly* 54 (October 1951): 430–451; Michael L. Collins, "The Callahan Expedition," *Texas Devils: Rangers and Regulars on the Lower Rio Grande, 1846–1861* (Norman: University of Oklahoma Press, 2008), 79–88, 271–72.

36. Earl W. Fornell, "The Abduction of Free Negroes and Slaves in Texas," *Southwestern Historical Quarterly* 60 (1957): 369–380.

37. Randolph B. Campbell, "Rachel Hamilton Hornsby," *Handbook of Texas Online* (http://www.tshaonline.org/handbook); Ruthe Winegarten, "Rachel Grumbles Enslaves Herself," in *Black Texas Women: A Sourcebook* (Austin: University of Texas Press, 1996), 12–13; James Grumbles, "Slave Narratives of Travis County," Austin History Center, Austin Public Library.

38. Campbell, *An Empire for Slavery*, 113.

39. Woolfolk, *The Free Negro in Texas*, 36.

CHAPTERS ONE THROUGH SIX

THE REPUBLIC OF TEXAS

1

ORIGIN OF FREE BLACKS IN THE REPUBLIC OF TEXAS

Harold R. Schoen

The term "free black" as applied in this paper is exclusively a legal term referring to those inhabitants of the Republic of Texas classified as "free persons of color" and subject to the special regulations enacted to govern them. There were never any strictly defined categories based upon ethnological considerations by which blacks were segregated from whites. Among the native Mexican population, there probably were some persons with large percentages of African blood, but none of these were technically "free blacks."

In a census of San Antonio recorded by Morfi in 1777, including the presidio, villa and the five missions, in a total population of 2060 persons, 151 are classified as "de color quebrado" [literally "of broken color," meaning colored].[1] Again, Morfi refers to the Spanish colonists of Texas as "una quadrilla de trapientos de todos colores," literally "a ragged crew of all colors."[2]

An official Spanish census of December 31, 1792, records 247 male mulattoes, 167 female mulattoes, 15 male blacks and 19 female blacks in a total population for Texas of 1617 males and 1375 females. An itemization of 308 household heads in San Fernando records 30 families in which both husband and wife were blacks, 33 families in which either husband or wife were blacks, and 35 widows and bachelors of black blood.[3] Of 69 blacks giving their nativity, 24 claimed San Fernando or vicinity, 10 claimed Adaes on the Louisiana border, 8 claimed Saltillo, one each claimed Guatemala, Guinea and the Canary Islands, and the remaining 24 claimed Mexican cities, mostly in bordering provinces.[4]

The complete disappearance of this large number of Texan Africans and their descendants, in the short period of forty-three years from 1792 to the declaration of Texan independence, probably cannot be explained through absorption, death or migration. Legally, however, these *de facto* free persons of color and their descendants disappeared with the organization of the Republic.

The fact that these persons were free Mexican citizens, owned Spanish names and spoke the Spanish language, doubtless was a consideration in their classification as other than free blacks. The widespread admixture of Spanish, Indian and African blood made accurate classification impossible and the presumption that these hybrids considered themselves Mexicans and were accepted by them as their relatives and countrymen, may account for the fact that nowhere do we find blacks of Spanish name and Mexican nativity complying or forced to comply by the laws of the Republic with the special regulations governing free persons of color.

Another large group of persons with black blood, virtually free though legally enslaved, demands some notice. The contact of black and white races everywhere has led to some intermixture, and Texas was no exception. The paucity of women in early Anglo-American Texas was an additional factor in leading white men to take black slaves as concubines and wives. The children of these unions, according to the common law, took their status from the mother and legally were slaves. Many of these children were actually free, and some fathers made attempts to have their progeny legally declared free persons of color.[5]

Benjamin Lundy, the abolitionist, on his second trip through Texas made note of "two brothers, named Alley . . . industrious immigrants from the State of Missouri. They have never married. They purchased, however, a handsome black girl, who has several fine-looking partly coloured children—specimens of the custom of some countries."[6]

An incident in Frank Brown's "Annals of Travis County" affords inferential evidence of both concubinal and marital arrangements between the races. A plantation owner offered any black on his farm for the recovery of his favorite horse which had been stolen by Indians. A young man, evidently white, devoted to the planter's youngest daughter, Dolly, inquired whether she was included in the offer, to which her father replied affirmatively. In romantic fashion, the young man recovered the horse, to the great delight of the owner, and although it is not recorded that the youth received his reward, "Dolly was married shortly afterward, and it is reasonable to suppose that he got her."[7]

Another marriage, more definite in character, was that of John F. Webber, the founder of Webberville. Webber had a child by a neighbor's slave. "Too conscientious to abandon his yellow offspring and its sable mother to a life of slavery, he purchased them from their owner, who, cognizant of the situation, took advantage of it to drive a sharp bargain." Webber built himself a fort in the unsettled prairie, "took his family home and acknowledged them before the world." Noah Smithwick, a friend and old-time partner of Webber, adds, "There were others I wot of that were not so brave."[8] Webber continued to live in Texas throughout the whole period of the Republic, but because of increasing social pressure, was finally forced to sell out and move to Mexico in 1851.[9] Mrs. Webber and her children probably retained their legal status as slaves, for at no time did they comply with the laws governing free persons of color.

In addition to the Texan-born slave children of white men, there were those of immigrants. William Primm, a white man, emigrated to Texas in 1835 from Louisiana and settled on an estate in Fayette County. He brought with him a part of his family, including five mulatto children, whom he owned as his natural offspring, but who were legally slaves.[10]

All the blacks in the cases thus far examined, in the broadest sense, might be considered as free blacks. Legally, however, the first group were Mexicans, the second, slaves.

The origin of legally free blacks, with which the body of this paper is concerned, may be attributed to many sources but falls conveniently into four divisions: (1) purchase of freedom by the slave; (2) manumission by the master; (3) escape of the slave from the master; (4) immigration of the black already free.

A clear case of purchase was that of Tomas Morgan, a black woman, who came to Texas as a slave in 1832 and "purchased her freedom with the proceeds of her own labor sometime during the year 1834."[11]

A note in Benjamin Lundy's diary indicates an indirect purchase of freedom by a black slave, who, for the price of his freedom, either served his master's term in a debtor's prison, or perhaps paid his debts.

> [August 24, 1833]. . . . There lives here in Bexar, a free black man, who speaks English. He came as a slave first from North Carolina to Georgia, and then from Georgia to Nacogdoches, in Texas. There his master died, and the heirs sold him to another person. This new master, being apprehended for debt, offered the slave his freedom if he would take him out of prison. The slave complied, but the master dying soon after, an attempt was made to re-enslave the man, which however proved unsuccessful. He now works as a blacksmith in this place. I have been [in] converse with him, he having seen me at Nacogdoches last summer, and knowing me again when he met me here. . . . Though he is jet-black, he says the Mexicans pay him the same respect as to other laboring people, there being no difference made here on account of color. . . .[12]

The second group of free blacks had its origin in manumission. A common cause for manumission was the blood or concubinal tie existing between owner and slave. Such manumissions, granted to relatives, were common throughout the South during the whole period of slavery. A grant of this kind in early Texas was recorded by Lundy on July 18, 1834.

> I became acquainted with a white man, named David Town, who originally resided in Georgia. Thence he removed to Louisiana, taking with him a black female slave, who was in fact his wife. She was a very capable woman, and had several likely children. Eight years ago, Town removed to Nacogdoches, where he emancipated his wife and children, who, up to that period, had been slaves, in the eye of the law. They all live together in harmony, are quite industrious, and make a very respectable appearance. The daughters are as fine looking as can be seen almost anywhere, and are free, in their whole demeanor, from the degrading restraint, so observable among coloured people in our country. The Mexican ladies of Nacogdoches are very sociable with them.[13]

The scarcity of labor in early Texas served to minimize manumission for meritorious services, but at least one such case is known. William McFarland brought his slave Fannie McFarland to Texas in 1827, and granted her freedom eight years later. Her four children, however, were held as slaves. Fannie lived at San Felipe and lost all her possessions there during the revolution. In 1837, she moved to Houston and by "industry, prudence and economy" gathered together a little property.[14]

A third group of free blacks had its origin in the successful runaway slave. The fact that Texas was under Mexican rule, in which the fugitive slave law was inoperative, probably induced many runaway slaves to head for Texas. There, on account of the scarcity of labor, they were welcomed without searching questions, and even protected against recapture by the friendly Mexican officials and the populace.

Runaway slaves were often successful in resisting capture and they doubtlessly received the aid of their employees in their efforts. On August 2, 1834, Lundy recorded the following:

> I reached the Trinity river, and having crossed it, I put up at the
> house of Nathaniel Robbins, who has on his farm a number of
> coloured people that are claimed as slaves, by a person in Louisiana,
> named Mays. Mays is at present in Nacogdoches, where he made
> up a party of nine men, a few days since, and came here to take the
> coloured people, *vi et armis.* Instead of succeeding, however, he
> and his whole band were taken prisoners. The . . . slave-shooter,
> Williams, was among the number; and it is said that he was the
> most easily captured of all.[15]

Some slaves who escaped, enlisted in the Mexican army and so insured
their continued liberty. Colonel Bradburn, a Mexican officer, harbored
two runaway slaves from Louisiana, enlisted them in his detachment and
refused to surrender them on the owner's demand.[16]

One case of an Alabama slave who fled to Texas before the declaration
of independence indicates that others were not uncommon. W. E. Primrn,
a slave owner of Alabama, in order to regain control of his man, Cuggoe,
prayed the Texas legislature for the

> passage of A law . . . that all persons of color that was slaves
> Before they came to Texas Eather By absconding or Runing away
> from the legal owner and came to Texas Before the Declaration of
> Independence of Texas shall Be Delivered up to the Legal owner
> with Damage and Satisfactturoy proof that such negro was Realy
> A Slave Before he came to Texas and that his Being in Texas
> before the Independence shall not Be so construd as to give him
> his freedom.[17]

Not all the successful runaway slaves came from the United States. Some
slaves owned by American colonists in Texas were equally successful in
making good their freedom by running away to Mexicans who harbored
and protected them. One case is revealed by Lundy when he stopped at
the Gonzales home of Francis Berry, "who was originally from Virginia,
and came last from Missouri." "He has no slaves," Lundy wrote, "all he

formerly had having run away, as he [Berry] states, 'to the Spaniards.'" Berry was philosophical enough to think himself "best off without them."[18]

The fourth and chief origin of the free black person in the Republic of Texas, however, was emigration from the United States. Essentially, this migration was a part of the general westward movement of population. It is difficult to determine with any accuracy, the time at which this immigration began but it is reasonable to suppose that the purchase of Louisiana gave it sharp acceleration. An entry in Lundy's diary, written in San Antonio on September 29, 1833, would place the date as early as 1807.

> I walked out this forenoon with Matthew Thomas, to see the cane patch, ground, &c., of his father-in-law, Felipe Elua, a black Louisiana creole, who was formerly a slave, but who had purchased the freedom of himself and family. He had resided here twenty-six years, and he now owns five or six houses and lots, besides a fine piece of land near town [Bexar]. He has educated his children so that they can read and write, and speak Spanish as well as French. They are all fine looking smart black people. He has a sister, also residing in Bexar, who is married to a Frenchman. The sugar cane, of which there is a patch of about an acre on Elua's land, looks as well as that which grows in Hayti, and the land is evidently well adapted to it. . . . Besides the cane, we saw some fine looking cotton, a large patch of sweet potatoes, together with beans, and other garden vegetables, the property of the same black man, and all in beautiful order.[19]

William Goyans was living in Nacogdoches at least as early as 1821. Eleven years later, when Lundy became acquainted with him, Goyans was married to a white woman, a native of Georgia. According to Lundy, they appeared "to live happily together, are quite wealthy, and are considered as very respectable." Two brothers of Mrs. Goyans, who, like their sister, were white, came to visit her during Lundy's stay. "They appeared well satisfied with their coloured brother-in-law, whom they had not seen before; and they took a very friendly leave of the family. . . ." Goyans

was of considerable help to Lundy on his trips to Mexico for the purpose
of establishing a free black colony in Tamaulipas.[20]

Emanuel J. Hardin came to Texas in 1822, settled in Brazoria County,
evidently as a farmer, and by living an "industrious and orderly" life,
he "acquired a considerable amount of property in the County besides
supporting himself and family." Hardin married Tomas Morgan, an
"industrious and useful negress" who had purchased her freedom and
held in her own name "a considerable amount of Real Estate in the
Country as well as personal property."[21]

A quadroon, Jean Baptiste Maturin, by name, received a grant from the
Mexican government dated Leona Vicario, October 20, 1823, conceding
to him one *sitio* of land in Nacogdoches County "about four leagues West
from the Town Nacogdoches." Maturin emigrated with his "wife and
numerous family of children" at the time of the grant and made "valuable
improvements" which enabled him to support his large family over a
period of at least fifteen years.[22]

In 1827, David and Sophia Gowns came to Nacogdoches with their
six children, to whom three more were added in a short time. Sophia
Gowns was a negress, but her husband, David, probably was a white
man, as no reference is made to him as a black man. The two oldest
daughters married and between them added five more free blacks to
the population.[23]

Robert Thompson, a black man of "prudence and industry," came
to Texas in 1831, at a later date purchased 200 acres of good land in
Montgomery County for which he paid $600 "in par money," stocked it
with a considerable number of horses, cattle and hogs, and found himself
so situated that he could live "independent and happy."[24]

In 1832, at the age of sixty, James Richardson came to Texas from
Philadelphia. A man of "industry, sobriety and correct deportment," he
made his living from the "habit of entertaining travellers between Velasco
and San Luis" and he was guaranteed a monopoly of the business on this

thoroughfare since he was in "a location where a white person equally serviceable could not be expected to reside." He was without descendants and without a wife, if he ever had one. The entertainment he provided consisted of serving "oysters and refreshments," the exact nature of the latter being undetermined.[25]

Samuel McCullough, a white man, came to Jackson County in 1835, bringing with him two black women, Peggy and Rose; his three daughters, Harriet, Jane and Mahaly; a son, Samuel McCullough, Jr., and another member of his family, a free black girl named Ulde. Samuel McCullough, Jr., was handicapped in life "by reason of an unfortunate admixture of African blood, which he is said, without any fault of his, to inherit from a remote maternal ancestor." No mention of the mother of this family was made, unless she was either Peggy or Rose.[26]

Moses Ashworth came to San Augustine previous to the declaration of independence, bringing with him four sons and a daughter. Moses was a white man but his children were free blacks and described as "people of mixed blood though nearly white." His daughter was married to Elisha Thomas, a black man.[27]

John Bird, his son Henry, and his son-in-law, Edward Smith, together with their three large families, emigrated to San Augustine County previous to the declaration of independence, "believing they would be received as citizens under the colonization laws of Mexican United States." John Bird claimed to be the grandson of General Bird of Virginia. He had previously lived in Logan County, Kentucky, and later at Courtland, Alabama, where for "many years" he was known to be a "truly honest man."[28]

At least three free blacks were accepted by Stephen F. Austin as colonists, two of whom definitely received title to their land. Lewis B. Jones, "a man of Color the Descendant of African Parents," emigrated in 1826 and was received by the Empresario as a colonist. He was a farmer from Mississippi, and brought with him his wife, Sarah, two daughters and a "dependent." In December, 1829, he applied for a half league of land on Fish Pond Creek to adjoin Jared E. Groce on his east boundary.[29] He claimed to have been given a league of land on March 25, 1831, which he selected and settled in 1834. In 1837, he was still in possession of the land and attempting to have his title legally recognized.[30]

Greenbury Logan, a blacksmith from Missouri, arrived in Texas in February of 1831. On December 22, of the same year, he applied for a quarter league of land on Chocolate Creek in Brazoria County, to which Stephen F. Austin granted him legal title.[31]

Samuel H. Hardin brought his family to Texas from some part of the United States, arriving in March of 1822. On March 12, 1831, he applied for a half league of land in Austin's colony. Samuel M. Williams, Austin's agent, reported that Hardin had lived in Texas nine years with his family, that Austin had accepted him as a colonist with permission to select a half league of land, that Hardin had always conducted himself well, that he was very industrious and active, and that he was worthy of the land. On April 25, 1831, Hardin was given title to half a league of land in Waller County.[32]

Immigration of single free black women was not uncommon. Harriet Newell Sands, a free woman of color, emigrated from Michigan in 1834, "with a Mr. Manton and remained in his employment, and in that of Edward Manton, his son, during which time she gave birth to two mulatto girls and a black boy."[33]

Zelia Husk, a "good and industrious" black woman, emigrated from Richmond County, Georgia, previous to the declaration of independence. Her location up to 1838, is unknown, but in that year she was living in Houston, "peaceably earning her livelihood" by "exercising the Industry of a washerwoman."[34]

Diana Leonard emigrated to Texas in 1835 and gained employment with Colonel James Morgan for a year, after which she also "exercised the industry of a washerwoman" in Houston, so supporting herself and her child.[35]

That there were other free blacks in Texas previous to the formation of the Republic is adduced largely from evidence presented by them in later years to establish their right to special residence privileges which were extended to early black settlers. Little else is known about the early activities of many of them except that they came to Texas previous to the declaration of independence. In view of the lack of census figures, their number can only be estimated. Men, women and children, the free black population at the time of Texan independence was in the neighborhood of 150 persons.

In addition to the blacks for whom there is some account, many of whom had a large percentage of white blood, it is possible that there were others who were able to pass the color line. Few places afforded a better opportunity for success than the frontier, and along that frontier in no place was it easier of accomplishment than in Texas with its large Mexican population. Blacks who intermingled with persons of Spanish ancestry, as we have seen, were accepted by the Mexicans as their countrymen and relatives, and were likewise accepted by the Anglo-American settlers. It is not to be inferred that blacks from the United States would encounter no difficulty in passing the color line among the Mexicans, but the difficulty would be considerably less.

If any of them were wholly successful in passing the color line, necessarily there would be no evidence. Noah Smithwick, in an account of the marriage of David Holdeman, "Bastrop's principal merchant," to Sam Craft's stepdaughter, reveals a partially successful attempt of two blacks to pass as white men. "This [wedding] being an extraordinary occasion, all the elite in the country were invited, and few regrets were sent."

> There were a couple of strangers present who attracted a good deal of attention—an elderly man, with a professional handle to his name, and his son a lad of twenty or thereabouts. They had money for which they were seeking investment. Both of them were well dressed sporting gold watches and shirt studs, and the young man was cutting a wide swath among the girls, laying us buckskin boys quite in the shade. But by and by old Aunt Celie, a mulatto

woman who was looking on through the open door, beckoned to her young mistress, Miss Harriet Craft, and taking her aside said:

"Miss. Ha'it, wat you in dar dancin' wid dat niggah To'?" "Hush, Aunt Celie; that isn't a nigger," said Miss Craft.

"He is niggah, Miss. Ha'it; he jes as much niggah as I is. Look at his ha' and his eyes," urged the indignant old woman.

. . . Later developments proved the keenness of the old woman's perception.[36]

No planned African American immigration from the United States ever materialized, but a number of schemes to colonize free blacks in Texas was suggested by Anglo-Americans, Mexicans and African Americans.

The chief exponent of such proposals was Benjamin Lundy, who contemplated the establishment of a colony of free blacks in Texas as early as 1830. His chief purpose was to demonstrate that the cultivation of sugar, cotton and rice could be engaged in profitably by the use of free labor. To this end, Lundy hoped and worked for the repeal of the law of April 6, 1830, which prohibited emigration from the United States to Texas, but finally, upon the advice of Almonte, Texas Commissioner of Colonization from Mexico, shifted his efforts to Tamaulipas, and there received a large grant of land, which, however, he was never able to develop.[37]

Lundy's plan received publicity, if not encouragement, in both northern and southern newspapers, and apparently it was a subject of discussion and debate among white men as well as blacks. *The New York Commercial Advertiser* of April 27, 1833, according to the *African Repository,* "holds the following sensible language in regard to . . . this visionary scheme" of colonization in Texas:

It is understood that the delegates [to a proposed Convention of Free People of Colour] are generally, if not altogether opposed to the Colonization Society—adverse to going to Liberia—and that they have in contemplation to plant a colony in Texas.

. . . if it can be *clearly* shown that a settlement in Texas would answer the purpose of the blacks, we would not lay a straw in their path. We are quite certain, however, that they will find [a number of] obstacles in their way, much more difficult to overcome than a settlement in Liberia. [These obstacles are as follows :]

. . . a conveyance to the Texas [*sic*] would be more expensive, on an average, than a passage to Monrovia. . . .the price of land is vastly dearer than in Africa.

. . . they must conform to the Catholic religion (if they would have any religion at all) whatever may be their particular creed, or they will live in constant inquietude, as well from the jealousies of the Government, as of their neighbors around them.

. . . very few of our colored people are acquainted with the Spanish language, and this they must acquire if they would hold any intercourse with the present population of that region. . . .

. . . admitting all these difficulties susceptible of removal, there is another which we presume will be found to be insurmountable. The presumption is founded upon the belief that their purpose will be to emigrate over land; for if they should proceed by water, the navigation would be almost as long, and altogether more dangerous than the voyage to Liberia. If they over take [*sic*] it over land, how will they get to Texas? They must pass through Louisiana, which is a slave State, and will never suffer any facilities to be given for the establishment of a black colony on her borders. Laws would be passed to seize them on their way, and thus to frustrate their object. Indeed there is such a community of feeling among all slaveholding States, that we are much inclined to think that in the apprehension of the Texas colony becoming a refuge for runaways, they would contrive ways and means to prevent their emigration even by sea.

> At all events the . . . embarrassments we have alluded to are such
> that we trust the Convention will ponder the matter well, in all
> its bearings, before they venture upon a measure fraught with so
> many obvious and appalling discouragements.[38]

The Richmond Whig, in the same vein, declared :

> It can never be shown that Texas will answer the purpose of the
> free people of colour of this country. The country does not exist,
> which from its social and political conditions, is more unsuitable
> for the location of the blacks. Already entered by great numbers
> of adventurers from the United States, and the refuge of all who
> avoid justice from Mexico, the blacks will stand as little chance for
> peace, quiet, and the protection of laws, among a population thus
> fierce, turbulent, and often lawless, as the lamb for quarter in the
> fangs of the wolf. Can they contend with the treacherous Spaniard
> and Creole, or those hardy and law despising adventurers who are
> sure to be found on the skirts of civilization? They cannot, and a
> brief space would see their settlement invaded, their possessions
> rifled, and themselves expelled from their chosen city of refuge.[39]

Efforts to secure land for African American colonization nevertheless
continued, and they were not confined to Lundy nor to white men. In
April, 1834, Nicholas Drouett, a mulatto and a retired Mexican army
officer, who, for a time, was associated with Lundy in his efforts to
gain a land grant in Tamaulipas, came to Texas seeking the privilege of
introducing five hundred black families from New Orleans, where he
had many relatives and friends.[40] After several conferences with Drouett
and two of his aids, Almonte decided that the project was impractical,
since the greater part of blacks in New Orleans were artisans, and would
not be permitted to live in the cities because of the peculiar aversion
Texans had for blacks. In a letter to the Minister of Relations at Mexico
City, Almonte outlined his reasons for rejecting the land grant, and at the
same time informed the minister that he had heard of two conventions
of free blacks held in New York City and Philadelphia in which they
endorsed emigration to Texas, but lacked means to transport themselves.

He believed this immigration to be advisable and suggested that the matter be taken up with the *charge d'affaires* in Washington.[41]

Colonization projects were warmly discussed, although usually rejected by African American conventions. The third annual convention for the improvement of the free people of color, held in Philadelphia in June, 1833, to which Almonte alludes, was originally called "for the purpose of giving aid and encouragement to a settlement of coloured people in the province of Upper Canada, in consequence of the revival of certain oppressive acts of the Legislature of the State of Ohio."[42] Contrary to the expectations of the newspapers and the belief of Almonte, the convention neither proposed nor endorsed any colonization plan. The committee on the Canadian report gave as its opinion that "there is not now, and probably never will be actual necessity for a large emigration of the present race of free coloured people, they therefore refrain from recommending any emigration whatever, but would respectfully say to such as may be desirous to go, that the fertile soil of Upper Canada holds out inducements far more advantageous than the desolate regions of Africa, where the scorching rays of a meridian sun, blasts by its withering influence the enlivened growth of successful vegetation."[43] This committee proposed two resolutions which were unanimously adopted :

> *Resolved,* that this Convention most respectfully Recommends to their constituents, to devote their thoughts and energies to the improvement of their condition, and to the elevation of their character, in this their native land, rejecting all plans of colonization any where.

> *Resolved,* that should any State by Legislative enactments, drive our brethren from its jurisdiction, we will give them all the aid in our power to enable them to remove and settle in Upper Canada, or elsewhere, that they may not be compelled to sacrifice their lives in the insalubrious climate of Liberia, provided for them by the American Colonization Society.[44]

A communication from Benjamin Lundy relative to his proposed colony in Texas was read at the convention and ordered to be printed in *The Genius of Universal Emancipation,* but no endorsement was given to the plan.[45]

All this discussion did not occur without official recognition by the Mexican Government. Three months previous to Almonte's suggestion to the Minister of Relations to encourage black immigration, the Mexican *chargé d'affaires* at Washington had already been informed by his government of the desirability of such immigration to Texas. He was ordered to make it known to all blacks in the United States that equality of rights was guaranteed them in Texas, that lands and tools were available for cultivation, and that protection would be given them in order that they might pursue their work peacefully.[46] The development of the Texas Revolution prevented this plan from being put into operation. Whether or not it would have had any great effects is problematical but improbable.

At any rate, none of these plans succeeded in organizing black immigration to Texas, or in planting a separate black settlement within its borders. But even the limited publicity and encouragement resulting from them, may have influenced individual African Americans and their families to move to Texas. Long before any plans were conceived, however, some free blacks from the United States were, as we have previously seen, already settled in this Mexican province.

The migration of blacks westward took on the same spontaneous and individualistic character as the westward movement of their white brethren, and their motives were probably very similar. Black immigrants to Texas were a cross section of free blacks in the United States. They came from the East and the South, from slave states and free states without distinction. Rich and poor, old and young, bachelors, spinsters, families and whole groups of related persons trudged their way west. Free-born black, self-emancipated slave, manumitted slave, and runaway slave came side by side. Many of them made intermediate stays, often for periods of years, as they came, and then resumed their march westward.

White men and black men often came hand in hand. Farmer, housewife, blacksmith, stockman, laborer, washerwoman, merchant and servant, free black immigrants included them all. Black, mulatto, quadroon and octoroon, all shades they came, with varying degrees of proof that they were close to the civilization they had adopted as it was marching west.

Despite the long subjection of their race to slavery, these African Americans certainly partook of the pioneering spirit in full measure. They were a part of the vanguard and it is evident that they easily learned methods of solving the problems of frontier life. In fact, they learned the lessons of frontier life in Texas so easily and well that they often were able to live in places where Anglo Americans could not be expected to survive. They were encouraged in their efforts by white men who often helped them migrate, employed them as laborers and mechanics upon their arrival, accepted them as farmers and colonists, and by these means advanced and strengthened this thin but significant stream of black pioneers.

Notes

1. Castañeda, C. E. (editor), *History of Texas, 1673–1779, By Fray Juan Agustin Morfi, Missionary, Teacher, Historian. Translated, with Biographical Introduction and Annotations,* I, 99.

2. Morfi, "Viaje de Indios y Diario del Nuevo-México," in *Documentos para la Historia de Mexico,* Series 3, Vol. 1, 459.

3. Nacogdoches Archives, VI. Texas State Library.

4. Memorial No. 139, File 74, no date; No. 250, File 18, no date; No. 63, File 15, January 11, 1848. Texas State Library.

5. *Ibid.*

6. *The Life, Travels and Opinions of Benjamin Lundy, Including His Journeys to Texas and Mexico; with a Sketch of Contemporary Events, and a Notice of the Revolution in Hayti,* 41. Benjamin Lundy was born in Hardwick, N. J., on January 4, 1789. While yet in his twenties he organized an anti-slavery society, and in January, 1821, began the publication of an abolition paper, *The Genius of Universal Emancipation.* During the next decade he became deeply interested in the colonization of blacks in some place more accessible and suitable than Liberia. He spent much time trying to find such a place to plant a colony, making two journeys to Hayti, one to Upper Canada, and three to Texas in 1830–31, 1833–34, and 1834–35. On the last trip he secured a large grant of land in Tamaulipas. Lundy intended to proceed with his settlement there and had "a large number of respectable persons in different States who proposed to accompany" him. But the Revolution in Texas caused him "to defer it a little" and subsequent events resulted in his abandonment of the grant. During the Revolution Lundy took the opportunity presenting itself of exposing, with the cooperation of John Quincy Adams, what they both regarded as a slaveholders' "vile project" of wresting Texas from Mexico. Meanwhile, after an uncertain and irregular existence, The Genius had expired toward the end of 1835, and for his new purpose Lundy began

the publication in Philadelphia of *The National Enquirer and Constitutional Advocate of Universal Liberty* which he published from August, 1836, until March, 1838, when he sold out to John G. Whittier, who changed the name to the *Pennsylvania Freeman*. The following summer Lundy left for Illinois, where he revived *The Genius* and published twelve more issues before a brief illness resulted in his death on August 22, 1839. The essence of his vitriolic attack on the Texas revolutionists is preserved in his pamphlet, *The War in Texas*, published in 1836. *Life of Lundy, passim*; Dumas Malone (editor), *Dictionary of American Biography*, XI, 506-507.

7. Frank Brown, "Annals of Travis County," IV, 68. University of Texas Library.

8. Noah Smithwick, *The Evolution of a State*, 224–226.

9. Brown, "Annals of Travis County," VI, 85.

10. Memorial No. 139, File 74, no date; No. 23, File 94. November 11, 1841.

11. Memorial No. 18, File H, no date.

12. *Life of Lundy*, 48.

13. *Life of Lundy*, 116.

14. Memorial No. 16, File 65, October 30, 1840.

15. *Life of Lundy*, 117–118.

16. Eugene C. Barker, "The Development of the Texas Revolution," in *Readings in Texas History*, 165.

17. Endorsed "Rejected." Memorial No. 71, File 73, December 14, 1859.

18. *Life of Lundy*, 44, August 11, 1833.

19. *Life of Lundy*, 54–55.

20. *Life of Lundy*, 116. Congressional Papers, Second Congress, File 11, No. 999, Texas State Library. Senate Journal, Fourth Legislature, 340.

21. Memorial No. 18, File H, no date.

22. Memorial No. 13, File M, April 23, 1839. No record has been found in the Land Office.

23. Memorial No. 13, File 32. October 18, 1840. David Gowns probably is the man to whom Benjamin Lundy refers as David Town.

24. Memorial No. 5, File T, December 13, 1840.

25. Memorial No. 23, File 75, October 19, 1840.

26. Memorial No. 101, File 67, no date; No. 102, File 67, October 29, 1841. *House Journal,* Fifth Session, 35. Harriet Smither (editor), House Journal, Sixth Session.

27. Memorial No. 19, File 49, September 19, 1840. *House Journal,* Seventh Called Session, 65.

28. Memorial No. 33, File 80, January 3, 1841; No. 15, File 5, September 20, 1836.

29. Listed as Levi B. Jones. Austin's Colonists, II, 91. State Land Office, Austin.

30. Memorial No. 5, File 49, October 8, 1837.

31. Spanish Titles, VIII, 581. Austin's Colonists, II, 105. State Land Office.

32. Samuel H. Hardin appears as Samuel Harding. Spanish Titles, IV, 1022.

33. Memorial No. 121, File 82, January 5, 1853.

34. Memorial No. 380, File 45, December 14, 1840; No. 122, File 40, December 11, 1841. In the 1841 petition her name is given as Zylphia Husk.

35. Memorial No. 16, File 54, December 14, 1840.

36. Noah Smithwick, *The Evolution of a State,* 156.

37. *Life of Lundy,* 63, 66, 69, 79, 80, 86, 128, 130, 145, 117, 149, 152, 162, 164, 167, 168, 183, 188, 189.

38. *African Repository,* IX, 86.

39. *Ibid.,* 86–87.

40. *Life of Lundy,* 113, 164.

41. Juan Nepomuceno Almonte to E. S., Secretario de Estado y del Despacho de Relaciones de los Estados Unidos Mexicanos, April 13, 1834. University of Texas transcripts, Dept. of Fomento, Leg. 8, Exp. 65.

42. *Minutes and Proceedings of the Third Annual Convention for the Improvement of the Free People of Colour in these United States Held by Adjournment in the City of Philadelphia, from the 3d to the 13th of June inclusive, 1833,* p. 22. No record of a free Negro convention in New York City previous to April, 1834, has been found.

43. *Ibid.,* 22–23.

44. *Ibid.,* 23.

45. *Ibid.,* 29. The letter appears in *The Genius of Universal Emancipation,* Vol. III, No. 8, third series.

46. Francisco Vidaurri y Villanselior to Joaquin Maria del Castillo, January 17, 1834. University of Texas transcripts, Dept. of Fomento, Leg. 8, Exp. 66.

2

FREE BLACKS AND THE TEXAS REVOLUTION

Harold R. Schoen

The affairs of free blacks in Texas were interminably bound up with those of their white friends, neighbors and countrymen. They rightly considered the welfare of all Texans to be their own, and they might expect the restitution of good government to fall with grace upon their own heads. They probably heard a great deal of discussion about the unjust burdens which Mexican misrule was forcing them to bear, and some of them, doubtless, felt the injustice of the decree of April 6, 1830, which prohibited their relatives and friends in the United States from joining them in Texas. The collection of duties which resulted from the administration of this decree increased the price of imports and it was as delicate a matter to collect taxes from black as from white men, particularly from those in Austin's colony who had grown accustomed to having their goods duty free. At any rate, it was as easy for the black as for the white man to place all his grievances, real and imaginary, at the door of the Mexican Government, and when the outbreak of hostilities threatened his life and property and the safety of his family, all of which he held as dearly as his neighbors, he was willing to risk his life in their preservation.

On the other hand, it was natural enough that the white man should accept the services of the black man in defense of the rights and privileges which had been extended to him, particularly since every man was sorely needed to oppose the overwhelming forces which it seemed certain the Mexicans would send to subdue, what they considered to be, an insurrection.

When a volunteer company was hastily organized near Matagorda early in October, 1835, for the purpose of driving away some Mexicans alleged to be committing outrages at Victoria, Samuel McCullough, a free African American, was among them. The company under Captain James Collingsworth did not rest at Victoria but continued on to Goliad. Collingsworth estimated that there were 60 to 100 Mexican troops at Goliad and he believed his "47 Good and Effective men," of whom McCullough was one, "all Sufficient to take that place."[1] On October 9, the company stormed the fort. In a letter urging Captain Benjamin Smith to reinforce him, Collingsworth explained his position and reported the battle in which one Mexican was killed, three wounded and captured, and three officers and 21 soldiers surrendered. He wrote, "I had one of my men wounded in the shoulder."[2] This man was McCullough. He was the only one of the Texan troops wounded in that battle, and claimed to be "the first whose blood was shed in the War of Independence." McCullough paid dearly for this unique distinction, as his shattered shoulder left him a helpless invalid for nearly a year and a cripple for life.[3]

The news of the capture of Goliad kindled a flame of enthusiasm throughout the country. On the tenth of October, Stephen F. Austin was elected commander-in-chief, and Greenbury Logan, a free black man, was among those who answered his call for volunteers to march on Bexar.[4] He

joined Captain Fannin's company in the middle of October, and marched
with the detachment of ninety men from Austin's main army of some 350
troops, when they met and defeated a much larger force of Mexicans near
Mission Concepcion on October 28. A council of war was then called to
consider the advisability of storming Bexar, but owing to the strength of
the fortifications and the lack of artillery to breach them, it was decided
not to make the attempt, but to lay siege to the town. The Texan army
continued to receive reinforcements, but there was much disorganization
in the ranks, and men, discontented with the long siege, were leaving
constantly. The siege was continued until December 3, when it appeared
to be about to end in disorder. On that morning, three prisoners, who
had been detained under surveillance since the beginning of hostilities,
made their escape from the city and reached the Texan camp. On the
basis of information given by them as to the strength of the city, a call
was made for volunteers to attack it early the next morning. The plan of
assault proposed that three hundred troops should be led into the town
in three divisions. Deaf Smith, J. W. Smith, and Hendrick Arnold, a free
black, were to act as guides to the three divisions.[5]

During that day and night, preparations were made for the assault, and
the men waited impatiently for the hour to advance. General Burleson,
who replaced Austin as commander-in-chief, called a council of officers,
and this council decided to postpone the attack. The value attached to
Hendrick Arnold may be judged by the fact that his absence was given
as the main reason for postponing the assault, the officers of one of the
divisions refusing to march without him.[6]

Early in the afternoon an order was issued to abandon the siege that
evening and set out for La Bahia. Meanwhile, a deserter from the Mexican
Army betrayed the weakness of the garrison and encouraged the Texans
to the assault, and Arnold, the absent black guide, returned. Colonel
Benjamin R. Milam, taking advantage of the sudden enthusiasm among
the men, made a stirring call for volunteers to follow him into the town.
Greenbury Logan, a free black man, stepped forward with a part of

Captain York's company to which he then belonged, to join the rest of the storming party. Milam was immediately elected to the command and selected the rendezvous to be met at dark. The attacking party was divided into two divisions, the first under the immediate command of Colonel Milam, with Hendrick Arnold as guide, and the second under Colonel Frank W. Johnson, with Deaf Smith and John W. Smith as guides.[7] On the morning of December 5, the assault was made; Arnold according to the plan "acted as pilot to Col. Milam in conducting his Troops in the Town,"[8] and they began fighting their way in from house to house with great courage and determination, finally forcing General Cos to capitulate five days later. Hendrick Arnold performed his service well. F. W. Johnson, who was left in command upon Milam's death on the third day, in his official report of the battle, wrote:

> All [of the men] behaved with the bravery peculiar to freemen, and with a decision becoming the sacred cause of liberty. To signalize every individual act of gallantry, where no individual was found wanting to himself or to his country, would be a useless and endless effort. Everyman has merited my warmest approbation, and deserves his country's gratitude.

Yet Johnson did not end his report without giving a special citation to Hendrick Arnold, who, he said, "performed important service."[9]

On the first day of this action, Greenbury Logan was badly wounded in the right arm, "by a ball's passing through it" while storming the town. Greenbury Logan served his adopted country "with distinguished alacrity and great credit to himself," but his glory was not unmixed, for his arm was so seriously wounded as to disable him for life.[10] At a later date, in order to enlist his Congressman, R. F. Forbes, in his effort to gain certain land privileges, Logan took his pen in hand and wrote his personal narrative:

> it is well known that Logan was the man that lifted his rifle in behalf of Texas as . . . [it was a free man's right]. it is also known that Logan was in everry fite with the Maxacans during

the campaign of 35 until Bexhar was taken, in which event I was
the 3rd man that fell. my discharge will show the maner in which
I discharged my duty as a free man and a solier . . . .[11]

The plight of the Texans aroused much sympathy in their native
country and the news of war brought volunteers from many parts of the
United States. Among them, in the company of white men and "under
their promise of protection," came Peter Allen, "a free man of color
residing in the State of Pennsylvania at the time the Texas Revolution
began; and a man of family."[12] These groups of volunteers, fresh from
the United States, made up the greater part of Fannin's troops in his ill-
fated plan to attack Matamoras.

After the fall of Bexar, serious differences arose among the Texan
leaders concerning the most advisable plan of war. Should they assume the
offensive by sending an expeditionary force to Mexico, or the defensive
and await attack on Texas soil? As it finally resolved itself, Fannin
was authorized to lead an expedition against Matamoras. Houston was
opposed to sending the main force of the army to the frontier, and it is
doubtful if he would have led the expedition in any case. At the time
he was engaged under a commission from the provisional governor,
Henry Smith, to negotiate a treaty with "the Cherokee and associated
Indian tribes." The purpose of the mission was to insure Texas against
a rear attack by the Indians during the difficulties with Mexico, and
if possible to "enlist . . . a force from them to act against our common
enemy [Mexico]."[13] With him, Houston took William Goyans, a free
black, as interpreter, "which appointment . . . he filled with much credit
to himself."[14]

On January 8, 1836, Fannin published a call for volunteers to undertake
the expedition to Matamoras, naming San Patricio as the rendezvous
between January 24 and 28. Peter Allen, late from Pennsylvania, intended
to be there at the appointed time, so he "joined the army and served
therein as a musician in Captain Wyate's company under the command
of Col. J. W. Fannin."[15]

What kind of an instrument Peter Allen owned, we are not told, but he played as Fannin marched to Goliad. It was by this time known that the Mexicans were invading Texas in force and Fannin decided to await them in the Goliad fortress. The main force of the Mexicans besieged the Alamo from February 23 to March 6, when they took it by storm without quarter. About the middle of March, Fannin received orders from Houston, who had meanwhile been appointed commander-in-chief of all armies, to fall back to Victoria, and on March 19, he started his retreat. He had gone but a few miles when his force was surrounded by Mexicans, and a fight ensued which ended only with nightfall. The next morning, finding himself in a hopeless situation, Fannin surrendered. A week later the prisoners were marched out under guard and shot down without warning. Although some few were fortunate to escape, not so Peter Allen, who shared the fate of the rest of his white companions. The bodies of the murdered men were piled in heaps, covered with brush and burned.[16]

Meanwhile the Declaration of Independence had been signed and the convention, having been given plenary powers, prepared for a more vigorous prosecution of the war. Among the measures which they passed was a draft law, making all able-bodied men between the ages of seventeen and fifty years subject to military duty. Officials were appointed for each municipality to compile a list of all available men within their respective boundaries. The names were to be drawn until the required number at any time was obtained, and those drawn were bound to serve under severe penalty.[17] Under this law, Robert Thompson, a free man of color, "stood a draft for a tour in the army and though not drafted he furnished a valuable mare and rifle gun for the use of the army of Texas for which he has [expected and] received no remuneration."[18]

Robert Thompson's contribution was not inconsiderable in view of the great need for rifles and a greater need for horses. The Government soon recognized that money and supplies, as well as patriotism and soldiers, were necessary to sustain the war, and a committee was early appointed by the council to negotiate for loans and to receipt for public monies. The several committees of safety busied themselves collecting more money and supplies by subscriptions and donations.[19] All who could, black and white, lent their private aid. Among these were the free African American brothers, William and Abner Ashworth, who gave freely of their property and "contributed generously to the advancement of the Revolution."[20]

Men, money and supplies would avail nothing, however, unless means of communication and transportation could be had to coordinate and join them together. This was a particularly difficult task in a frontier country and every conceivable conveyance and means of locomotion was pressed into service. Two slaves who were manumitted soon after the close of the war, largely on the basis of aid rendered during it, may properly be considered as free blacks which they soon became. Thomas F. McKinney's slave, Cary, "during the Revolution . . . was of much service in carrying expresses, &c."[21] Wyly Martin's slave, Peter, received early recognition for his services:

> Among the many who have contributed their services in once vanquishing our enemies, a valuable servant (Peter) who hires his own time, was pressed into service, with his wagon and team, to carry provisions to the army last fall; he has as yet received no compensation. Thus we see the operation of the war carried on no less by the weak than the strong.[22]

After Goliad, the retreat eastward before the Mexican forces continued without Fannin and his men, and without the music of Peter Allen. For nearly six weeks it continued, finally coming to an end on the San Jacinto. The retreat, of course, left the settlements defenseless. Every human being that could go, fled before the prospect of being captured by an invading army whose reputation preceded it in tales of the Alamo and Goliad. Free African Americans, black slaves, and white masters fled together, rendering to each other such aid as they could afford. James Richardson's "habit of entertaining travellers between Velasco and San Luis" was abruptly interrupted, and although some sixty years of age, he enrolled in Captain Thomas Bell's garrison at Velasco.[23] It was in this flight that Fannie McFarland, a free black woman, lost all her possessions at San Felipe.[24] Many of these Texans never stopped until they reached the safety of United States soil. The army itself came to rest on the San Jacinto. On the morning of April 20, the Mexicans came in sight and on the following day, the Texans in a surprise attack routed the Mexican army. At least two free blacks distinguished themselves through participation in this action. Hendrick Arnold, who successfully piloted Colonel Milam into Bexar when he stormed the town, appeared at the final battle. Arnold was "One of the most efficient members of Deaf Smith's Spy Company and an active participan[t] in the battle of San Jacinto."[25]

The other free African American who participated in the battle, Dick, was like Peter Allen, a musician. "By the effective beating of his drum . . . this gray headed descendant of Ham carried consternation into the ranks of Santa Anna's myrmidons." On the occasion of the San Jacinto dinner in May, 1850, "the venerable drummer" was present "and seemed to live his early days over again when witnessing the ceremonies of this joyous occasion." The *State Gazette* gave "Honor to the patriotic old man" and predicted that "his name will be handed down to posterity associated with those of the immortal heroes who wear the well-earned laurels plucked upon the deathless plains of San Jacinto."[26]

The battle of San Jacinto was hailed as a great victory. A treaty of peace was signed with the captured Mexican President and General, Santa Anna, and although it was soon repudiated, Mexican authority was never again extended over the Texan settlers. The new Republic continued in comparative peace the ten-year career which it began in the throes of a very dubious war.

The free African American contributed in full measure to making at first, good government, and at last, independence, a reasonable hope; and with his strength and his property, his blood and his life, he helped to remove all doubt that the Republic of Texas would survive the Revolution. In the performance of this service, the free black served in a wide variety of capacities with bravery and distinction; as messenger and drayman;

guide, spy and interpreter; musician and fighting man. He had come from distant parts to lend his aid, he had bestowed his property on the cause, he had fought shoulder to shoulder with his white companions, bled and suffered together with them, laid down his life at their side, and smouldered on the same funeral pyre.

Notes

1. C. M. Collingsworth to Stephen F. Austin. Eugene C. Barker (editor), *The Austin Papers,* III, 164.

2. James Kerr to Council of War. *Ibid.*

3. Congress recognized McCullough as "among the first to shed his blood in the war of independence." Congressional Papers, Fifth Session, No. 1677, File 19; No. 1527, File 17; Memorial No. 101, File 67, no date.

4. Congressional Papers, Sixth Session, No. 2349, File 25; No. 2582, File 28; Memorial No. 3, File 54, March 13, 1837.

5. Papers of the Third Legislature, Joint Resolution No. 43, File 47. H. Yoakum, *History of Texas from Its First Settlement in 1685 to Its Annexation to the United States in 1846,* II, 24.

6. *State Gazette* (Austin), September 1, 8, 1849. Yoakum, *History of Texas,* II, 25.

7. Yoakum, *History of Texas,* II, 25.

8. Papers of the Third Legislature, Joint Resolution No. 43, File 47.

9. F. W. Johnson to General Burleson, December 11, 1835. J. H. Brown, *History of Texas, from 1685 to 1892,* II, 417–421.

10. Congressional Papers, Sixth Session, No. 2349, File 25; Memorial No. 3, File 54, March 13, 1837.

11. Greenbury Logan to R. M. Forbes, November 22, 1841. Congressional Papers, Sixth Session, No. 2582, File 28.

12. *House Journal,* Seventh Legislature, 499.

13. Samuel Houston to Colonel Bowl or Tewulle, February 5, 1835. *Lamar Papers,* I, 317. Sam Houston and John Forbes to Henry Smith, February 29, 1836. J. H. Brown, *History of Texas,* I, 551–553.

14. William Goyans "served in the army of Texas during her dark hours of the revolution, shoulder to shoulder with the white man." *Senate Journal,* Fourth Legislature, 340.

15. *House Journal,* Seventh Legislature, 499.

16. *Ibid.,* Yoakum, *History of Texas,* II, 100.

17. Ordinance of the Convention, March 12, 1836. H. P. N. Gammel, *The Laws of Texas,* 1822–1897, I, 849–853.

18. This petition is signed by 30 citizens of Montgomery county. Memorial No. 5, File T, December 13, 1840.

19. Eugene C. Barker, "The Finances of the Texas Revolution," in *Political Science Quarterly,* XIX, No. 4, p. 614, 622–623.

20. Apparently the Ashworth brothers also served in the army. Joseph Grigsby, chairman of a select committee, reported to the House of Representatives that the Ashworth brothers contributed to the achievement of independence "both by personal Service and by their substance Generously bestowed without fee or reward." Committee Reports, Sixth Congressional Session, No. 2582, File 28. A later report of the House committee on the state of the Republic records "that they sustained the Government in her struggle for Independence with their property and personal service in the field." *House Journal,* Seventh Called Congressional Session, 63.

21. Thomas F. McKinney to Cary, November 11, 1839. Williams Papers, Rosenberg Library, Galveston.

22. *Telegraph and Texas Register* (San Felipe de Austin), March 5, 1836. Committee Reports, Fourth Congress. Peter and Cary were the only two adult slaves manumitted during the Republic, but they were not the only slaves to participate in the war. James Robinson came to Texas in March, 1836, bound by indenture to Robert Eden Handy. Upon his arrival, he joined the army with Handy, refusing a passport which was offered him to return to his home and friends, and "begged permission to remain and share the fate of those who met the enemy . . ." He did remain, and "While thousands . . .

of citizens were retreating in panic and confusion to the United States this single minded black boy, though unacknowledged as a patriot and bound by no *ties* of interest; still rose superior to every selfish consideration and bravely breasted the storm of Mexican invasion at the gloomiest hour of our fortunes . . ." In his petition to Congress, Handy "respectfully hopes that as his [Robinson's] color did not prevent the acceptance of his services in the hour of your utmost need, it will not now debar the payment of his reward." Robinson was at the battle of San Jacinto, remaining at the upper encampment in obedience to orders. Attested by Wyly Martin, then Chief Justice of Fort Bend County. Memorial No. 11, File 75, April 26, 1838. When a pension was provided by the State of Texas for veterans of the Texas Revolution, William T. Austin complained that no provision had been made for Thomas Stephens and Mark Smith, "who served and did good service in said revolution, but whose names do not appear in the muster-rolls, for the reason that they were slaves." Stephens served in the action against Bexar, and Smith fought at the battle of San Jacinto. Memorial No. 215, File 84, April 27, 1871.

23. This petition is signed by 23 citizens of Brazoria county. Memorial No. 23, File 75, October 19, 1840.

24. Memorial No. 16, File 65, October 30, 1840.

25. Papers of the Third Legislature, Joint Resolution No. 43, File 47.

26. Dick later served in the capacity of drummer during the Mexican War at the battles of Monterey and Buena Vista. *State Gazette* (Austin), May 25, 1850.

3

Manumissions

Harold R. Schoen

Although the Mexican government reluctantly tolerated slavery in the early years of Texas colonization, it could never be reconciled to the institution. Mexican statesmen of this period learned their political philosophy from the French Revolutionists. "Liberty, Equality and Fraternity" characterized the spirit of their own Great Revolution and provided them with an aurora of generosity and benevolence which seems inseparable from reform movements. Liberty became a part of their religion and they joined it with God to glory in their national motto —"God and Liberty." That it was merely a word without significance to the Indians and mixed-bloods living in peonage, we could hardly expect them to see or admit. In the abstract and by its proper name, they abhorred slavery as the antithesis of liberty.[1]

This philosophy expressed itself in a long series of conflicting laws designed to extend the blessings of liberty to all slaves, but in each case by various subterfuges, the Texans were able to circumvent the wholesale operation of the law. After the establishment of the Texas Republic, the status of some blacks was affected by these Mexican laws under which they once had lived, and a few of them were actually freed. In order to understand these aspects, it is necessary to review briefly Mexican legislation on the subject of emancipation.[2]

The abolition of slavery as an important reform sought by the Mexican Revolution may rightly begin with the movement initiated in Mexico by Miguel Hidalgo, self-styled Generalissimo of America. Although he never promulgated a definite scheme for the government of emancipated Mexico he did issue a decree of December 6, 1810, abolishing the evils against which he fought. The first provision required all slave owners to manumit their slaves within ten days of the decree on penalty of death.[3] Six weeks later Hidalgo's army was decisively defeated and forced to disperse, and soon after, Hidalgo, at the hands of a Spanish firing squad, met the fate he had decreed for recalcitrant slave owners.

The successful Revolution of 1821, followed by the establishment of a Mexican Empire made it necessary for all acts and grants to be affirmed by the new Emperor, Agustin de Iturbide. Among these was the colonization contract of Stephen F. Austin, and for the purpose of confirming it he traveled to Mexico City. When he arrived in April of 1822, a new colonization policy was already under consideration, and after considerable delay it emerged as the Colonization Law of 1823. Article 30 clearly stated the slavery provisions:

> After the publication of this law, there can be no sale or purchase of slaves which may be introduced into the empire. The children of slaves born in the empire, shall be free at fourteen years of age.[4]

Iturbide signed the law on January 4, 1823, but General Santa Anna had already proclaimed a republic. On July 13, 1824, the republican congress passed a law prohibiting forever the "commerce and traffic" in slaves and declaring all slaves introduced to Mexico in violation of the law, free by the mere act of treading Mexican soil.[5]

When the colonization law of Coahuila and Texas of March 24, 1825, failed to place a favorable meaning on "commerce and traffic" in slaves, Austin consulted his friend, the secretary of state, at Saltillo, about the effects of this federal statute and received the opinion that it could be reasonably interpreted as prohibiting only the slave trade, and therefore, that settlers introduced under colonization contracts could bring in slaves for their own use.[6] Erasmo Seguin, Texas representative in Congress, soon afterward offered the suggestion that the state legislature might be induced to interpret the act favorably to the colonists.[7]

For this purpose Austin addressed a memorial to the legislature proposing that until 1840, colonists, but no others, should be allowed to take slaves to Texas for their own use and property; that, in accordance with the federal law, trading should be strictly forbidden, except that colonists might buy from each other; and that after 1840 introduction should be prohibited under all pretexts. In order to make this interpretation more palatable to the liberty-loving Mexicans, Austin prepared as a part of his desired law an elaborate scheme of gradual emancipation, the main feature of which provided that grandchildren of slaves introduced by the colonists should be free, the males at twenty-five and the females at fifteen. This scheme if adopted would delay complete emancipation to the twentieth century and Austin anticipated objection to it, but believed that a less remote emancipation would discourage desirable immigration.[8]

This interpretation of the federal laws was never sanctioned by the state legislature but immigrants continued to bring slaves to Texas. In order to circumvent the law which clearly prohibited the purchase and sale of blacks, the master, wishing in fact to sell a slave, in consideration of his value "hired" him to the new master for a term of years which would exceed the slave's lifetime, and if the slave was a woman, in consideration of the maintenance of any children she might bear, the new master was to have the full use of the children as long as the old master would have been entitled to it had he kept possession of the woman.[9]

In July, 1826, the state legislature had completed the framework of a new constitution and was occupied with the general provisions. Article 13, dealing with slavery, as reported by the committee on the constitution read:

> The state prohibits slavery absolutely in all its territories, and slaves now in the state shall be free from the day the constitution is published in this capital. A law shall regulate the mode of indemnifying those who owned them at the time of publication.[10]

Austin prepared a memorial declaring the act most unjust. The law authorizing the settlement of the first three hundred families permitted the introduction of slaves and guaranteed property without distinction. To free them would be an act of bad faith, the enormity of which could not be concealed by recognizing the obligation to compensate the owners, since this indemnity could only come by levying a heavy tax on the slave owners to pay for their own indemnification. The law if enacted would deprive the colonists of their laborers and turn Texas into a wilderness, and the blacks, moreover, if liberated would become vagabonds, a nuisance and a menace. The *ayuntamiento* of Bexar prepared a similar petition, making a *"Warm"* representation against the proposed law.[11]

Rumor among the colonists of the intention to abolish slavery caused much anxiety to slaveholders and many talked of returning to the United States. Under these circumstances Austin addressed another memorial to the legislature, making judicious concessions to the Mexican love of liberty in order to prevent the absolute emancipation which faced Texas. This time he begged that introduction of slaves be allowed for five years and that children of slaves be emancipated at the age of twenty-five.[12]

When finally passed on January 31, 1827, the slavery article recognized existing slavery and allowed introduction for an additional six months, but declared free children born to slaves after the promulgation of the constitution.[13]

To give the constitutional provision effect, a decree was issued on September 15, 1827, setting up elaborate machinery for the registration of children born of slave parents and of all deaths of slaves, and for the education of free black children. In addition the decree provided that slaves of a master who died without apparent heirs—and adopted children—were not to be considered heirs, should be liberated and that when there were heirs one-tenth should be freed by lot, but manumission should not take place if the master or heirs were murdered by one of the slaves.[14] There is no evidence that this law ever effected the liberation of a single slave. No provision was made for the care of children born of slaves who naturally remained with their mothers under the care of the master, and before any of these children reached nine years of age they were no longer under Mexican laws. Few Texans owned ten slaves and the provision for the liberation of one-tenth could not apply to owners of less, while division of ownership among the members of a family could reduce the holdings of a single individual below this point. From available sources it cannot be determined that any Texas slave-holder died without apparent heirs, but if any did, creditors could make use of a subterfuge yet to be considered.

Austin, who visited Saltillo shortly after this decree was passed, argued for repeal[15] but only effected an amendment providing that emancipation should not take place when a master was "assassinated or poisoned by an unknown hand or die[d] in any unnatural way."[16] This amendment obviated the necessity of proving that a slave had murdered the master in order to deprive slaves of the liberty provided them under Decree No. 18. No stretch of the imagination is necessary to see that creditors of a slaveholder who died without apparent heirs might claim that he had been poisoned or died "in an unnatural way" in order to seize his slaves to satisfy their claims.

At the same time that the legislature passed this amendment it also legalized domestic trading by providing that a slave "for the sake of convenience" might "change his master" if the new master would indemnify the old for his cost. While there is no documentary evidence that Austin influenced this provision, it is reasonable to suppose that he was aware of it and favored it. The government had already recognized its obligation to compensate owners in case of emancipation. If Austin did not propose the provision could it have been part and parcel of the emancipation policy of the government, which, through a gradual and comparatively painless process, might acquire slaves at cost and then set them free? Whatever the intent of the law, by the mere assertion that the slave wished to change his master, the federal law of July 13, 1824, prohibiting commerce and traffic in slaves was circumvented, and the bill of sale familiar to the colonists in the United States replaced the less satisfactory contract for the "hire" of slaves.

One impediment still prevented the full operation of the slave system as the colonists wished it—the importation of slaves was prohibited. Evasion from the operation of this law was sought and gained by the passage of an act in the legislature validating labor contracts between master and servant made before entering Texas. Passage of this act was secured before the members of the legislature understood its effect. Jose Antonio Navarro and Miguel Arciniega, Texan representatives, both believed that if its operation were understood it might not have passed, and Arciniega thought that it might be repealed.[17] This law provided that: "All contracts not contrary to the laws of this State made in foreign countries between emigrants to, or inhabitants of, this State and servants or hirelings introduced by them are guaranteed as valid in this State."[18]

This law, in effect, legalized the importation of slaves through the execution of a simple indenture contract. Before emigrating to Texas, master and slave appeared before a notary, the master declared the value of the slave, the slave declared his wish to be free. Once in Texas the slave would be free, but the master would lose the value of the slave.

In consideration of this loss to the master and gain to himself, the slave contracted to work at stipulated wages after removal until he had repaid his value. Minors and unborn children were included in the contract and the wages were so low that there was no possibility of the slave or the slave's children ever achieving their liberty.[19]

As a subterfuge this procedure was reasonably effective but because of the possibility of its repeal, Austin continued unsuccessfully to agitate for the repeal of the constitutional prohibition on slavery or at least a suspension of its operation for ten years.[20]

Colonists continued to bring in blacks under these indenture contracts until the laws of the Texas Republic legalized the importation of slaves. This system of indentures was also extended to blacks who had been brought to Texas previous to November 29, 1827, and who were legally slaves,[21] either to avoid a possible emancipation decree or to keep in bondage children of slaves decreed free by the constitution. Slave and master appeared before the Alcalde, the slave acknowledged receipt of the full sum of his value for the purpose of purchasing his freedom. In consequence of this advance made to him by his master, he bound himself to labor for him at stipulated wages until he discharged the debt and legal interest thereon as well as the cost of clothing, medical assistance and such other things as he might consume, with the exception of food which his former master provided free.[22]

President Guerrero, in August, 1829, was invested with extraordinary military authority in order to concentrate the resources of the nation to repel a Spanish invasion; and by virtue of this military dictatorship he issued on September 15, in commemoration of Mexican independence, a proclamation abolishing slavery throughout the Republic, except in the Isthmus of Tehuantepec.[23]

The Texas Governor, Jose Maria Viesca and the political chief at San Antonio, Ramon Milsquiz, sought to suppress the decree until exception could be had for Texas. They represented to the national secretary of state that the publication and enforcement of the decree would draw upon the state disturbances which could only be quelled by using violent and costly measures.[24] When Austin learned of the decree he was determined to resist its execution. Basing a projected revolution on constitutional grounds he declared that colonists had "taken an oath to defend the constitution, and are bound to do so. That the constitution of the state expressly recognizes the right of property in slaves by allowing six months after its publication for their introduction into the state. That they will defend it, and with it, their property."[25]

The decision to except Texas from the decree came in a private letter from the president to General Teran, commandant general of the Eastern Interior Provinces and military chief of Texas, in reply to one of his own in which he represented that it would never be obeyed in Texas unless it was enforced by an army greater than Teran had at his disposal.[26]

In April, 1832, the legislature of Coahuila and Texas passed a new colonization law, repealing that of 1825. Two of its articles touched the slave question. The first subjected immigration to existing and future laws of slavery; and the other limited indenture contracts to ten years' duration.[27]

Before the expiration of the ten years, Texas had won its independence and made constitutional provisions restoring slavery as a legal institution. The fragmentary journals of the plenary convention to frame the constitution do not reveal the full history of the slavery provision which reached its final form as General Provisions, Section 9:

> All persons of color who were slaves for life previous to their emigration to Texas, and who are now held in bondage, shall remain in like state of servitude; provided, the said slave shall be the bona fide property of the person so holding said slave as aforesaid. Congress shall pass no laws to prohibit emigrants from bringing their slaves into the republic with them, and holding them by the same tenure by which such slaves are held in the United States; nor shall congress have power to emancipate slaves; nor shall any slaveholder be allowed to emancipate his or her slave or slaves without the consent of congress, unless he or she shall

send his or her slave or slaves without the limits of the republic. No free person of African descent either in whole or in part, shall be permitted to reside permanently in the republic, without the consent of congress; and the importation or admission of Africans or negroes into this republic, excepting from the United States of America, is forever prohibited, and declared to be piracy.[28]

The circumspect language of the first sentence in this section may in part be explained by a committee recommendation. In considering the subject of the African slave trade, this committee suggested that "as a nation just ushered into existence, it most eminently becomes our duty and policy to adapt our measures to the genius and spirit of the age. We must be governed by the opinions of others—we must so regulate our infant steps as to deserve the kind and watchful solicitude of older Nations. But while advocating the broad and abstract principle of justice, let us not . . . interfere with or violate the just rights of our citizens."[29]

This feeling that the constitution must not offend the sensibilities of older nations by too obviously enslaving legally free persons and yet that such respect should not interfere with or violate the just rights of Texans perhaps explains the substitution of the obscure language in the first sentence of the article for the clearer preliminary draft which appears in the proceedings of the convention:

> All persons of color who were slaves for life, previous to their emigration to Texas, and who are now held as bonded servants or otherwise, shall remain in the like state of servitude in which they would have been held in the country from which they came; provided the person or slave be the bona fide property of the person holding the same, either by purchase or otherwise.[30]

The fluctuating and unsettled legislation of Mexico on the subject of slavery showed a disposition to put an end to it, and the various subterfuges used by Texans to circumvent it gave rise to great uncertainty regarding the tenure by which they held dominion over their black slaves. Although the owner might honestly believe that his legal title had not been destroyed or impaired by Mexican legislation he could not feel secure. But it is clear that whatever may have been the legal effect of this legislation on the relation of master and slave in Texas, that relationship never ceased for a moment to exist in fact. The proviso therefore stated that the black enslaved must be the *bona fide* rather than the legal property of the person holding him either by purchase or otherwise. Blacks, as we have seen, were held as slaves in fact under three different tenures : (1) as slaves, (2) as indentured servants, and (3) as "hired" servants. If a master held a black by any of these titles, if he believed it to be right and good, although it might not as a legal document stand the test of Mexican legislation, that *bona fide* title was confirmed and made legal by this proviso. The term *bona fide* was clearly not used as a synonym for legal. To give it that interpretation would destroy not only its own effect but the effect of the preceding sentence to which it is appended.[31]

The manifest intention of the convention, then, in framing this provision was to return all blacks to the same status they would have held, had they remained in the slave states of the United States. Yet this interpretation was not always placed upon the provision, and some blacks gained their freedom because under Mexican law their masters did not have a legal title to them. Among them was Harriet Arnold.

In the winter of 1826, Catherine Arnold emigrated from Mississippi to Texas with her son, Daniel, his wife, Rachel, his two sons, Hendrick and Holly, his two daughters, and five slaves, among them Dolly, and settled on the Brazos in Austin's colony.[32] Hendrick and Holly were African Americans,[33] and although there is no evidence that they were ever formally manumitted by their father, they acted in all capacities as free persons.[34] Shortly after their arrival in July or August, Dolly by Hendrick Arnold gave birth to a mulatto girl, Harriet.[35] During the Texas Revolution Hendrick Arnold, described as "one of the oldest and boldest pioneers of the west," joined the army and fought valiantly for his adopted country.[36] Sometime before January 4, 1836, Arnold married a daughter of a captain, in whose company he served for a part of the Revolution. At the time of his death in 1849, he was married to a woman by the name of Martina, but whether she was the same wife he had in 1836, is uncertain.[37]

On August 9, 1846, Hendrick conveyed and set over to James Newcomb, his daughter Harriet, on condition that Newcomb should in the course of five years emancipate and set her free. In the early part of 1849, both Hendrick Arnold and James Newcomb fell victims to the cholera which raged in Bexar county. George M. Martin administered the estate of Newcomb, who had not yet taken any steps for the purpose of carrying out his contract with Arnold. Although Martin still had two years within which to fulfill the contract, on December 29, 1849, he had introduced into the House of Representatives a joint resolution to permit Harriet to remain in the State as a free woman of color.[38] The resolution passed the House on January 9 of the following year,[39] and was sent to the Senate where on a second reading it was laid on the table until the fourth of July, a witty disposition in the fifties.[40]

After Arnold's death, his son-in-law attempted to gain possession of Harriet from Martin, but he died some time before September, 1851, without gaining his purpose. Arnold's brother, Holly, then took up the cause of recovering Harriet, claiming that Arnold had no right to sell her, that she belonged to him. At the *time* of the sale, according to Martin, Holly was present and made no objection. Martin wrote to Col. Thomas W. Chambers that if the Arnolds persisted in prosecuting suit against him, he would like to send Harriet to him and let her stay there until the matter was settled. Harriet had a Mexican for a husband, "one of the best I ever saw and is Just as Good a Servant as I would wish as correct and honest as anybody I ever Knew. Harriet is as Good a house servant as can be found any place."[41]

Two months later, at which time the stipulated five years to emancipate Harriet allowed Newcomb and his administrator, Martin, had expired, Martina Arnold, as the administratrix of her husband's estate sued Martin in the Bexar County Court to recover Harriet. Pleading poverty and the necessity of educating several minor children, Martina begged the Court to *give* her judgment against Martin for a two thousand dollar penalty incurred by the terms of the contract for not freeing Harriet, $750 for her hire for the five years, and for the recovery of Harriet. After the commencement of the suit, Martin was informed that Harriet was born a free person "under the Mexican Laws"[42] and could not be claimed as a slave, and prayed for a dismissal of the suit.

The jury found "that the constitution of the State of Coahuila and Texas of the 11th March 1827 was published and promulgated in the Month of April or May AD 1827 in Texas . . . that the colored Girl Harriett who is the subject of this suit was born in Texas of Slave parents in the fall of 1827 and after the promulgation of said constitution and is not the property [of any person]." Martin appealed the case on the grounds that the verdict of the jury was contrary to the law and evidence.

At the Supreme Court trial, Oliver Jones, prominent in early Texas legislatures, testified that "There were no Slaves born in the Country prior to the adoption of the constitution of the Republic in 1836." There was a law, he thought, that guaranteed property to immigrants and colonists, which was thought by some to protect the title of the master to slaves brought into the country, but that if this law did not protect slave property, he knew of no other. Antonio Manchaca, a native of San Antonio, testified that "Slavery did not exist in the Province of Texas during the existence of the Mexican Government over this Country. That a slave brought from the United States and escaping [in Texas] would not have been delivered up by the authorities unless claimed as a peon. There were no children born Slaves in Texas. He recollects one person brought as a Slave from the United States who was set free here by the authorities or rather there was no Law to authorize the Masters to claim her as a slave."[43]

The judgment of the Bexar County Court was "in all things affirmed," and Martin was ordered by the Supreme Court to "proceed with all convenient dispatch" to convey Harriet to a state or country where she could be free, or to proceed "to act in any manner" by which "full emancipation can be soonest and best" completed.[44]

Martin prepared a bill "To relieve and do justice to Harriet Arnold" which he presented to the extra session of the fourth legislature to secure permission for Harriet to remain in Texas "until she dies."[45] The bill was read the first time on January 13, 1853, and referred to a committee on the following day.[46] The session adjourned on February 7, without taking further action. Before the convening of the next legislature Martin probably discovered that under the law of December 12, 1840, Harriet already had permission to remain in the State since she was residing in Texas previous to the declaration of independence.[47] At any rate, we hear no more of her.

The effect of this decision was to declare free all children born of slave parents after May 29, 1827, and previous to the adoption of the constitution of the Republic. The decision, however, would not automatically free these blacks if their freedom was contested by their masters. There is no evidence that any black other than Harriet secured freedom under this decision, nor did any subsequent cases, if there were any, reach the Supreme Court. A survey of county court records might reveal some cases in which blacks sued for their freedom on the basis of this decision, but because blacks were barred from citizenship and from the use of the courts by the constitution,[48] it would be necessary for them to enlist a white man to sue for them, an obvious difficulty. A relief law passed by the fourth Congress of the Republic appears to have been an early recognition by a master of these children's right to freedom. By the provisions of this act, Albert Mitchell, recognized as a free boy of color, was permitted to remain in the family of John M. Clifton until he was twenty-one years of age, at which time Mr. Clifton, in the language of the bill, was "required" to give the boy his free papers. During the Republic, children free under the Mexican law would have ranged in age from infancy to not more than eighteen years of age, and it is difficult to see any way in which they could have immediately become free. The Albert Mitchell act, allowing Mr. Clifton the use of the boy until he became of age, in return for the necessary care given him during his minority, seems to have been a practical solution.[49]

A second Supreme Court decision[50] recognized the freedom of another group, the black concubines of white men. In February, 1836, Adam Smith purchased Margaret from a master who regarded her as a slave. The evidence is not clear whether she paid for herself or was paid for by Smith, but the evidence is rather full that from the time of the purchase or nearly so to 1846, Smith lived with her as his wife. During all that time he disclaimed being her owner but said on all occasions that she was free. She claimed and exercised ownership of property in her own right, Smith always called it her property and never exerted any control over it or her actions. For a part of this time she kept a boarding house; she bought and paid for the supplies and boarders always settled with her. In 1840, some disagreement took place between Smith and Margaret, at which time Smith told her to take her child and go away; that he wanted nothing more to do with her. When she left him Smith gave her a paper which read, "The bearer, Margaret, a negro woman, about thirty years of age, is free and at liberty to go and do the best she can to make an honest livlihood in the world. Given under my hand this 19th day of March, 1840. Adam Smith." The manumission papers were, of course, illegal, since Smith had never secured the consent of Congress and Margaret did not leave the country. After Smith's death his administrator claimed Margaret and a ten-acre lot held by Smith as the trustee of Margaret as the property of his intestate.

The Supreme Court held that the laws of Mexico placed no restrictions on manumission and although Smith may have been at one time Margaret's master, since he disclaimed that relationship and did not claim to be her master and did not hold her in bondage when the constitution was adopted, her status was that of a free black.[51] The implication of this decision would seem to be that slaves living in concubinage with white men, and not actually held and used as slaves at the time of the adoption of the constitution, were free. The question of their status was never raised, however, except upon the death of the master and then only if claimed by administrator or creditors.

The status of a third group of blacks, those who were brought into Texas subsequent to November 29, 1827,[52] and previous to the adoption of the constitution, who were not indentured under the law of May 5, 1828,[53] was brought into question by Samuel McCullough, Sr. On October 29, 1841, he set forth in a petition to Congress that he had immigrated in 1835, previous to the declaration of independence, with two black women, Peggy and Rose, "desiring that they should be and remain free." He did not require an indenture from them, and he considered that they had acquired freedom under the laws regulating the introduction of such persons into Texas. "Being desirous of securing them a permanent home," he prayed for a law authorizing him to record in the County of Jackson a deed of emancipation, and begged for an act enabling Peggy and Rose to continue their residence in Texas.[54]

Three months later, the committee to which the petition was referred, recommended an enabling act on the grounds that "Peggy and Rose were welcome under the thirteenth article of the constitution of Coahuila and Texas[55] as free persons, and as such were introduced by the petitioner in good faith, as an evidence of which he declined requiring of them their indentures and has in no instance exercised ownership or control over them. Your committee feel no hesitancy in deciding in favor of the passage of the law prayed for as it was not the design of the framers of our constitution to enslave free persons."[56]

There can be no doubt that Peggy and Rose had gained their freedom under Mexican law by crossing the Texas border as slaves and treading Mexican soil. Their freedom under the Texas constitution, the committee believed, depended upon whether McCullough considered them as his *bona fide* property, that is, upon his intent and usage. It was convinced of intent by the lack of an indenture, and of usage by the claim that McCullough had exercised neither ownership nor control over them.

Evidently Congress was not so easily persuaded, as no Congressional action followed the report, and apparently in the eyes of the law, Peggy and Rose continued to be slaves.[57] Records of the debates on the committee report are not available, if there were any, but certainly evidence could be introduced which would cast some doubt upon the allegations of McCullough and the conclusions of the committee. No attempt was made at the time of the adoption of the constitution by either Peggy or Rose to gain the consent of congress necessary for their continued residence[58] although McCullough's own son applied for the right.[59] A joint resolution of June 5, 1837, extended the right of residence to all free persons of color who had emigrated to Texas previous to the declaration of independence, but on February 5, 1840, another law was passed requiring all free persons to remove from Texas, from which exception had been asked and given to Samuel McCullough, Jr., his three sisters and another relative by the name of Uldy.[60] The omission of the names of Peggy and Rose from this petition, which included the names of all other blacks introduced by Samuel McCullough might indicate that he did not even at that late date consider Peggy and Rose to be free.

The cases thus far considered arose from a series of Mexican laws, which, despite what appears to have been the intent of the constitutional convention, were not wholly invalidated by the basic law of the Republic of Texas.

The Constitution placed two restrictions upon the manumission of slaves subsequent to its adoption: first, Congress was specifically denied the power to emancipate slaves; second, slaveholders were required to gain the consent of Congress to manumissions unless the manumitted slaves were sent out of the Republic. The first restriction seems to have been wholly unnecessary, but developed in part out of a long experience with legislative bodies which showed a disposition to interfere with slave property. The object of the second restriction was probably two-fold—

to prevent the manumission of old, crippled or infirm blacks who might become a burden on the State, and to prevent the increase of what was considered to be an undesirable free black population.

The first of a long series of requests for the consent of Congress to the manumission of slaves was presented by Joseph A. Parker, Houston representative to the third Congress, in behalf of his constituent, Joseph Walling, who had emigrated in the belief that he could emancipate three black slaves whom he had brought with him. These slaves he described "as followeth, To Wit One woman of yellow complection named Moriah about 23 or 24 years of age, allso her 2 childring—a girl named Hariet about 4 years old and a boy about 1 year old named Thomas—which Slaves I wish to emancipate and set free for many Good causes first because the said woman has long since made to me full and ample satisfaction for her freedom and allso the freedom of her children—allso I have conscientious scruples of holding in Bondage said woman and her two children . . ."[61]

E. L. Holmes, of Matagorda, chairman of the Judiciary Committee, to whom the petition was referred, reported to the House that the committee deemed it "highly impolitic and contrary to the genius and spirit of the constitution to emancipate slaves and suffer them to remain within the limits of the Republic; that the principal reason urged by the petitioner in asking this authority, to wit: that he has conscientious scruples in holding in bondage said slaves, is not sufficient to induce your committee to report favorably to his prayer."[62]

The report was both ambiguous and self-contradictory. First, it declared the residence of manumitted slaves an unwise policy; second, to manumit slaves and allow them to remain was contrary to "the genius and spirit of the Constitution;" and third, conscientious scruples were not a sufficient reason for manumission. If it were both unwise and unconstitutional to allow manumitted slaves to remain within the Republic, then obviously, no reason could be sufficient to induce Congress to grant such a privilege, and the third proposition, that conscientious scruples did not constitute a sufficient reason, was superfluous. But despite the ambiguity of the statement, the House accepted the committee's report as its judgment, and Joseph Walling was refused the right to manumit his slaves.[63]

Two months later, in January, 1839, Congress received a petition from Edward Teal in which he asked authorization to manumit his slave, Fanny.[64] A bill for the purpose was introduced in the House, and, after an unsuccessful attempt to postpone action indefinitely, the House passed the bill. The reasons for emancipation outlined by Teal are unknown, but evidently they were sufficient to induce that body, in the opinion of the Judiciary Committee, to forsake a judicious policy and violate the "spirit and genius of the Constitution."[65] In the Senate, the bill was indefinitely postponed a few days before the adjournment of the third congress.[66]

Wiley Martin, who was now "a verry old man, between sixty and seventy," found himself in his old age with no heirs and no near kindred to whom he might leave his property. Before his death he wished to manumit his slave, Peter, and he referred the fourth Senate to two of its own members, Oliver Jones and Thomas Barnett,[67] for substantiation of the good character of Peter, who had served his master honestly and faithfully for nearly thirty years from his boyhood to the date of this petition. In a postscript, Wiley Martin asked the "friendly aid and influence" of "Colonel Lawrence and Colonel Burton,"[68] as well as of Jones and Barnett in "bringing about the objects contemplated" in his petition.[69]

Wiley Martin's memorial was duly introduced in the Senate by Oliver Jones, and referred by the president of the Senate to a special committee of which Jones was made chairman.[70] The committee reported that Peter had resided in Texas for sixteen years, "the most part of which he has transacted business on his own account by Consent of his master, and his deportment at all times has been that of an Industrious, Humble and useful subject."

The report continued, "That during our struggle for Independence he rendered material aid to the government by Hauling (with his own team and at his own expense), military stores and provisions for the use of the Army during the period they were stationed before Bexar in 1835—" In consideration of these facts the committee recommended the passage of an act enabling Peter to remain in the Republic after manumission.[71]

A long debate ensued in which interpretations were placed upon the original constitutional provision necessitating Congressional sanction of private manumissions, and particular reasons were offered for rejecting and approving the act accompanying the committee report, giving Peter the right to remain in the Republic after manumission.

Stephen H. Everitt, of Jasper and Jefferson, opened the debate by offering his objections to the committee report. He said that he was willing to emancipate slaves to be transported out of the country but on no other consideration. Such action would not require an act by Congress. Admitting the merit of the case, Everitt did not believe that the sympathies of the Senate should be excited to the point of justifying the infringement of the law and the Constitution, which he pointed out specifically denied to free blacks the right to remain in the Republic. He failed to mention the fact that the same Constitution specifically gave Congress the right to grant residence rights to blacks. Everitt went so far as to admit that justice might claim for the petition a favorable reception in the Senate, and that some partial good might result to Wiley Martin and Peter. He could not overlook the fact that an evil of the deepest dye might result from favorable action on this petition, and he announced his intention of opposing and voting against the bill. If destruction and bloodshed were to be brought upon his country through the creation of a free black element, Everitt declared that he would not be responsible for it, and he called the attention of the Senate to the ruinous brink of dissolution from which the United States had more than once been rescued. Looking upon the awful spectacle of insurrection, for which the free black was largely responsible, he begged the Senate to profit by the experience and example of the United States before they should give their vote to sustain a measure so baneful in its consequences, and establish what he regarded as a dangerous precedent.

Oliver Jones, as chairman of the committee reporting favorably upon the bill, stated in reply that Everitt's position was erroneous and his apprehensions unfounded. Jones saw that the Constitution undoubtedly contemplated such cases as the one under debate, by giving Congress the power, at its discretion, to allow emancipated blacks to remain in the Republic. He made it clear that he was as much averse to free blacks as any man, and should, except under very extraordinary circumstances, use his best efforts to keep Texas clear of them. This case, however, was one of very extraordinary circumstances. Jones stated that he had known Peter for sixteen years, during which time Peter had engaged in business for himself and accumulated a fortune of perhaps $16,000, and that Peter had always been faithful, honest and humble. Peter's master, he stated, was a kind old man and in gratitude for Peter's fidelity was desirous of setting him free, so that he would not be the slave of another after his present master's death.

Extending democracy to race, Jones declared that justice should be done alike to black, yellow and white, without regard to color; and that since this slave, Peter, had done so much service to the State during her hours of danger and invasion, he hoped the Senate would not deny Peter the right to remain in the Republic he helped to create and defend. He saw no danger in creating a precedent. He did not think the present Congress so much wiser than all future congresses might be, as to believe that its proceedings would be regarded as a controlling example.

George W. Barnett, who was one of the four Congressmen Wiley Martin had asked for special consideration in the postscript to his petition, rose at this point to second Everitt's motion for indefinite postponement of the bill. He remarked that he did so to give time for deliberation, but his further remarks and final vote indicate that he would have been satisfied with an indefinite postponement as a satisfactory final disposition. He stated that he had already often expressed his opposition to free blacks and that he would never vote to emancipate a slave unless to be sent out of the country. Under those circumstances, of course, no vote of Congress would be necessary. Barnett had long known Peter and admitted that he knew his character to be as had been represented. He had, furthermore, taken part in the campaign at Bexar, when Peter had gratuitously furnished supplies to the army, and stated that he was willing to reward Peter doubly for his services, but that he could never consent to a bill allowing Peter to remain in Texas as a free citizen. Interestingly enough, Barnett saw in the very fortune which Peter held, a further danger in his emancipation, as he could, should he choose to interest himself, exert an influence in cooperation with the abolitionists, and so strike at the very roots of Texas' most useful domestic institution, and at the peace and security of Texans and their families.

Francis Moore, Jr., arose to remark that he perceived a very laudable feeling of gratitude had gained the ascendancy over the better judgment of Mr. Jones. Since Jones knew both the slave and his master, Moore thought Jones's support of the bill rather natural. In the evidence that Mr. Jones presented in favor of Peter, particularly in his accumulation of a sizable fortune, Moore was willing to admit that the strongest ground of slaveholders used in refuting the abolitionists, was swept away, because slave-holders had always insisted that slaves and free blacks were incapable of self-support and self-government. Mr. Moore concluded, nevertheless, that if Peter were set free with the privilege of remaining in Texas, upon the grounds of obedience and fidelity, others might claim the same treatment, and failure to get it would cause in them dissatisfaction, insubordination, and finally insurrection. Moore recommended that Peter be emancipated, allowed to go with his fortune to Africa or some other country, but under no circumstances should an example be set so deleterious as that demanded by the act under debate.

The question to postpone the bill was called and defeated by a vote of seven to five. Barnett, Everitt, John A. Greer, Moore, and Beden Stroud voted affirmatively; Burton, John Dunn, Richard Ellis, Oliver Jones, James S. Lester, Harvey Kendrick, and Juan N. Seguin defeated the motion, with Anson Jones not voting and James Gaines absent.

Burton, who was one of the Congressmen from whom Wiley Martin had asked special consideration, summed up the debate, pointed out that the Constitution and the law permitted owners to manumit their slaves only on condition that they were removed from the country, but Mr. Martin wished to emancipate Peter with the privilege of remaining within the country, and that under the circumstances the only course to be pursued was to pass a special law for the relief of this old, humble and faithful slave.

Ellis and Lester, who had not participated in the debate, threw their votes with the five senators in favor of postponement, and the bill was laid on the table by a vote of seven to six, Anson Jones voting with those who wished immediate action.[72]

No further debates on this bill are available, but when it was taken up a few days later, it passed by a vote of nine to three, only Barnett, Moore and Stroud voting against it.[73]

The House Committee on the State of the Republic, reported the bill back to the House with an amendment providing that Wiley Martin enter into good security to the value of one thousand dollars with the chief justice of Fort Bend county, to guarantee that Peter would never become a public charge. The House passed the bill with the amendment which was concurred in by the Senate on December 20, 1839, and the act was duly signed by the president.[74]

Peter was the first emancipated slave allowed to remain within the country, and undoubtedly the favorable action on his petition brought forth a number of similar requests.

But before any action was taken upon the bill emancipating Peter, Cary, who had been a slave of Thomas F. McKinney for ten years, had begun negotiations for the purchase of himself and family, and had started from Galveston to Austin, evidently to plead his own cause.[75]

After a delay of more than a month, Cary arrived in Austin on December 14, 1839,[76] bringing with him a letter from his master, Thomas

F. McKinney. This letter, addressed to Cary, himself, certified that he had
been the slave of McKinney for about ten years during which time he had
been faithful and honest, and that during the Revolution he had been of
much service in carrying expresses. McKinney's letter further stated that
Cary had accumulated means and desired to purchase himself, together
with his wife and child, and that McKinney would be glad if a law was
passed authorizing the purchase and making valid any contracts Cary
might make touching the subject of manumission.[77]

A bill for the purpose of allowing Cary to remain in Texas as a free
man was introduced on December 28, and passed the House on January
2, 1840.[78] On January 10, 1840, Anson Jones, on behalf of the Committee
of the Judiciary, recommended the passage of the Cary bill.[79] On January
22, it was postponed indefinitely on motion of Francis Moore, by a
seven to six vote. Stephen H. Everitt, who we have seen was the first
to speak against the emancipation of slaves, and later voted for the
manumission of Peter, now moved for a reconsideration of the Cary bill,
and by changing his vote passed the bill to a third reading and final
passage on the following day.[80]

A proviso, similar to the amendment attached to the act relieving Peter,
was embodied in the Cary act making it necessary for Cary to post a
bond of one thousand dollars within six months to guarantee the State
against his possible dependency. No provision of the act specifically gave
the right to remain in Texas to Cary's wife and child, and although this
right may have been implied, there is no evidence that Cary's wife and
child were ever freed.[81]

Mrs. Houstoun later met "Captain" Cary in Galveston where she
found him keeping "what is courteously termed, a livery stable." Horses
described as "not very bad," were to be hired from him for half a dollar
including "a sort of carriage." According to Mrs. Houstoun, Cary had
saved up a thousand dollars, a great portion of which he had earned
by hunting deer, and with this money had purchased his freedom. No
mention is made of Cary's wife or child. Mrs. Houstoun describes him

so: "A drunken rascal he was, with a head covered with black wool and shaped like a sugar loaf."[82]

While the bill pertaining to Cary was under consideration, a petition in the form of a bill was received from Sterling McGraw asking permission for the manumission and continued residence in Texas of six slaves, and offering a six thousand dollar deposit with the president of the Republic to guarantee their good conduct. No reasons for the manumission were given and the bill was rejected.[83]

Taking renewed hope from the favorable action taken by the Senate on the bills for the benefit of Peter and Cary, the House again passed upon the petition of Edward Teal granting his slave, Fannie, permission to remain in Texas after manumission, this time in the form of a joint resolution.[84] The concurrence of the Senate was asked and a favorable report of a special committee received by the Senate, but the joint resolution never passed.[85]

On January 25, 1840, the Senate passed a bill to permit Diana Baxter to emancipate Lythe, a colored woman, and her three children. Congress adjourned on February 5, before the House could take any action.[86]

The faithful conduct of a mulatto woman and her five children induced Bartholomew Manlove to promise the woman and her children freedom at the time of his death. The operation of the Constitution and the law prevented him from fulfilling his promise, and he begged Congress to give him its necessary sanction.[87] William Menefee, chairman of the committee on the state of the Republic, after "due reflection" on the part of the committee, reported a bill to the House enabling Rosine and her five children to remain in Texas after manumission.[88] The House passed the bill, but it was indefinitely postponed in the Senate.[89]

On December 9, 1840, Ben Fort Smith, representative from Montgomery County and well-known slave dealer, introduced a bill to enable him to manumit his own slave Mocklin, Mocklin's wife, Pamola, and their three children. The bill was reported back from the committee with a rider, permitting Dr. Samuel Thompson to manumit his slave Cynthia and her daughter Molly together with "all their future increase." No record of the debates on this bill is available, but on a final vote it was rejected by 15 to 14.[90] The bill was recommitted to a select committee which recommended an amendment striking out provision for the manumission of Samuel Thompson's slaves, but the House refused to accept the recommendation and on a clear-cut issue permission to manumit slaves was denied by the House to one of its own members.[91] The Senate disposed of the same bill by laying it on the table to May 10, 1841, at which time Congress was not in session.[92]

Peggy Rankin of Montgomery county, on October 25, 1841, petitioned the Sixth Congress for authorization to manumit her slave, Sinez, together with her three children. The mother of Sinez, when yet a child, had been given to Peggy Rankin by her father, and by her raised. Sinez had been born the property of Peggy Rankin, during the whole of her life had been a faithful and obedient servant, and was remarkably kind and attentive to her mistress in her infirm old age. Peggy Rankin, who was now eighty-six years old, felt that she would not live long and was anxious to reward her slave. Mr. Rankin, who had recently died, had also intended to manumit Sinez, but had delayed action too long. Mrs. Rankin with unintentional humor assured Congress that all of her children were of age. The six of them consented to the manumission of Sinez and were willing to enter into such obligations as might be required by Congress to guarantee that Sinez and her children would never become public charges.[93]

When the bill was introduced into the House, a motion was made to amend it by providing that the slaves manumitted should leave the country three months after manumission. The amendment, of course, defeated the purpose of the bill, but the House did not choose to evade the issue. The amendment was rejected and the bill lost.[94]

This long series of unfavorable consideration to bills for manumission seems to have had the desired result of stopping petitions begging such privilege. For more than three years, apparently, no petitions were received and no bills introduced pertaining to the manumission of slaves.[95]

During the last session of the Texas Congress, a bill authorizing G. H. Harrison and Ann C. Harrison to manumit a black boy, Shadrack, successfully passed the House but was defeated in the Senate,[96] while Edward Teal made a third futile attempt to manumit his slave Fannie.[97]

The last request for the right of manumission submitted to the Texas Congress came from an early settler, Thomas Cox, and holds particular interest. Cox emigrated from Alabama, arriving in Texas in March, 1822. At the time he was thirty-eight years of age and with him he brought his wife Cynthia and one child.[98] In 1845, he was living in Harrison county and from there he petitioned Congress for the right to manumit his two natural children who were slaves. The petition was referred to a select committee which rendered a favorable report and the bill passed the House, but no action was taken in the Senate.[99] Three years later, at which time the number of his children had increased to four, Cox, then sixty-four years of age, wrote a forthright and sincere statement of his peculiar position:

> To the Honorable the senate and House of Representatives of the Legislature of the State of Texas.
>
> Your petitioner would respectfully represent unto your Honorable Body that he is the father of the following children, Lotty, Commodore, Perry and Frederick, who under the Institutions and laws of the Country are Slaves—That since his emigration to this State, now several years, he has done and performed all the duties required of him as a citizen—in no instance disregarding the laws of the Country, or the rules of moral conduct, except, the one which forces him to ask at the hands of your Honorable Body the favor and indulgence herein prayed for — Your petitioner will not attempt a justification of his conduct herein, or enumerate any of the circumstances by which, in consequence of his early settlement in the Country, he was surrounded, and which, were they known, might perhaps, form some excuse for his non-obser-

vance in this behalf of the laws of moral restraint — He sincerely regrets the situation in which he finds these his only children and notwithstanding their position in society, he entertains for them, to its full extent, the attachment of the parent for his offspring — and submits, whether they should be held to the mortification and disadvantages of a situation into which they have been thrown, by no agency of their own, but by the improper action of the authors of their existence.

Your petitioner, therefore most respectfully prays, that, an act be passed by your Honorable Body, allowing him to emancipate said children, promising to bind himself, in any way directed, that they shall not become a public charge —And your petitioner as in duty bound will ever pray &c—

Thomas Cox[100]

On January 28, 1848, Cox's petition was laid on the table where it rests to this day. A self-righteous committee report on a similar petition from William Primm nine days previously was a sufficient answer to Cox's request. It had declared, in part,

The committee have a duty to discharge to the State, and although a *Father* has appealed to their sympathies in behalf of his *children* and although they have no right to control the peculiar taste of any individual, who may regret the unfortunate position in which he placed himself, by the indulgence of his feeling; they do not feel disposed to encourage others, to put themselves in a similar situation. When a man places himself by his own act, in a disagreeable situation, contrary to the laws of the country, in violation of public sentiment, and in opposition to the moral feelings of the people among whom he resides, he ought to bear his misfortunes with the resignation of a martyr, or migrate to a country whose institutions are more in accordance with his situation and feelings.[101]

During the ten years of the Republic, fifteen requests were made for the manumission of thirty-eight slaves. All but two of these requests were refused, although six petitions involving the manumission of fourteen slaves were favorably acted upon by one house of Congress without the concurrence of the other.

Only two slaves were manumitted with the right to remain in Texas.[102] Both favorable actions were taken by the same Congress, the Fourth, but this same session refused three other petitions and only granted the first, Peter's, after a long struggle. The two manumitted slaves, Peter and Cary, were the property of Wiley Martin and Thomas F. McKinney, respectively, both prominent in the public affairs of Texas. Thomas F. McKinney, during the Revolution, was an agent of the provisional government, and had purchased the first vessels for the navy. The firm of McKinney & Williams, of which he was a partner, transacted nearly all the financial business of the Government and later McKinney represented Travis county in the state legislature. Wiley Martin had been an Alcalde in Austin's colony, had raised a company of soldiers and acted as its Captain in the Revolutionary Army, and had served a term as Chief Justice of Fort Bend county. Subsequent to Peter's manumission he was elected a member of Congress.

Both Peter and Cary had demonstrated their ability to govern them-selves, and had accumulated considerable sums of money. Both of them had been of assistance to the State during the Revolution, and both were owned by prominent Texans, who recommended their manumission.

Which of these three qualifications played the greatest part in their manumission, it is difficult to determine, but no other slaves for whom manumission was asked were the property of prominent men, had accumulated fortunes, or been of assistance to the State during the Revolution. Probably all of these facts had some weight in the deliberations of Congress, and apparently Peter and Cary had a better claim and were better qualified to receive their freedom than other candidates.

NOTES

1. We should not, however, accuse the Mexicans of insincerity. This type of ideology based on a blind use of antonyms is not unusual particularly in revolutionary movements for freedom. The Mexicans, at least, were not forced into the rationalization of their northern neighbors that blacks were not of the human species in order to logically exclude them from the benefits of that noble but meaningless proclamation that "all men are created equal."

2. For a full discussion of the status of slavery in Texas from 1821 to 1835, see Eugene C. Barker, "The Influence of Slavery in the Colonization of Texas," in *Southwestern Historical Quarterly*, XXVIII, 1–33.

3. Dublan y Lozano, *Legislacion Mexicana*, I, 339–340.

4. Gammel, *Laws of Texas*, I, 30.

5. Dublan y Lozano, *Legislacion, Mexicana*, I, 710.

6. Juan Antonio Padilla to Austin, June 18, 1825, *Austin Papers*, I, 1135.

7. Erasmo Seguin to Austin, July 24, 1825, *Austin Papers*, I, 1156.

8. Bill and argument concerning slavery, August 18, 1825; Austin to Governor Rafael Gonzales, August 20, 1825, *Austin Papers*, I, 1170, 1180.

9. Bill of Sale for Slaves. *Austin Papers*, I, 969.

10. Quoted by Austin in his memorial to the Legislature, August 11, 1826, *Austin Papers*, I, 1407.

11. Austin to State Congress, August 11, to Padilla, August 12, and to Ayuntamiento of Bexar, August 14, 1826; J. E. B. Austin to Austin, August 22, 1826, September 3, 1826, *Austin Papers*, I, 1407, 1409, 1422, 1430, 1445.

12. Austin to Members of the Legislature, November 20, 1826. *Austin Papers*, I, 1507.

13. The constitution was published May 29, 1827, so that children born of slave parents after that date, and blacks brought to Texas after November 29, 1827, were to be free. Article 13. Gammel, *Laws of Texas*, I, 424.

14. Decree of No. 18. Gammel, *Laws of Texas*, I, 188–189.

15. Austin's argument against law regulating slavery. *Austin Papers*, I, 1716.

16. Decree No. 35. Gammel, *Laws of Texas*, I, 202.

17. Navarro to Austin, May 17; Arciniega to Austin, May 17, 1828. Austin Papers, MS.

18. Decree No. 56, May 5, 1828. Gammel, *Laws of Texas*, I, 213.

19. Copy of a contract prepared by Austin in May, 1828. Austin Papers, MS. In another form the slave agreed to serve the master for a specified term of years which would exceed his lifetime. University of Texas transcripts, Department of Fomento, Mexico, Legajo 7, Expediente 56.

20. Austin to J. M. Fiesta, February 19, 1829. Austin Papers, MS.

21. Indentures as a method of evading emancipation was suggested by Ellis H. Bean [Peter Ellis Bean] in 1826. "But there is a way your Settlers can stop it all [emancipation] But the sooner the Better that is to Gow in Presens of and Alcalde stating that this nigro cost you so much and when he Pays it by labor Don you have no charge against him he Discounts so much a month and other hirid Persons a small sum so that he will be the same to you as Before and it will be no more notised. . . ." *Austin Papers*, I, 1368.

22. Emancipation and indenture contract, February 9, 1933. W. T. Williams Papers, University of Texas Library.

23. Dublan y Lozano, *Legislacion Mexicana*, II, 151.

Governor Viesca to the secretary of state, November 14, 1829. *Texas Gazette*, January 30, 1830.

25. Austin to John Durst, November 17, 1829. Austin Papers, MS.

26. Teran to Elosua, December 18, 1829. General Land Office of Texas, LVII, 130. The correspondence on this subject between Teran and Guerrero has not been located. The contents are partially revealed in a confidential report of the Secretary of State, Lucas Alaman, to a secret session of Congress. *Biographic Necrologica del Exmo. Señor Lucas Alaman, apendice al tomo primero del Diccionario Universal de historia y geographic,* 49–50. The exception was officially confirmed on December 2, in a letter from the secretary of relations to the Governor, December 2, 1829. General Land Office of Texas, LVII, 131. Alaman's confidential report was the basis for the new colonization law of April 6, 1830. This law confirmed slavery legislation already passed, but made no new provisions. Dublan y Lozano, *Legislacion Mexicana,* II, 238–240.

27. Articles 35 and 36, Decree No. 190. Gammel, *Laws of Texas,* I, 303.

28. Gammel, *Laws of Texas,* I, 1079.

29. Gammel, *Laws of Texas,* I, 896.

30. Gammel, *Laws of Texas,* I, 872.

31. Compare Guess v. Lubbock, 5 *Texas* 535.

32. Arnold v. Martin, Supreme Court Records, Austin. This case has never been published. Austin's Colonists, I, 53. State Land Office, Austin.

33. Arnold v. Martin. Joint Resolution No. 43, File 47. Papers of the Third Legislature.

34. Hendrick owned and transferred property in a slave, petitioned the General Council, and his name was entered on the muster rolls of the Volunteer Army. Holly applied to Austin for a league of land. Memorial No. 4, File 1; Comptroller's Military Service Records; Stephen F. Austin's Application Book, II, 75.

35. Arnold v. Martin. Joint Resolution No. 43, File 47; Papers of the Third Legislature; *House Journal,* Third Legislature, 422.

36. See chapter II, "The Free Negro and the Texas Revolution," in *Southwestern Historical Quarterly*, XL, 26. Joint Resolution 43, File 47, Papers of the Third Legislature.

37. Memorial No. 4, File 1, January 4, 1836; Proceedings of the General Council in Gammel, *Laws of Texas*, I, 750-751; Arnold v. Martin.

38. *House Journal*, Third Legislature, 385.

39. *House Journal*, Third Legislature, 473.

40. The Legislature adjourned February 11. Joint Resolution No. 43, File 47. Papers of the Third Legislature.

41. George M. Martin to Col. Thomas W. Chambers, September 10, 1851. Chambers Papers, University of Texas Library.

42. The constitution of Coahuila and Texas promulgated on May 29, 1827, declared free all children of slaves born after that date. Article 13. Gammel, *Laws of Texas*, I, 424.

43. Arnold v. Martin.

44. Supreme Court Minutes, Austin Sessions 1849-1856, Arnold v. Martin.

45. House Bill No. 54, File 60. Papers of the Fourth Legislature, Extra Session.

46. *House Journal*, Fourth Legislature, Extra Session, 87.

47. Gammel, *Laws of Texas*, II, 648.

48. General Provisions, Sec. 9. Gammel, *Laws of Texas*, I, 1079.

49. The details of this bill are not revealed in the Congressional Papers nor in the *Journal*. *House Journal*, Fourth Congress, 193, 208, 212, 228, 285, 288, 310; Congressional Papers, Fourth Congress, No. 1367, File 15; The relief laws of the Fourth Congress do not appear in Gammel's *Laws of Texas*. See Harriet Smither (editor), *Reports and Relief Laws*, published as volume III of *Journals of the Fourth Congress of the Republic of Texas, 1839–1840*, to which are added the relief laws, 249.

50. Guess v. Lubbock, 5 *Texas* 535.

51. Guess v. Lubbock, 5 *Texas* 535.

52. Article 13, Constitution of Coahuila and Texas. Gammel, *Laws of Texas,* I, 424.

53. Decree No. 56. Gammel, *Laws of Texas,* I, 213.

54. Memorial No. 102, File 67, October 29, 1841.

55. Constitution of the State of Coahuila and Texas, 1827, Article 13: From and after the promulgation of the constitution in the capital of each district, no one shall be born a slave in the state, and after six months the introduction of slaves shall not be permitted. Gammel, *Laws of Texas,* I, 424.

56. Committee Reports, Sixth Congress.

57. No further reference in the Congressional Records or *Journals* have been found, and Gammel's *Laws of Texas* records no *act* recognizing the status of Peggy and Rose as free persons of color.

58. Gammel, *Laws of Texas,* I, 1079.

59. Memorial No. 101, File 67.

60. *House Journal,* Fifth Congress, 35, 93. Gammel, *Laws of Texas,* II, 468.

61. Memorial No. 6, File W, October 15, 1838.

62. *House Journal,* Third Congress, 54, 57.

63. *House Journal,* Third Congress, 57.

64. This petition has not been found.

65. *House Journal,* Third Congress, 372.

66. *Senate Journal,* Third Congress, 118.

67. Evidently George W. Barnett.

68. Apparently Major I. W. Burton, senator from Nacogdoches and Houston, and Major William Lawrence, representative from Harrisburg, both members of the Fourth Congress.

69. Memorial No. 22, File 59.

70. Harriet Smither (editor), *Senate Journal,* Fourth Congress, 55, 56, 57.

71. Committee Reports, Fourth Congress. A report of Peter's services at the time appeared in the *Telegraph, and Texas Register,* March 5, 1836.

72. *Austin City Gazette,* December 25, 1839.

73. *Senate Journal,* Fourth Congress, 74, 80.

74. Congressional Papers, Fourth Congress, No. 1272, File 13. *House Journal,* Fourth Congress, 86, 91, 150. *Senate Journal,* Fourth Congress, 143, 159. Harriet Smither (editor), *Reports and Relief Laws,* 231–232.

75. Thomas F. McKinney to Samuel M. Williams, November 11, 1839. Williams Papers, Rosenberg Library, Galveston, Texas.

76. Samuel M. Williams to Mrs. P. Williams, December 14, 1839. Williams Papers, Rosenberg Library, Galveston, Texas.

77. Thomas F. McKinney to Cary, November 11, 1839. Williams Papers, Rosenberg Library, Galveston, Texas.

78. *House Journal,* Fourth Congress, 235, 254, 259, 305.

79. The Albert Mitchell bill, already referred to, was recommended for passage at the same time. A third bill granting permission to James Young, a free black, to remain in Texas was also recommended. James Young was not, however, a manumitted slave, and his case is reserved for a subsequent chapter. Committee Reports, Fourth Congress, No. 1367, File 15.

80. *Senate Journal,* Fourth Congress, 193, 199, 208, 212, 228, 229, 285, 288, 310. Harriet Smither (editor), *Reports and Relief Laws,* 238.

81. Congressional Papers, Fourth Congress, No. 1367, File 15.

82. Mrs. [M. C.] Houstoun, *Texas and the Gulf of Mexico or Yachting in the New World,* I, 291-295.

83. Congressional Papers, Fourth Congress, No. 1269, File 14.

84. *House Journal,* Fourth Congress, 265, 268, 271.

85. The exact disposition of the bill is unknown *Senate Journal,* Fourth Congress, 270. Committee Reports, Fourth Congress.

86. This bill not been found. The Senate as a committee of the whole amended the bill on January 24, before passing it to a third reading. The nature of the amendment is unknown. *Senate Journal,* Fourth Congress, 233, 237, 292, 296.

87. Memorial No. 54, File 60, November 9, 1840.

88. Committee Reports, Fifth Congress, No. 2200, File 23. Congressional Papers, Fifth Congress, No. 1628, File 18.

89. *House Journal,* Fifth Congress, 155, 172, 189. *Senate Journal,* Fifth Congress, 78, 80. Congressional Papers, Fifth Congress, No. 1705, File 19.

90. Congressional Papers, Fifth Congress, No. 2036, File 22. *House Journal,* Fifth Congress, 222, 376, 496, 550, 583, 592.

91. *House Journal,* Fifth Congress, 550, 583.

92. *Senate Journal,* Fifth Congress, 187.

93. Memorial No. 28, File 75, October 25, 1841

94. Congressional Papers, Sixth Congress, No. 2336, File 25.

95. No entries have been found in the *House Journals* or *Senate Journals* for the seventh or eighth congresses, and no petitions or bills have been discovered in the Congressional Papers for those same sessions.

96. Congressional Papers, Ninth Congress, No. 2939, File 32. *Senate Journal,* Ninth Congress, 205.

97. *House Journal,* Ninth Congress, 329.

98. Austin's Colonists, I, 44.

99. This petition has not been found. Congressional Papers, Ninth Congress, No. 2972, File 32. *House Journal,* Ninth Congress, 202.

100. Memorial No. 63, File 15, January 11, 1848.

101. *Senate Journal,* Second Legislature, 176.

102. Slaves who were manumitted and sent out of Texas, for the most part, would leave no records behind them, if indeed, there were any. Some rejected petitioners may have arranged for the transportation of manumitted slaves who were denied residence in Texas, but because of the obvious difficulties this was not likely. Monroe Edwards, the slave trader, published a statement in the Northern papers that he had manumitted all his slaves in Texas. No evidence exists that he owned a single slave in Texas at the time, but if his statement was true, he had necessarily removed the slaves from Texas shortly after manumission. *Telegraph and Texas Register,* July 8, 1840.

4

LEGAL STATUS

Harold R. Schoen

The Mexican government in Texas recognized two social classes, the free citizen and the slave. The Republic of Texas added to these a third, free persons of color, and established for them a separate and distinct legal status. These persons of color were defined, in an act which incapacitated them from testifying in court except against each other, as persons with one-eighth or more black blood.[1] Actually, not all persons with this degree of admixture complied with the regulations enacted to govern free blacks. Some Mexicans, doubtless, had larger fractions of black blood coursing in their veins, yet all of them retained their status as free white persons.[2] Some blacks, like Thomas Cevallos, lived in the Republic during the ten years of its existence and were only brought under free black regulations by the state government which succeeded the Republic upon annexation to the United States.[3] Others, actually free, retained their slave status under benevolent masters, in many cases their own fathers, and only found it necessary to claim their true status upon the death or approaching old age of their masters.[4] Still others denied their black ancestry, among them a daughter of William Primm married to David L. Wood, both white men. Wood, in the impersonal third person, tells his own story.

> "In the fervour and integrity of his heart, and in conformity to the usages of all the civilized world, he espoused and married a wife (the daughter of William Primm of Fayette County) to be his bosom companion and the co-partner of his future destiny. By doing which he was not aware that he was rendering himself obnoxious to any law whatever; but rather that he was obeying the divine precepts and laws of morality. But, in the midst of all his expectations of future happiness he was assailed by the grand jury, and a bill of indictment found against him, upon less than a shadow of testimony (an incompetent witness) that his wife was of African descent."[5]

Wood prayed that Congress might place him "beyond the reach of any future attempts against his private peace and happiness by passing an act to legalize his marriage, lest he should be driven by the spirit of persecution to seek a home with his wife in a foreign land, where they would be as exiles from the society of all those who are most dear to them in life." Wood may have been ignorant of his wife's descent, or he may have been technically right in asserting that she was a white woman. Certainly she must have been nearly white in order for him to make the claim, and perhaps she had less than one-eighth black blood. But however remote her African ancestry, subsequent testimony by her own father proves she was born a slave and legally remained one.[6]

The difficulty of accurately determining the proportion of black blood, which might easily run into sixteenths and thirty-seconds, in a class of people who were generally ignorant of their ancestry is assurance that the legal definition could not have been strictly obeyed. The status of a person with remote African progenitors depended upon his ability and desire to pass as a white man, rather than upon a mathematical calculation.

Consequently, persons with more or less than the legal proportion of black blood could be found on both sides of the theoretical color line.

The first legislation which segregated the free black as a special class, even before a black was legally defined, was an emergency act passed by the provisional government shortly after the outbreak of the Texas Revolution. This came about in response to a letter from the Beaumont committee of safety urging upon the General Council the necessity of adopting some measures to prevent the immigration of free blacks to Texas. In the absence of this letter[7] we can only surmise the fears which led the committee in the midst of a revolution to recommend restrictions on what must have been an insignificant migration of free blacks. Particularly after the insurrections led by Denmark Vesey in South Carolina and Nat Turner in Virginia, preventive measures against repetitions were considered to be a public concern. These uprisings left an ineradicable distrust of free blacks, created a desire to keep the country clear of them, and cast suspicion over all their movements.

Even in peaceful times the danger of insurrections was always present. Plantation rules restricting movements and activities of slaves were in part based upon this fear, and Austin's amendment to a law of Coahuila and Texas to prevent the manumission of slaves of a master who "died in any unnatural way" was a tacit admission that slaves might murder their masters in order to gain their freedom.[8] How much did the danger increase with the approach of the Mexican army? Rumor at least had it that the Mexicans intended to free the slaves, and a broadside addressed to the public declared it to be the intention of the Mexican government to "put their slaves free and let them loose upon their families."[9] Anglo-Americans began to put the question to one another, "Would there not be a great danger from the blacks should a large Mexican force come so near?"[10]

The question proved to be not an idle one. In the middle of October, a week after the battle of Goliad, B. J. White reported from that place to Stephen F. Austin, recently elected commander-in-chief, that "the blacks on Brazos made an attempt to rise." Major Sutherland came to Goliad to take a few soldiers back with him to preserve order which apparently had been restored. Nearly one hundred Blacks who were believed to be implicated in the plot, "had been taken up many whipped nearly to death some hung, etc." According to White's report, an elaborate plan had been adopted contingent upon the success of the revolt. "The blacks above alluded to had divided all the cotton farms and they intended to ship the cotton to New Orleans and make the white men serve them in turn."[11]

The direct connection of a free black with the insurrection was apparently not established, but a day previous to the report of the uprising, the Permanent Council had given Captain Stephen Miller "an order to arrest Bob (a free black) alive if possible or dead if it be impracticable to take him alive—he having made violent threats against the whites."[12] Bob was never brought before the Council for trial, but his threats against the whites immediately previous to the insurrection might easily have been considered more than a coincidence. Nor was the General Council unaware of the presence in Texas of dangerous free blacks. On December 11, it gave orders to Captain Miller to arrest "one William Francis a colored man and bring him forthwith before this council on a charge of high crimes and misdemeanors."[13]

When the General Council received the recommendations of the Beaumont committee of safety it was "strongly impressed with the necessity of adopting some measures as recommended in said letter to prevent the importation and emigration of free blacks and mulattoes into Texas." The committee report looking forward to an independence which had not yet been declared continued to lay down what was to become the settled policy of the Republic:

> the residence of such free blacks and mulattoes among us, would prove an evil difficult to be remedied should it once be tolerated. To the slave-holder nothing could be of deeper interest than the timely adoption of some measures that will prove effectually preventive of a course so much to be dreaded in a country, whose

soil, from the nature of its productions must be cultivated by slave labor. The infusion of dissatisfaction, and disobedience into the brain of the honest and contented slave, by vagabond free blacks, who, denied the society of whites, from necessity or choice, associate with persons of their own color, can not be too promptly and strongly guarded against.[14]

The report was eminently unfair to many free blacks who, at the time it was made, had already proved their devotion to the Texan cause. Samuel McCullough and Greenbury Logan had been crippled in action; Hendrick Arnold had taken a leading part in the storming of Bexar; Peter Allen was just then making his long journey from Pennsylvania to meet his death with Fannin; William Goyans had been of considerable aid to Houston on his mission to placate the Indians; and many other blacks had generously contributed money, food, equipment and supplies to the cause.[15] These facts could hardly have been known to the Council in the confused conduct of the war, but probably the imminent danger of insurrection, if it was thought to exist, would have outweighed consideration for a handful of soldiers and a basket of provisions.

On January 5, 1836, four days after the committee made its report, the General Council passed an ordinance and decree to prevent the importation and immigration of free blacks and mulattoes into Texas. This act made it illegal for any free black to come within its limits on penalty of being sold into slavery to the highest bidder at public auction. To enforce the decree every citizen of Texas was made a deputy, one-third of the proceeds from the sales of apprehended blacks was to be paid to the arresting citizen and the remainder to the State treasury. A fine of five thousand dollars (or imprisonment until the fine was paid) was to be imposed upon all persons bringing, aiding or inducing free blacks into Texas. The new law was ordered to be "regularly given in charge to Grand Juries throughout Texas," and was to be inserted three times in the New Orleans *Bulletin.*[16]

Although this ordinance was violated,[17] there were no prosecutions between January and September, 1836, when the ordinances of the provisional government were superseded by the constitution of the Republic of Texas.

The first draft reported to the convention at Washington by the committee to frame the Constitution, excepted only slaves and Indians from the franchise and would have entitled free blacks resident in Texas on the day of the declaration of independence to all the rights and privileges of citizenship.[18] But this was an oversight soon to be corrected. An amendment offered by George C. Childress, of Milam, providing that no free person of color should ever be permitted to reside in the Republic, was rejected.[19] The final provision, appearing in the Constitution as section 10, barred "Africans, the descendants of Africans and Indians" from citizenship.[20] The exclusion of blacks from the privileges of citizenship threw considerable doubt upon their right to hold property already acquired, upon the claims of black veterans to bounty lands for service in the Revolution, and upon the prerogative of black residents to headrights. The ninth provision of the Constitution made it necessary for all free blacks to apply to Congress for the right to make their residence "permanent," a vague term which was never clarified.[21]

The adoption of the Constitution left the free blacks with three main grievances: (1) citizenship which they had previously held was denied; (2) property rights were insecure, and (3) residence could not be permanently continued without Congressional consent. These three complaints singly and in combination became the subjects of numerous petitions praying for relief. The first of these rather naturally came from the veterans of the war, who, by their participation in the battles which resulted in the establishment of the Republic, had a strong claim for special consideration.

John Bird and his son, Henry, prepared a petition two weeks previous to the convening of the first Congress, in which they outlined their peculiar position and the injustice which would accrue to them unless they were excepted from the constitutional regulations. Both of them were men of families who had emigrated and settled in Texas, believing they would be received as citizens under the colonization laws of Mexico, "but as we are colored people . . . doubt may exist [as to our rights] altho we emigrated prior to the Constitution." They asked for a special act granting them citizenship; and requiring the land commissioner to order a survey of the land upon which they settled, and confirm to each title to a league and labor of land, to which they were entitled by the Mexican colonization law. Henry Bird set forth his service in the army as a volunteer, "for which he has an honorable discharge," and added that "he finds himself ever ready to meet the enemies of Texas—when called on to do so."[22]

This petition was referred to the House committee on public lands who reported that they were of the opinion "that part of their petition is reasonable and ought to be granted." Reviewing the constitutional provisions, the report continued, "Without giving our opinion of the justice or policy of that provision, we think, in cases where we are satisfied that they are honest, industrious, and peaceable persons, that the congress ought, at least, to let them remain in this country, as long as they remain so." Taking up the particular merits of John and Henry Bird, the report continued, "One of them is too old to do military duty; the other has served a tour of duty in the volunteer army, and has an honorable discharge from his captain, and both produce testimonials of good character."[23]

The committee could not constitutionally recommend citizenship for the Birds but by reporting that part of the petition was reasonable, and omitting any reference to the land titles which were sought, their unstated conclusion was that the appeal by free blacks for the right to hold land was unreasonable. In consideration of the facts and philosophy uncovered by this report, the committee contented itself to recommend the passage of a resolution permitting John and Henry Bird to reside in Texas "during their natural lives, provided they do and perform all things which may be required of them by the laws of the republic."[24]

This resolution was read a first time on December 2, 1836, and ordered to be read again "tomorrow," but it seems to have been one of those tomorrows that never came.[25]

The question of black rights, however, was not to be answered with quiescence; additional petitions on the subject arrived in quick succession. Previous to the Revolution, Greenbury Logan had worked at his trade as a blacksmith. A wound in his right arm had incapacitated him and after his discharge from the army, thirty-eight years of age and "infirm in body," he and his wife opened a boarding house in Brazoria in order to gain a livelihood. Logan "had hoped that after the zeal and patriotism evinced in fighting for his adopted country, and his willingness to shed his blood in a cause so glorious, he might be allowed the privileges of spending the remainder of his days in quiet and peace." In a petition addressed to Congress for the purpose of gaining these ends, Logan outlined his military service with a note to the effect that Colonel W. G. Hill and Captain William T. Austin could certify to the truth of his statements. Twenty-three prominent Texans, including Henry Austin, endorsed his petition[26] which received prompt attention from Congress when it met in an adjourned session in Houston, in May. Colonel Hill, now senator, introduced the petition on May 15, and was made chairman of a special committee to examine its merits.[27] "In consideration of the good character, respectability and honesty of said Greenbury Logan, as well as of his various services in and for this Republic," the committee recommended that he and his wife, Caroline, be "authorized to remain permanently and enjoy all the rights, priviliages [sic] and immunities of free Citizens," with the proviso, "so far as compatible with the Laws and constitution of the Republic."[28] No opposition to the bill was voiced, making possible a suspension of the rules and passage of the bill on the day of its first reading.[29] A message was immediately sent to the House informing that body of the Senate's action.[30] The House, meanwhile, had received petitions from William D. Stewart praying for land and residence rights, and from James Richardson, begging the privilege of remaining in Texas.[31] The committee on the judiciary to whom these petitions had been referred, recommended an inclusive joint resolution allowing all free blacks who were residing within the Republic at the time of the adoption of the Constitution "the privilege of remaining in any part of the republic, as long as they choose, on the condition of performing all the duties required of them by law."[32] Upon second reading in the House, it was amended by striking out "time of the adoption of the constitution," and inserting "date of the declaration of independence."[33] A further amendment to extend the privilege of residence to the "natural issue" of all free blacks who might be granted the residence privilege was accepted.[34] With these amendments the joint resolution passed in the House with an unrecorded vote, in the Senate by a vote of seven to three, and was approved and signed by President Houston on June 5, 1837.[35]

While this resolution was pending in the Senate, another petition begging special privileges was received in the House from the pen of Samuel McCullough, Jr., also a veteran of the war. McCullough outlined his services in the army, and stated that under the laws of Mexico he had been a citizen but that he had never made application for any land. Since the war he had "by marriage become the head of a family" and "desirous of settling in life and performing the duties of a citizen; but he unhappily finds that by the Laws of the Country, for the Independence of which he has fought and bled, and still suffers, he is deprived of citizenship by reason of an unfortunate admixture of African blood, which he is said, without any fault of his, to inherit from a remote maternal ancestor." Since he could not receive the land to which he believed himself entitled "without the beneficent action of Congress," he prayed for that action and for the privilege of remaining in Texas with his children.[36] A day previous to the final passage of the joint resolution, the committee on claims and accounts, to whom McCullough's petition was referred, "deeming it impossible to take any action on the petition ask[ed] to be discharged from its further consideration."[37] Since the House had already passed an inclusive resolution which gave McCullough the right of permanent residence, the committee in fact rejected his plea for land and citizenship, but not for residence rights.

Thus by June 5, 1837, all free blacks resident in Texas previous to the declaration of independence could legally remain; their right to hold, possess and convey property must yet be established. Free blacks who immigrated subsequent to the declaration of independence must first establish the privilege of permanent residence. The barrage of petitions had just begun.

Lewis B. Jones petitioned Congress on October 8, 1837, complaining that by reason of his black blood he found himself "barred by the Constitution of the Republic from exercising the privileges of a Citizen." He had, to be sure, been granted the right to remain in the Republic, but he had not received title to a league of land granted to him by Austin on March 25, 1831, and he was barred by the operation of the law from receiving title, although he had selected and settled his land and was "in peacible possession for three years from 1834" to the date of his petition. No action was taken by Congress at this time to clear his title.[38]

Edmund J. Carter, "a man of family," emigrated from Carowee county, Arkansas, to Red River county in Texas during the latter part of 1837. Under the law it was necessary for him to secure from Congress the right to remain permanently. Carter, however, was not so modest as to request the least. He asked that he be given the right "to enjoy unmolested the privileges of a citizen so fer as to be portected by the Laws of the Country and to Hold Land and other property." Fifty-five citizens of Arkansas endorsed the request of this "well disposed Industrious man" and believed him to be "fully Competent to discharge faithfully any of the privileges of citizen Ship." In addition, forty citizens of Red River county, in Texas, prayed that "he be entitled to the privileges of citizenship." Together with these two petitions, he sent to Congress an honorable dismissal from the "baptist Church of Christ at new hope" which was effective as soon as he was "joined to another Church of the Same faith." This imposing array of secular and ecclesiastical testimonials made no impression upon Congress, and his plea was ignored.[39]

The sitio of land which Jean Baptiste Maturin had received in Nacogdoches county by grant of the Mexican government had never been
surveyed, and he had "never been formally put in possession thereof in
the manner in which the laws then required, as of right he might have
been." His title to the land was therefore imperfect, and under the then
existing laws, inoperative. He would suffer great wrong if deprived of
his property, upon which he had lived for fifteen years, so supporting
his "wife and numerous family of children," and he appealed to "the
dictates of *Justice* and enlightened *benevolence* which ever influence the
deliberations of your Honorable Body" for a "full and perfect title in *fee*
simple." Twenty-five citizens of Nacogdoches county signed the petition
with Maturin, but without affecting the "enlightened *benevolence*" of
Congress.[40]

Nelson Kavanaugh had been manumitted in Richmond, Kentucky,
in the spring of 1837, coming to Houston soon afterwards. He was a
single man, "without wife or children," and "a barber by profession." He
asked Congress for "the privilege of residing permanently in the Republic
& providing for his holding such property as his industry and honest
endeavor may enable him to acquire." He claimed to have "Testimonials
from many of the most respectable gentlemen of Texas who have honored
me with their names," and went so far as to say that he was "no friend
of the abolitionists who he is well aware, more than even the ill conduct
of some of his colour and condition, have drawn down upon us the
ban of the Republic." Memucan Hunt, James Reily, and Robert Wilson
believed that he was "worthy of exemption, should be allowed most of
the privileges of a white man, such as holding real estate, suing and
being sued." Only a second judgment induced the crossing out of "and
the right to swear in court." Kavanaugh's petition, despite the high praise
accorded him by "many of the most respectable gentlemen of Texas,"
was rejected by the judiciary committee to whom it was referred.[41]

At the adjourned session of the second Congress, in 1838, Senator
I. W. Burton presented the petition of William Goyans, praying for a

headright.[42] Two days later, on May 23, the petition was referred to a select committee, which on the same day made a report in the form of a bill authorizing William Goyans to apply to the land commission and secure a certificate for a league and labor of land upon proof of residence, marriage and emigration previous to the declaration of independence and adherence to the government during the campaign of 1836. The bill was amended to give the same rights to Jeremiah Goen of Jefferson county, and John Bird, Henry Bird and Edward Smith of San Augustine county. In an effort to rush the bill through before adjournment, which was set for the following day, the rules were suspended and the bill passed.[43] It was immediately sent to the House, but that body refused to be rushed into a decision and adjourned without taking any action. No property rights were guaranteed to free blacks at this time.

Two petitions had been received from blacks who had immigrated subsequent to the declaration of independence, one of which was apparently ignored, and the other definitely rejected. Although the policy of the government towards early black settlers was becoming more liberal as evidenced by the joint resolution of June 6, 1837, and the willingness of the Senate in May of the following year to grant them headrights, no official encouragement was given to further immigration of free blacks. Individually, they did receive positive encouragement from their patrons and employers, as is evidenced by the endorsers of the petitions of Edmund J. Carter and Nelson Kavanaugh.[44] Negative encouragement was officially given to new arrivals in two ways. First, the Constitution provided that no free black could reside "permanently" in the Republic without the consent of Congress. Thus, a black who was visiting his friends or relatives could claim that his residence was temporary, although his stay might be extended for years. Second, although the Constitution forbade permanent residence, no penalties had been imposed and no enforcing agent named.

The third Congress, in 1838, attempted to remedy these defects. The session was hardly a week old, when a bill was introduced requiring all free blacks who had immigrated to Texas subsequent to the declaration of independence to quit the country within sixty days. The sheriffs were ordered by the provisions of this bill, to arrest all violators and sell them into slavery to the highest bidder.[45]

Before this bill could be submitted to a vote, it was substituted by another, less harsh, but calculated to effect the same result. This bill provided that all free blacks who had migrated to Texas after the declaration of independence must leave the country or post a satisfactory bond within four months to guarantee removal. Failure to post bond prohibited further residence, making removal necessary before the expiration of an additional sixty days, at which time a warrant would be issued, the offending black arrested, and sold into slavery for twelve months at public auction for cash to the highest bidder. On failure to leave the country sixty days after his release from twelve months of slavery, a second arrest would result in his sale into slavery for a period of five years. If the black failed to remove himself from Texas within sixty days after his second release, at a third auction he would be sold into slavery for life.[46] This bill passed the Senate on December 21, 1838, but was indefinitely postponed in the House eight days later, and never revived.[47]

Nine days later the House, by a vote of 19 to 11, was willing to permit William Gladden and Burril Coleman, two newly arrived blacks, to remain permanently in Texas.[48] The committee to whom their petitions were referred reported that they had satisfactory evidence that these two blacks were "of good moral character, and very useful to the community." The report continued that "notwithstanding the right . . . vested in Congress by the constitution to grant the prayer of said petitioners, they would not recommend it in ordinary cases, but from the peculiar facts of this case your committee would recommend . . ." that these blacks be permitted to remain.[49] Congress adjourned on January 24, 1839, before any action was taken in the Senate.

The failure of the third Congress to provide legislation which would rid the country of late black immigrants, left the problem in the hands of the local communities. The largest center of population, both black and white, at the time was Houston. Here the white laborer was brought into direct competition with the black, in which he usually lost the contest, for the reason that the black's standard of living was lower and he was willing to do more work for less wages. Social contacts between the races, moreover, were closer and more frequent in the cities, and racial prejudices keener than in the rural districts.[50] Francis Moore, Jr., was at this time mayor of Houston. He had often shown his antagonism to the free black class and as a senator had expressed his fear lest the extension of privilege to free blacks would result in "dissatisfaction, insubordination, and finally insurrection" among the slaves.[51] It is reasonable to suppose that Moore lent his office to any move which would rid Texas of this great danger.

Searching about for some act under which free blacks might be prosecuted, the ordinance of the General Consultation of January 5, 1836, was resuscitated. This ordinance provided for the sale into slavery of all free blacks who immigrated to Texas subsequent to the passage of the act, and was similar in most respects to the bill which Congress had failed to pass during its last session.[52]

On April 9, 1839, between eight and twenty blacks were brought before the Recorder's Court by constable McGee as violaters of this Ordinance.[53] Beyond a doubt, it had been superseded by the Constitution, which placed no restriction on immigration, and the joint resolution of June 5, 1837, which granted residence privileges to all blacks living in Texas on March 2, 1836. Further evidence that the ordinance was a dead letter lies in the fact that two congresses had considered bills similar to the ordinance and defeated them. A reporter of the trial, obviously hostile to the free black man, admitted the invalidity of the ordinance of the General Consultation when he said:

> This Ordinance of the General Consultation has never been attempted to be put in execution since its passage to the present time—and probably would have remained inoperative but for the rapidly growing evil of a free black population, particularly within

this City. It has become known to the magistrate that there are some thirty or forty persons of this description within the limits of the Corporation, prowling about with no ostensible means of subsistence; and, as a necessary consequence, corrupting and rendering turbulent and dissatisfied the slaves among whom they associate.

That *free blacks* are a very serious evil when suffered to commingle with slaves, is a truth known and admitted by all anywise conversant with the institution of slavery. It was a wise and judicious foresight of those composing the Consultation to embrace that early period of the political existence of the Republic, to take strong and efficient measures to prevent forever the existence of so great a curse.[54]

At the trial, S. S. Tompkins, A. M. Tompkins, and Henry Thompson, counsel for the black defendants, based their plea on constitutional grounds, denying the competency of the court to try the case. The tenth article of the Constitution, by excepting Africans and the descendants of Africans from citizenship recognized their existence within the State and according to the defence, "was intended to be a repeal of the Ordinance which had been previously enacted by the Consultation." The prosecution argued that, quite to the contrary, the ninth article of the Constitution requiring the consent of Congress to the permanent residence of blacks within the Republic, was "predicated upon, and was drawn up with a view not to conflict with the previous act of the Consultation."[55]

One of the defence counsel argued that the ninth article of the Constitution did not strengthen the previous act, inasmuch as "it was susceptible of being construed *into an invitation held out to free blacks to emigrate to the Republic!—For,*' said he, 'how can they petition Congress for permission to remain, unless they first emigrate to the country?'" Finally, the defense urged upon the Court that the Constitution having been created subsequent to the Consultation did away with all its acts, and that no law in existence would authorize the sale of free blacks into slavery. The Court, after some deliberation, dismissed the black defendants on the ground that it was incompetent of jurisdiction. The prosecution, dissatisfied with the decision, signified its intention of bringing the case before another magistrate with a view of *appealing* to the District Court.[56]

Frustrated by their defeat in the Court, the Houston city council immediately passed a rash ordinance, which, contrary to the provisions of the Consultation, the Constitution, and the laws of the national government, provided:

> That if any person of African descent, in whole or in part, be found within the city of Houston at the expiration of thirty days after the publication of this Ordinance, it shall be the duty of the City Constable to arrest said person or persons, and take them before the District Judge of the second judicial district, to be dealt with according to law.[57]

The thirty days expired but the blacks remained, further evidence that they were not foot-loose vagabonds or guilty culprits who would flee the city to avoid arrest and prosecution. A few weeks after the termination of this period of grace, the Grand Jury returned an indictment against "the free Blacks residing in Harrisburg county, contrary to the provisions of the ordinance passed by the Consultation, and contrary to the express declaration of the Constitution."[58] The Recorder's Court had declared the ordinance of the Consultation voided by the Constitution and the laws adopted by the Republic, and while this decision was in no way final, it was well grounded and never reversed. By the provisions of the Constitution an indictment would not lie against blacks who immigrated previous to the declaration of independence. No law existed which prevented free blacks immigrating to Texas and remaining within the country so long as their residence, lacking the consent of Congress, did not become "permanent." The Grand Jury presentment, to conform with the law, should have presented the names of free blacks who immigrated subsequent to the declaration of independence with evidence that they had made their residence permanent without the consent of Congress. Since this offence was not punishable under the laws of the Republic, the

Grand Jury introduced the ordinance of the Consultation which punished illegal residence by sale into slavery. The view that the ordinance of the Consultation was still in force might well have been taken. In that case the Grand Jury should have presented the names of blacks who had immigrated subsequent to January 5, 1836. It was sworn "to enquire of, and present all treasons, murders, felonies and other misdemeanors whatsoever" committed within the county.[59] If any blacks had committed offences in addition to illegal residence, indictments should have been returned against each black person separately, together with the evidence resulting from the Grand Jury inquiry.

That the Grand Jury did none of these things, but resorted to a blanket charge against all free blacks as a class, raises a strong presumption that they were aware the evidence and the law did not exist which would justify the extermination of the free black population upon which they were evidently intent. The mass of sweeping generalities contained in the presentment falls conveniently into six broad indictments.

The first charge, that "as a population they are worse than useless since they neither perform any productive labor nor exercise reputable callings" and that they were indolent and dishonest cannot be taken seriously in view of the multitude of petitions signed by numerous Texans who certified to the reputable callings in which many of them were engaged, and who wished to have blacks residing permanently near them, chiefly on the grounds that they were honest and industrious and performed productive labor.

The second charge, that "with scarcely an exception, they are addicted to vice and commission of petty crimes" is entirely unsupported in the indictment and in the facts so far as we know them. Crimes committed by free blacks in the Republic are most conspicuous by their apparent infrequency. Newspaper reports of crimes committed by them are rare and it is reasonable to suppose that crimes themselves were few. Only three offences are contained in the newspaper files of the Republic previous to the date of the indictment. On May 2, 1837, Texans were warned against harboring Thomas Beale, a free black who had enlisted as a seaman on board the *Brutus* and had deserted his ship,[60] but two weeks previous to Beale's desertion, S. Rhoads Fisher, Secretary of the Navy, described conditions aboard the schooner as "miserable" and reported that rations would not last more than two weeks.[61] In the one available payroll report of the *Brutus,* nine desertions are recorded between August 30 and October 16, 1837.[62] Beale's disappearance simultaneously with the food supply may have been more than a coincidence.

One case of some free blacks allegedly harboring a runaway slave is gained from an advertisement inserted in the *Telegraph.* Leander H. M'Neel offered one hundred dollars reward for the return of his twenty-five-year-old slave, Buck. "He run off from me about a month ago and was caught in Houston where he was harbored by some free blacks."[63] The fact that the indictment did not list any offence of this kind throws some doubt upon its truth.

A street brawl between two blacks, humorously reported in the newspaper, indicates that such events were neither frequent nor serious.

> An Affair of Honor—A black barber of this city [Houston] recently received a challenge from a "colored gemman," but being ignorant of the *"code of honor,"* he neglected to make "l'amende honorable" to the satisfaction of his opponent, a street brawl ensued, but owing to the timely interference of the city constable, neither was enabled to obtain "de satisfaction ob a gemman" and both were immediately dragged before the mayor; by whose order they were severely whipped. They have since showed an entire aversion to "de wulgar practice ob dulin."[64]

Other violations of the law by free blacks, doubtless, would be discovered in an examination of the court records but the charge that free blacks with few exceptions were addicted to crime is unsupported in the indictment and refuted by the signatures of numerous prominent Texans who certified to the honesty and law-abiding character of most free blacks.

The third charge, to which the Grand Jury invited special attention, and the chief cause of complaint, was "the mischievous influence which free blacks exert over our slaves." This danger seems to have been felt throughout the whole South, and was essentially based upon the ubiquitous fear of insurrection. Because of the free black's greater freedom of movement and because of his wider experience and keener intelligence the general belief existed at least since Vesey, a free black, organized an insurrection in South Carolina, that in any important insurrection the free black might furnish the inspiration, the weapons and the organization. Perhaps even more feared than armed rebellion, because more difficult to combat, was the insidious influence of the free black, which, it was felt, would render the slaves with whom he came in contact dissatisfied, disobedient and restless, thus undermining the peculiar institution of slavery through a campaign of passive resistance. From the vantage point of the present time, this danger seems to have been more fancied than real, but there can be no doubt that slaveholders were convinced of its existence. Admittedly, evidence of this nefarious, intangible influence would be difficult to gather, yet no crime had been committed even if the charge were as true as the Grand Jurors doubtless believed it to be, and it was not properly the subject of an indictment. The charge, moreover, was not true of all free blacks. Many Texans, in petitions yet to be considered, specifically declared that the exemplary conduct of certain free blacks could in no way exert a malicious influence on the slaves with whom they came in contact.

The fourth charge, "that free blacks being addicted to Gambling, initiate the slaves, who supply the means of pursuing it by stealing from their masters," if true, could have been punishable under the law. The receiver of stolen goods, if convicted, was required to restore double their value to the lawful owner, and in addition to receive thirty-nine lashes on the bare back. If the Grand Jury was in possession of indictable evidence, on this charge, it would seem that the punishment was adequate to deter its continual repetition. The *Telegraph* at a later date placed the responsibility for thefts by slaves at the door of the masters rather than at the threshold of the free black. It believed the practice of letting blacks hire their time, always common in Texas, to be responsible for many crimes of this kind.

> We have known some masters to require the blacks who thus hired their time, to bring them every evening or Saturday night, the sum for which they engaged their time, and if the money was not forthcoming, the black was severely flogged . . . they are compelled to get money . . . and if they cannot get it honestly, they will steal. At all events, the temptation from this source is so great, that it is by no means surprising that thefts are frequent.[65]

That one free black "at least, is in correspondence with the abolitionists of the north, if not an emissary of theirs," constituted the fifth charge. Correspondence with abolitionists of the North was no criminal offence, unless indeed the Grand Jury classified it as "treacherous correspondence" with the enemies of Texas.[66] Communicating with abolitionists, of course, would be highly distasteful to most Texans and particularly to slave owners, but if the black were an emissary and actually was a menace he could have been charged with attempting to incite insurrection and if proven guilty would have suffered death.

The sixth charge that "a family of free blacks commonly presents the impersonation of ignorance and was often an irresponsible instrument in the hands of white men" appears to have been a true one. Ignorance, however, was no crime in Texas. The charge, moreover, could not honestly be made on the basis of color, since some free blacks were actually able to write intelligent letters, while numerous documents give mute testimony that many white Texans signed their papers with a cross.

In conclusion, the Jury declared that they were "aware that they have not even alluded to several very important points which suggest themselves in the consideration of this subject." Significantly enough they stated, "It is not deemed necessary to do so in this community," an open admittance of existing prejudice.

This bitter indictment of a whole people seems to have been scarcely warranted. The sweeping accusations, the absence of specific names and specific charges, and the tendency to place all evils at the door of the free black seems to have been the product of the high feeling in Houston against the black at this time, rather than of a cool, dispassionate investigation by a Grand Jury.

Some of the accusations may have been true of particular persons, but the presentment made no charges upon which individual persons could be tried according to their separate offences. The indictment seems to have held the whole group jointly responsible for the acts of each one and its object seems to have been the extirpation of the free blacks rather than a desire to give them justice under the law. The Grand Jurors, doubtless, were sincere when they stated that "in their presentment of this subject, they have acted under a sense of imperative duty," but perhaps they did not weigh heavily enough their sworn duty to "present no person through malice, hatred or ill will."[67]

The exact disposition of the presentment is unknown, but no evidence has been found that the indicted blacks were ever brought to trial. An editor in *The Morning Star* some ten weeks after the publication of the indictment, praised the prohibitory city ordinance of April 10, but admitted that free blacks were still in the city. The observation that an example could be made of them to deter other blacks from coming to Texas, indicates that nothing had yet been done.

> It affords us peculiar satisfaction to be able to direct the attention of our citizens to the ordinance recently passed by the City Council, relative to free blacks. It provides that they shall be dealt with according to law. It is not necessary for us to explain *why* the provisions of the law should be enforced in this instance. Everyone must be aware of the evils arising from a frequent intercourse between slaves and free persons of color; and being aware of them, must rejoice when any effectual remedy is devised and upheld. We have—fortunately for us—but few of this class amongst us; perhaps not more than twenty or thirty in the whole Republic, the

majority of whom are in this city; an example can therefore be easily made of those, which will effectually deter others coming here. Our northern brethren are welcome to them all. We will not quarrel with them for a division.[68]

With the convening of the fourth Congress on November 11, 1839, the scene of the battle being waged for the extermination of the free black shifted to Austin. Beden Stroud offered an act in the Senate, the terms of which required the chief justices throughout the Republic to notify all free blacks to leave within a certain length of time to be determined before the bill became law.[69] The bill was laid on the table, but on the following day referred to the committee on judiciary.[70]

On the same day, Francis Moore presented a petition from the citizens of the city of Houston praying that Henry Tucker be permitted to remain permanently.[71] Tucker was one of the culprits indicted by the Houston Grand Jury for illegal residence, but doubtless he was considered an exception to its intemperate presentment. The petition related that he had come to Houston in July of 1838. Since that time he had "been acting in the capasity of a barber, and as such gives entire satisfaction to a respectable and numerous patronage." Tucker was portrayed as "a man of good and industrious habits" and "of the most respectable character." Thirty-four of the leading citizens of Houston, including Ashbel Smith, foreman of the Grand Jury, "cheerfully" recommended him "as having always demeaned himself as a peacible and useful individual in this community."[72]

The petition was referred to the committee on judiciary which was already considering the bill introduced by Stroud, for the expulsion of all free blacks.[73] On the following day the committee made a joint report of the bill and petition in which they clearly stated their position. "The committee believe that the spirit and intention of the framers of the Constitution was not to permit any free Black to Emigrate to this Country under any Circumstances and Your Committee conceive that the prayer of the petition should not Be Granted in this Case, but would Recommend, the passage of a law to punish all free blacks who are found within the limits of this Republic who are not permitted to remain here by Law."[74]

The committee's report, it will be observed, was directed only against those blacks "who are not permitted to remain here by Law," referring to the joint resolution of June 6, 1837, which gave such permission to all blacks resident in Texas on March 2, 1836. The report was consistent with the policy thus far pursued by Congress, as no free black who had immigrated subsequent to that date had ever received the permission of Congress to remain. It was evidently approved by the Senate, Tucker's petition was rejected, and the committee began drawing up the legislation it had recommended.

The formulation of new restrictive measures did not, however, interfere with the granting of special privileges to particular blacks. An act permitting Peter, the emancipated slave of Wiley Martin, to remain in Texas became law on December 20, 1839; Thomas McKinney's emancipated slave, Cary, and the black boy, Albert Mitchell, were given permission to remain in the following month. These three bills are treated more fully in the chapter on Manumissions.

On December 4, 1839, Robertson presented to the House a petition of sundry citizens of the county of Bastrop praying Congress to pass an act granting James Young permission to remain in Texas.[75] The petition was first referred to the committee on judiciary, which, engaged in drawing up legislation for the expulsion of all blacks, decided that a plea for exception more properly belonged to the committee on the state of the Republic. That committee reported favorably upon the petition and recommended that the desired legislation be passed. The report was accepted but laid on the table on December 11, 1839. On January 10, 1840, the Senate committee on judiciary reported favorably upon three bills for the relief of Cary, Albert Mitchell and James Young, and recommended the passage of acts enabling them to remain in Texas. The acts for Cary and Albert Mitchell were ultimately passed, as we have seen, but Young's bill was lost somewhere in the parliamentary machine.[76] The action of Congress in refusing the petition of James Young was in line with previous policy, but the consent to the residence of manumitted slaves was a new departure. Strangely enough, this liberal tendency in creating more free blacks was the work of the same Congress, at the same time, planning the most restrictive measures enacted during the ten years of the Republic. As a further contradiction of policy, an initial concession was made to the claims of free blacks to their share in the public domain.

On November 13, 1839, a day previous to Stroud's original proposal to remove all free blacks from the Republic, Stephen H. Everitt presented to the Senate a petition from Joseph Tate begging for the privilege to remain in Texas and for the grant of bounty land to which his four months of service in the army entitled him. Tate had lived in Jasper county "for many years before and since the declaration of independence," and under the joint resolution of June 6, 1837, already acquired residence rights. Along with the petition came a statement from Thomas Gales Forster, chief clerk of the War Department, that Tate had served in Captain Cheshire's company and that his certificate for bounty land had not been issued. Ninety-two residents of Jasper county endorsed Tate's plea for land.[77]

The petition was referred to the committee on public lands which reported a bill favorable to the issuance of bounty land to Tate.[78] On the bill's third reading, John A. Greer proposed an amendment striking out the words "land due him." Such an amendment, of course, emasculated the bill and in explanation Greer stated that he knew of no law authorizing Africans to hold land within Texas. He based his opposition to such a law on the fact that the Constitution expressly denied citizenship to blacks and should, he thought, preclude their ownership of land. He was willing to give Tate money, but not land, and he objected mainly because it would be setting a bad example. Stephen H. Everitt, Oliver Jones, I. W. Burton, and Francis Moore advocated the propriety and justice of granting the land to Tate, but George W. Barnett joined Greer in the opposition, conceiving it to be unconstitutional to grant or give land to free blacks.[79]

In the final vote, the opposition prevailed and the bill was amended to authorize a payment of $213.50 in treasury notes of the Republic in lieu of bounty lands. On November 21, 1839, the Senate informed the House of the passage of the bill, and the House concurred without recorded debate.[80]

Meanwhile, both the Senate and House committees on judiciary had been formulating laws for the regulation of free blacks, in accordance with the constitutional provision which forbade the permanent residence of free blacks in Texas without the consent of Congress. No penalties had been provided, and in the prosecution of a group of alleged offenders in Houston the Court had denied jurisdiction. Early in the session Stroud had offered a bill in the Senate requiring all free blacks to leave the Republic. The judiciary committee on November 16, 1839, recommended the passage of an act to punish all blacks who were found in Texas without permission to remain by law. On November 30, the judiciary committee had drawn up a bill to which Stroud and Greer found some minor objections, delaying its passage.[81]

The judiciary committee of the House, either in conjunction with the Senate committee or independently, submitted a similar bill to the House on January 7, 1840, which passed ten days later.[82] The House bill was referred by the Senate to its judiciary committee, which reported favorably on the bill and recommended its passage.[83] Three days later it passed the Senate, and on February 5, 1840, the day upon which Congress adjourned, this act concerning free blacks became law.[84]

This restrictive law, based upon the old ordinance of the General Consultation, embodied eleven sections, and was designed to rid Texas of free blacks forever. It provided that after its passage the immigration of free persons of color into the Republic was unlawful, and instructed sheriffs and constables to give such persons ten days' notice to quit the limits of the Republic. After the lapse of ten days, with no response on the part of the black so forewarned, the officer was to arrest the offending person, bring him before the Court, there to post a thousand dollar bond to guarantee his removal. If the black could not post the required bond, he was to be exposed to public sale, the successful bidder acquiring all rights of ownership for one year. At the expiration of the year, the released black must leave the country within ten days, post bond of one thousand dollars assuring his removal, or be subject to sale into slavery for life. Monies received from such sales were to be paid into the public treasury, "subject to appropriation by the District Court for public purposes."

The law further provided for the removal of all free blacks residing in Texas, allowing them two years to comply and at the end of that time subjecting them to the same procedure and punishment provided for unlawful immigrants. Any person inducing, assisting or bringing "directly or indirectly" any free person of color within the limits of Texas was to be deemed guilty of a misdemeanor and subject to a fine of not less than ten thousand dollars. This act definitely repealed the joint resolution of June 6, 1837, and if carried out, would exterminate the free black from Texas within the provided two years. The President was instructed to command all free persons of color then in the Republic to remove themselves before January 1, 1842. In order to leave no doubt as to its full meaning all laws contrary to the spirit of the new act were repealed.[85]

This basic solution of the free black problem was as simple as it was complete, but the problem was too complex to be solved so easily. Texans were of two minds regarding the free colored element in their midst. On public grounds they were apprehensive that in case tumult were plotted these people would make the efforts of the slaves more formidable. From this point of view they were not concerned with the virtues and vices of the colored freemen on their own score so much as the effect of their mingling with the slaves. They were well agreed that the free blacks as a class were an undesirable element to be well rid of, but they were not moved by personal dislike and rarely were they able to single out an individual black who exerted a vicious influence upon the slaves. The attitude of the Texans toward individual blacks was much more kindly. They found that blacks of their acquaintance were exceptions from their concept of the class, but they did not see what is evident today: these exceptions taken collectively comprised the whole black population. Some Texans took an attitude of amiable patronage toward certain free blacks, and when their favorites were threatened with removal exerted their efforts to forestall it. The problem before us is to discover the white men who were directly interested in exempting certain blacks from the law.

First were the white relatives of blacks. Most of the free blacks had a large admixture of white blood, and their expulsion would make necessary the migration of white persons or the severance of family ties. If all white men remained, fathers must lose their black children, white husbands would be separated from their black wives or concubines, husbands legally defined as blacks from their white wives. If on the other hand they migrated with their black families, some white men must leave their white wives and families. The severance would also work beyond immediate families and we might expect sympathy from grandparents, uncles, brothers and cousins against the execution of a law which would work hardship against their kin. From this group as well as from others we should also expect deep sympathy for black husbands who would be forced to leave their slave wives, free mothers who would lose their slave children and free children their slave mothers. Not all white persons supported their black relatives, to be sure, for some of them considered their acknowledgment a graver sin than their existence.

Veterans of the Revolution who fought "shoulder to shoulder" with black soldiers formed a second important group who opposed the full execution of the law. They had come to know of the services of the blacks in the struggle for independence and through a sense of fair play did not feel that banishment by the government was a proper reward for the men and relatives of men who had fought, bled and died to establish it.

A third important group were the masters who had manumitted or intended to manumit their slaves and who would practically lose that right if the law were enforced. The necessity of transporting manumitted slaves beyond the limits of Texas, for all practical purposes, would prevent masters from rewarding faithful service which in some cases they had already promised to do. Sympathy for this group was to be expected from all persons convinced of the inherent evils of slavery, who looked forward to gradual abolition as its ultimate solution, and did not wish to see this door closed.

Personal friends of certain free blacks, particularly old settlers who had accepted the blacks as colonists, found them to be good neighbors over a long period of years, and considered them to be no danger now. This fourth group, who as pioneers knew at first hand the difficulties these blacks had in establishing themselves in the wilderness, did not view with unconcern their forced migration and the consequent loss of the fruits of long years of struggle.

In addition to these four groups of sentimentalists, were those who had an economic interest in the retention of a free black population. Employers of free black labor, faced with a chronic scarcity of artisans, were not anxious to lose a good brickmason, mechanic, blacksmith or common laborer. Their wives wished to retain an efficient washerwoman, cook, nurse, or house servant. Some white men found an inn, boarding house, livery stable, dray service or barber shop owned by blacks, conveniences which they wished to be continued. To this group might be added merchants, lawyers, agents and others who found their black customers to be some source of profit and who wished to retain their trade.

These groups of white persons, many of them of considerable importance and influence, together with such friends as they could ally with them, while interested primarily in the granting of exceptions from the law of February 5, 1840, only to particular free blacks, were to storm the next Congress with such an avalanche of pleas that they not only restored the free black to his previous status, but embarked the Republic upon a more liberal policy than it had thus far pursued.

NOTES

1. An Act establishing the jurisdiction and power of the District Courts. Gammel, *The Laws of Texas*, I, 1265–1266.

2. See Chapter I, "Origin of the Free Black in the Republic of Texas," in *Southwestern Historical Quarterly*, XXXIX, 292–308.

3. Memorial No. 91, File 81. November 7, 1851.

4. See Chapter III, "Manumissions," in *Southwestern Historical Quarterly*, XL, 85–113.

5. The marriage laws prohibited the intermarriage of any person of European blood with Africans or their descendants. Such marriages were null and void, and the parties on conviction were to be deemed guilty of a high misdemeanor. Gammel, *The Laws of Texas*, I, 1294–1295.

6. Memorial No. 33, File 94, November 11, 1841; No. 139, File 74, no date; *Senate Journal*, Second Legislature, 186.

7. This letter has not been found. Reference to it is made in the Proceedings of the General Council. Gammel, *The Laws of Texas*, I, 720. The location of Beaumont has not been ascertained.

8. Austin's argument against law regulating slavery. *Austin Papers*, I, 1716.

9. Horatio Allsberry to the Public, August 28, 1835. *Austin Papers*, III, 107.

10. Thomas J. Pilgrim to Austin, October 6, 1835. *Austin Papers*, III, 162.

11. B. J. White to Austin, October 17, 1835. *Austin Papers*, III, 190.

12. E. C. Barker (editor), "Journal of the Permanent Council," in *Texas State Historical Quarterly*, VII, 249.

13. James V. Robinson to Captain Stephen Miller, December 11, 1835. Papers of the General Council, Texas State Library. William Francis, if arrested, was not brought before the Council.

14. Proceedings of the General Council. Gammel, *The Laws of Texas,* I, 720-721.

15. See Chapter II, "The Free Black and the Texas Revolution," in *Southwestern Historical Quarterly,* XL, 26–34.

16. Gammel, *The Laws of Texas,* I, 1024. The language in the printed act varies from the manuscript in the Journal of the General Council, 238. Texas State Library.

17. Peter Allen came to Texas sometime in January under the protection of some white men, and Thomas Cevallos came in a company of Mississippi Volunteers shortly after the battle of San Jacinto. *House Journal,* Seventh Legislature, 499–500. Memorial No. 91, File 81, November 7, 1851; *Weekly Picayune* (New Orleans), August 8, 1853.

18. Proceedings at the Convention at Washington. Gammel, *The Laws of Texas,* I, 871.

19. Gammel, *The Laws of Texas,* I, 874.

20. Gammel, *The Laws of Texas, I,* 1079.

21. An original provision, making it necessary for free Blacks to secure the consent of Congress to their immigation and residence in Texas, in the form of a special act which must specify each person by name, was considerably amended before acceptance. Proceedings at the Convention of Washington, Gammel, *The Laws of Texas,* I, 872. In its final form the provision placed no restriction upon immigration or temporary residence, and did not require individual acts specifically naming the beneficiaries. Much subsequent group legislation which afforded relief to free Blacks would have been greatly impeded under the original draft and the granting of special rights to unborn Blacks would have been unconstitutional.

22. Memorial No. 15, File 5, September 20, 1836.

23. These testimonials have not been found.

24. *House Journal,* First Congress, 219, 220.

25. *House Journal,* First Congress, 220.

26. Memorial No. 3, File 54, March 13, 1837.

27. *Senate Journal,* First Congress, Adjourned Session, 9, 13.

28. Bill No. 620, File 6, Congressional Papers, First Congress, Adjourned Session.

29. *Senate Journal,* First Congress, Adjourned Session, 14.

30. *House Journal,* First Congress, Adjourned Session, 46.

31. These petitions have not been found. *House Journal,* First Congress, Adjourned Session, 32.

32. *House Journal,* First Congress, Adjourned Session, 46. In the regular course of business, the bill for the relief of Greenbury Logan passed by the Senate, came up for action in the House. On November 29, 1837, the House rejected the Senate bill, but at this time it was superfluous, as the joint resolution had already become law. *House Journal,* Second Congress, 198.

33. This amendment excluded from its benefits blacks who immigrated to Texas between March 2, 1836, and September 5, 1836.

34. *House Journal,* First Congress, Adjourned Session, 71.

35. *House Journal,* First Congress, Adjourned Session, 73; *Senate Journal,* First Congress, Adjourned Session, 23, 29, 32, 39; Bills Nos. 643, 678, File 7, Congressional Papers, First Congress, Adjourned Session; Gammel, *The Laws of Texas,* I, 1292.

36. Memorial No. 101, File 67, no date.

37. In the committee report Samuel McCullough appears as Samuel Mullock. House Journal, *First Congress,* Adjourned Session, 105.

38. Memorial No. 49, File 5, October 8, 1837.

39. A petition from Emanuel Carter is filed with that of Edmund J. Carter. Emanuel Carter, probably a close relative of Edmund J., was born in Tennessee

and had emigrated to Texas previous to the declaration of independence. He was, therefore, entitled to residence under the provisions of the joint resolution of June 6, 1837, and no congressional action upon his petition was necessary. Memorial No. 6, File C, March 17, 1838.

40. Memorial No. 13, File M, April 21, 1838.

41. This petition is endorsed, "Judiciary 25th April Rejected." Memorial No. 1, File 52, April 25, 1838.

42. This petition has not been found.

43. The names of the five men appear here as they do in the bill itself. Congressional Papers, Second Adjourned Session, No. 999, File 11. The names in the *Senate Journal,* appear as follows: Wm. Going, Jermiah Goings, John Byrd, Henry Byrd, Edw. Smith. *Senate Journal,* Adjourned Session, 90, 98, 99.

44. Kavanaugh was still residing in Texas in 1842, when he renewed his efforts to gain official consent to his residence. Committee Reports, Congressional Papers, Sixth Congress.

45. Bill No. 1034, File 11, Congressional Papers, Third Congress.

46. Bill No. 1083, File 12, Congressional Papers, Third Congress.

47. *Senate Journal,* Third Congress, 64, 65. *House Journal,* Third Congress, 233, 241.

48. These petitions have not been found.

49. *House Journal,* Third Congress, 299.

50. Almonte, as early as 1834, recognized the great aversion to the free black person in Texas cities. On this basis he had refused to sanction the immigration of blacks from New Orleans since the greater part of them were artisans but at the same time he believed the immigration of free black farmers to be desirable and recommended that the government encourage it. Juan Nepomuceno Almonte to E. S. Secretario de Estado y del Despacho de Relaciones de los Estados Unidos Mexicanos. April 13, 1834. Dept. of Fomento, Leg. 8, Exp. 65. University of Texas transcripts.

51. *Austin City Gazette,* December 25, 1839.

52. Gammel, *The Laws of Texas,* I, 1024.

53. *The Morning Star,* (Houston), April 10, 1839.

54. *The Morning Star,* April 10, 1839.

55. *The Morning Star,* April 10, 1839.

56. *The Morning Star,* April 10, 1839.

57. The Constitution gave Congress the right to permit free Blacks to reside permanently in the country; they had exercised that right in the joint resolution of June 5, 1837, which gave to all Blacks resident in Texas on March 2, 1836, "the privilege of remaining in any part of the Republic." The ordinance of the Consultation prohibited immigration only after January 5, 1836. Under all existing laws the right of old Black settlers to reside in the Republic was affirmed, but the Houston ordinance ordered the arrest of every free Black within the limits of the city, without exception.

58. *Telegraph and Texas Register,* April 10, 1839; *The Morning Star,* June 3, 1839. The report was sent To the Hon. B. C. Franklin, Presiding Judge:

The Grand Jurors have directed their attention to the condition of the free blacks residing in Harrisburg county, contrary to the provisions of the ordinance passed by the Consultation on this subject, and contrary to the express declaration of the Constitution. After a very careful, patient, and full investigation of facts, they made a presentment to the honorable Court, of those blacks, who, in violation of the supreme law of this land, are residing within the limits for which your Grand Jury is sworn to make inquest. As a population, they are much worse than useless: in general, they neither perform any productive labor, nor exercise reputable callings. With scarcely an exception, they are addicted to vice and commission of petty crimes. They are often irresponsible instruments in the hands of white men. But it is chiefly the mischievous influence which the free blacks exert over our slaves to which Grand Jurors would invite special attention. Texas is a slaveholding country, and will, the Grand Jurors trust, ever remain such.

A family of free blacks commonly presents the impersonation of indolence, ignorance and dishonesty. Such a family, unless strictly and perpetually watched, and kept at a distance, will render the slaves of the plantations near which they are situated, dissatisfied, disobedient, restless, thievish and corrupt. In the towns where the facilities for dishonesty by slaves are much greater than in the country, the presence of free blacks is felt as a very great evil. In addition to their other vices and petty crimes, the free blacks being addicted to Gambling, initiate the slaves, who supply the means of pursuing it by stealing from their masters.

The Grand Jurors are aware that they have not even alluded to several very important points which suggest themselves in the consideration of this subject. It is not deemed necessary to do so in this community. And in the brief notice they have taken of one or two points, they are fully sustained by facts in the conclusion they have expressed. They would likewise mention, that they have been informed on undoubted authority, that one free black at least is in correspondence with the abolitionists of the north, if not an emissary of theirs. This subject too, derives a great addition at this time to its inherent importance from the fact, that one of the states of the Union adjoining this republic, has found the free blacks so great an evil, that it is expected she will soon expell [sic] them from her borders. In that event it may be confidently anticipated that they will attempt to disgorge themselves into Texas—a dark spot on this fair and sunny land. The Grand Jurors in their presentment of this subject, have acted under a sense of imperative duty. Ashbel Smith, foreman.

59. Section 33, An Act establishing the jurisdiction and powers of the District Courts. Gammel, The Laws of Texas, I, 1268. The Republic had adopted an act for the punishment of crimes and misdemeanors on December 21, 1836, (Gammel, The Laws of Texas, I, 1247–1255), and had supplemented it a year later by an act prescribing additional offences to be considered crimes when committed by slaves and free Blacks, and attaching to many of them more drastic punishment when committed by these classes. The first section of the act for the punishment of crimes and misdemeanors by slaves and free

persons of color designated seven capital offenses; namely, insurrection or the attempt to incite it; poisoning or the attempt to poison a white person; rape or its attempt upon a white woman; assault upon a white person with intent to maim or kill, or with a deadly weapon; arson; murder; and burglary. Burglary was not originally named as a capital offense but was added later in an amendment offered by Anson Jones. *(House Journal,* Second Congress, Called Session, 201.) Robbery seems to have been inadvertently omitted as a capital offense, but was already prescribed as one in the original criminal code and should therefore be considered as an eighth capital offence for free Blacks. (Section 9. An Act punishing crimes and misdemeanors. Gammel, *The Laws of Texas, I,* 1284.) As contrasted with the criminal code applicable to white persons, only five crimes were punishable by death when committed by a white person: premeditated murder, arson, slave stealing, rape, burglary and robbery. Assault with attempt to commit murder or rape by a white person was punishable with a one to five year prison sentence; maiming was punishable by a fine of one thousand dollars and thirty-nine lashes on the bare back. (Gammel, *The Laws of Texas,* I, 1247-1255.) The second section of this act made it illegal for free Blacks to inveigle or entice slaves away from their owners, assist them in leaving the country, or to conceal or render aid to runaway slaves with intent to prevent their return. The commission of any of these offences was made punishable by a fine equal in value to the slaves so aided. Inability or failure to pay such a fine, by the provisions of the act, resulted in the sale of the free Black into slavery for life. Sections 3, 4, and 5, applied only to slaves and are not of immediate concern here. By the provisions of Section 6, the use of insulting or abusive language or threatening any white person was made punishable by stripes not exceeding one hundred or less than twenty-five. (Gammel, *The Laws of Texas,* I, 1385–1386.)

60. *Telegraph and Texas Register,* May 2, 1837.

61. S. Rhoads Fisher to Col. A. S. Thuston, Commissary General, April 15, 1837. Navy Papers, Texas State Library.

62. Schooner *Brutus,* Payroll No. 3, Navy Papers.

63. *Telegraph and Texas Register,* November 17, 1838.

64. *Telegraph and Texas Register,* August 18, 1838.

65. *Telegraph and Texas Register,* August 4, 1841.

66. Section 1, An Act Punishing Crimes and Misdemeanors. Gammel, *The Laws of Texas,* I, 1247.

67. Part of the prescribed oath for Grand Jurors. Section 33, An Act establishing the jurisdiction and powers of the District Courts. Gammel, *The Laws of Texas,* I, 1268.

68. *The Morning Star,* August 13, 1839. The editor greatly underestimated the number of free blacks in the Republic which must have exceeded two hundred.

69. *Senate Journal,* Fourth Congress, 35. The *Austin City Gazette,* November 27, 1839, reported that, in addition, the bill prevented the Senate from receiving or entertaining petitions from free Blacks. In a later edition (January 8, 1840) the same paper reported that a "gag resolution" was adopted on November 29, 1839, but this report was erroneous as no mention of it was made in the Journals and the Senate received and considered numerous petitions during the session.

70. *Journal,* Fourth Congress, 37.

71. *Senate Journal,* Fourth Congress, 37.

72. The list of prominent Texans who signed this petition includes J. B. Ransom, Henry S. Foote, George Fisher, W. G. Hill, George W. Hockley, and A. C. Allen. Memorial No. 16, File T, no date.

73. *Senate Journal,* Fourth Session, 37.

74. *Senate Journal,* Fourth Session, 38.

75. This petition has not been found. *House Journal,* Fourth Session, 121.

76. *Senate Journal,* Fourth Congress, 228-229.

77. Memorial No. 1, File T, no date. *Senate Journal,* Fourth Congress, 32.

78. *Senate Journal,* Fourth Congress, 45.

79. The newspaper report erroneously goes on to say that the act was then amended by striking out the words "due him," and passed. *Austin City Gazette,* December 4, 1839.

80. *House Journal,* Fourth Congress, 47, 63, 69, 150. *Reports and Relief Laws,* 216–217.

81. Stroud and Greer wished to use convicted blacks for improving and opening roads. The bill provided for their sale into slavery to the highest bidder. *Senate Journal,* Fourth Congress, 83.

82. No debate is recorded and no amendments were offered. *House Journal,* Fourth Congress, 264, 295, 297.

83. Committee Reports, Fourth Congress. *Senate Journal,* Fourth Congress, 303.

84. *Senate Journal,* Fourth Congress, 308. Gammel, *The Laws of Texas,* II, 325.

85. Gammel, *The Laws of Texas,* II, 325–326.

5

THE LAW IN PRACTICE

Harold R. Schoen

The free black policy of the Republic of Texas, crystallized in the passage of the definitive act of February 5, 1840, which remained in effect until emancipation, was to prove more effectual in theory than in practice. Practical difficulties asserted themselves in the facts that the black wished to remain and his individual white friends were willing to use their influence in making this possible. By the terms of the law, immigration of free blacks was prohibited and black residents were required to remove themselves from Texas within two years on penalty of sale into slavery. Although these provisions were effectually designed to make color the universal badge of servitude by annihilating the free black class, there is no evidence that any free black left of his own free will and none that he left by force. The immediate result of this law was a deluge of petitions for exemptions endorsed by influential white men in favor of their disfranchised friends, neighbors and servants.

The provisions of the law at first were not clearly understood. Immediately after its passage, G. A. Pattillo of Jefferson county wrote to the president enclosing the petition of Jessee Ashworth,[1] "Praying Permission to remain quietly in this republic untill the next meeting of Congress," obviously for the purpose of gaining from that body consent to his continued residence. According to Pattillo "Mr. Ashworth is a man under a good Character and in good Standing in the country where he has migrated from. I have my Self been acquainted with him for the last fifteen years and know him to Be a quiet and unassuming good citizen, you will confer a favour by paying some attention To the petition. Mr. Ashworth is not unly [sic] a good Citizen but a man of some property and will be of some benefit to the Gourment."[2] Jessee Ashworth had probably immigrated previous to February 5, and under the law was entitled to the privilege which he asked, and no action was taken on his petition.[3]

Thomas J. Rusk, who was employed as attorney by a number of free blacks to aid them in their efforts to retain status and remain in Texas, expressed the opinion that the joint resolution of June 5, 1837, permitting blacks resident in Texas on the day of the declaration of independence to remain, was still in force and that the law of February 5, 1840, did not apply to them.[4] His contention, however, was hardly tenable since the eleventh section of the 1840 law specifically stated that "all laws contrary to the meaning and spirit of this act are hereby repealed."[5] Rusk probably had little hope that his interpretation would be accepted, since for his clients he resorted to the one clear avenue of escape which remained, an appeal to Congress to exercise its constitutional right and pass private acts enabling particular blacks to remain in the country.

Congress had adjourned on February 5, 1840, the same day that the new law was passed. The fifth Congress was to convene on November 2, and although two years were given them to comply with the law, free blacks, their lawyers and friends did not delay their pleas but spent the intervening months busying themselves in the preparation of petitions to be presented to the fifth Congress.

Among these were three from the citizens of Jefferson county praying for the relief of the four Ashworth brothers, Joshua [Abner], Aaron, David and William, and their brother-in-law, Elisha Thomas. Abner and William were early immigrants; their two brothers, Aaron and David, had arrived in Texas in 1838, and according to the petition had been "citizens for two years," although during that time they had neglected to apply for permission to remain in the Republic. Previous to February 5, 1840, possibly they considered themselves as their brothers' guests rather than as permanent residents and so circumvented the law. Sixty citizens of Jefferson county, nevertheless, signed their petition begging Congress to grant them permission to remain.[6]

A second petition accompanied the first, pleading the cause of Abner and William, but neglecting their brothers. Abner and William certainly had the stronger claim for relief and it was possibly with this in mind that a separate petition was prepared for them. If the first petition did not receive favorable consideration, the second might. The second petition stated that Abner and William had been citizens for the past six years, that they had "contributed generously to the advancement of the Revolution, that glorious struggle which resulted in bursting the fetters of Tyranny and which has elevated Texas to a string in the scale of nations." Seventy-one citizens of Jefferson county believed that the law of February 5, 1840, would "operate grievously by forcing them from the country, whose battles they have fought and whose independence they assisted in achieving."[7] The third petition, for the continued residence of Elisha Thomas, an early resident who had service in the army immediately after San Jacinto, received the endorsement of sixty-one citizens.[8]

Joseph Grigsby presented these petitions to the House on November 5, 1840, when the session was but three days old. They were immediately referred to a special committee of which Grigsby was made chairman.[9] On the following day, this committee reported that the Ashworths had resided in Texas for several years and that some of them had arrived previous to the declaration of independence. They had contributed towards the achievement of independence "both by personal service and by their substance Generously bestowed without fee or reward." The report continued, "they conduct themselves well and are men of good credit wherever they are known, having been at all times punctual to their engagements, upright in their dealings and peaceable in their disposition and Although your committee are well satisfied that as a general rule it is not the true policy of this Country to encourage the introduction of this description of persons among us Nor even to allow them to remain, yet your committee believes that the persons set forth in the petition . . . should be an exception."[10]

The committee report was accepted and a bill for the relief of the Ashworths passed its first reading without recorded opposition.[11] With this favorable action, James Reily believed the time auspicious for introducing the petition of Henry Tucker. Despite the long list of prominent Houstonians who had endorsed a previous petition for his relief, the fourth Congress had refused to grant his plea. The new petition commended Tucker highly for "his habits of Sobriety, Industry and Honesty." Thirty-nine prominent Texans including John R. Reid, late district attorney, after "attentive observation of his habits" testified "that notwithstanding they concur most heartily in the Law passed by the last Session of Congress, Compelling all free persons of colour to leave the Republic, by the first of January, 1842,[12] Yet the character and correct conduct of the said Henry Tucker is and has been such, that they feel satisfied that no injury can result from his example or conversation to the Slaves with whom he May associate, and on the other hand that this community is really benefitted by his Labour [and] they therefore cheerfully recommend" that he be permitted to remain.[13] The petition was subsequently referred to the committee on the state of the Republic which on November 10, reported that it was of the opinion "that all such petitions signed by such a number of respectable Citizens all testifying to his character should be complied with."[14]

It became apparent to T. Pillsbury of Brazoria that the House members concurred heartily in the principles of the 1840 law, but not in the application of them to blacks living in their respective districts. In an effort to conserve the time necessary to consider each petition separately he offered a resolution, adopted by the House, instructing the committee on the state of the Republic to "enquire into the expediency of providing by law for the continuance in the republic of free persons of color, who were in the country at the time of the adoption of the constitution, and to report by bill or otherwise."[15] Such a bill had precedence in the joint resolution of June 5, 1837, and if passed would dispense favorably with the great majority of black petitions and incidentally with the two for the relief of Samuel H. Hardin and James Richardson which Pillsbury carried in his pocket.

Not content to await the committee's report, Patrick Usher offered a resolution for the appointment of a special committee to take into consideration the propriety and expediency of exempting Samuel McCullough, Jr., his three sisters and Uldy, another member of the family, from the provisions of the law. The resolution was adopted and Usher was named chairman of the committee[16] which subsequently reported "their case is one of a peculiar and meritorious kind; and fully entitled to the sympathies of the nation . . . One of the individuals [Samuel McCullough, Jr.] proposed to be exempted as aforesaid was among the first to shed his blood in the war of independence, such being the case, your Committee are altogether averse to his removal from the bosom of the nation . . . [since] such a course . . . would . . . be worthy of the condemnation of all enlightened nations, therefore as the said individual has been disabled in the service of his adopted country," he and his relatives should be allowed to remain.[17] The recommended bill for the relief of the McCulloughs passed its first reading on November 9, the same day on which the Ashworth bill was engrossed.[18]

The committee on the state of the Republic, having so far ignored Pillsbury's resolution to grant residence rights to all free blacks living in Texas at the time of the adoption of the Constitution, the intention of Congress apparently was to dole out residence rights singly or in family groups. Pillsbury thereupon unfolded the two petitions which provoked his resolution. The first of these, endorsed by twenty-three citizens of Brazoria, prayed that James Richardson be allowed to remain.

Richardson was a "vendor of oysters and refreshments" and noted for his "industry, sobriety and correct deportment," and his sixty years had not prevented him from serving in the garrison at Velasco in the late war. "From the circumstance of his being in the habit of entertaining travellers between Velasco and San Luis, which is the only one on the road and midway between those towns, he is useful to the public in a situation suitable to his days and at a locality where a white person equally serviceable could not be expected to reside. . . . From his age and character and the fact of his having no descendants, as well as from . . . [the] isolated situation of his dwelling, he is not liable to cause or promote any of the evils for whose prevention the Laws" prohibiting residence were designed.[19]

In the second petition presented by Pillsbury the citizens of Brazoria county represented "that while they approve the policy which dictated the passage of 'An Act concerning free persons of color' by the last Congress, they believe there are some persons of that description in the Country who by their long residence, industrious habits, and general good conduct have strong claims to be exempted from the provisions of that act and among that number are" Emanuel H. Hardin and his wife, Tomas Morgan. Continuing, they said, "Your petitioners believe that it would be both arbitrary and unjust to require them to leave the country, since they came here under laws that invited their emigration, and acquired rights and property to a considerable amount before those laws were changed." Sixty-five citizens, including Wm. T. Austin, Henry Austin and Henry Smith, believed that if the law were applied to the Hardins a great injustice would be done them.[20]

The Richardson and Hardin petitions were both referred to the committee on the state of the Republic on November 9.[21] On the following day the Ashworth bill passed the House[22] and the bill for the relief of the McCulloughs was read a second time. At this reading attempts were made to amend the bill by adding the names of Lewis B. Jones and family; William Goens [Goyens] and Bredget; and Pleasant [Bious], a resident of Houston. The amendments were lost but the original bill passed.[23]

When the Ashworth bill came up in the Senate on November 20, it was amended by inserting after the named beneficiaries "and all free persons of colour together with their families, who were residing in Texas the day of the Declaration of Independence," and passed.[24] The amendment of the Senate was accepted by the House without recorded contest and became law on December 12, 1840.[25]

This law restored the privilege of residence to all free blacks who had immigrated previous to the declaration of independence "anything in the laws of the country to the contrary notwithstanding."[26] In addition, it conferred the same rights upon David and Aaron Ashworth who had immigrated in 1838. These two brothers were the first and only blacks to immigrate subsequent to the declaration of independence who were given Congressional sanction to remain. On December 15 a superfluous act gave the same privileges to the McCulloughs that had already been given to them in the Ashworth act of December 12, 1840.[27]

No further supernumerary acts were passed. Memorials already in the hands of committees and those which continued to come in were simply endorsed "provided for by law." Although these petitions were not actively considered by Congress in the formulation of the Ashworth law, the fact that a majority of the congressmen had received one or more of them from their constituents played a decisive role in its passage. The majority of these men, doubtless, would have upheld the principles of the 1840 law had it not been incumbent upon each congressman to sustain all similar petitions for the relief of free blacks in order to secure favorable consideration of his own. These petitions are a chief source of information about the colored population as well as a catalogue of the reasons given by white men for dispensations in favor of blacks.

Thomas J. Rusk prepared a petition for William Goyens and eight other unnamed persons, probably relatives of Goyens, representing that Goyens "has conducted himself as an honest industrious cit[i]zen and has accumulated considerable property in land etc. and has been of great servic[e] to the Country in our Indian difficulties." Fifty-four citizens of Nacogdoches county believed it would be "an act of Justice and magnanimity" for Congress to grant Goyens and these eight other blacks the right to remain in Texas.[28]

The nine children of David and Sophia Gowns represented that their parents had emigrated to Texas in 1827 with the six oldest children, the three youngest having been born in Texas. Their mother had died in 1838, which explains the absence of her name from the petition; their father was a white man.[29] The two oldest daughters, Louisa and Eliza, had been married for some years, evidently to white men, and between them had added five free blacks to the population. "Considering themselves secure in person and property under the Constitution of Coahuila and Texas," the petition continued, "and all their hopes and expectations in that particular being fully realized by an act for the relief of free persons of colour passed June 5, 1837, those of your petitioners who have arrived at an age of maturity have endeavored with what scant means have been at their command to improve their condition by the acquisition of some little personal property, and their most strenuous efforts have been to demean themselves in a proper and becoming manner, consequently it is with extreme sorrow that they find [by] an act of the last Congress, they are allowed but a short time longer to remain within the limits of this Republic." They asked Congress to relieve them from the operation of the law, "and by a measure of kindness and generosity permit them to remain in a land endeared to them by almost every tie that can bind the affections to any country." Sixteen citizens of Nacogdoches and Thomas J. Rusk, as attorney, signed the petition.[30]

Fannie McFarland had been brought to Texas in 1827 and had been manumitted in 1835, but her four children were held as slaves "so that all her hopes and prospects of life are here." Seventy-nine citizens of Houston urged upon Congress the untold hardships which Fannie would suffer from "being obliged in her *old age* to leave her children, to sacrifice her hard earned property, to be obliged to part from friends of years standing, to be obliged to leave her only home and be turned loose upon the wide world," and they prayed Congress to give her "permission to spend the few remaining days of her life as a resident and cit[i]zen of this republic."[31]

Thirty citizens of Montgomery county testified that Robert Thompson was "a man of prudence and industry" and cheerfully recommended that he be allowed to remain in the country. Thompson had purchased two hundred acres of good land for which he paid six hundred dollars "in par money" and upon which he made extensive improvements. He was "possessed of a considerable stock of horses, cattle and hogs and is in a situation to live independent and happy."[32]

Zelia Husk alleged that she came to Texas in 1835, and for two years previous to her petition lived in Houston "peaceably earning her liveli-hood" by "exercising the Industry of a washerwoman." Despite her industry, Zelia did not have the means of removing from Texas with her daughter Emily. Forty-one Houstonians were willing to have her stay indefinitely.[33] Diana Leonard, a competitor of Zelia, found herself in a similar position. She had come to Texas in 1835, worked one year in the service of Colonel James Morgan and for two years lived in Houston "exercising the industry of a washerwoman." She lacked the means for transporting herself and her child, and twelve citizens of Houston, including Joseph Baker and I. M. Moreland, prayed that she be exempted from the law.[34]

Five citizens of Rutersville "well acquainted with the old Free Black Wooman Patsey" joined John Robb, with whom she lived, in a declaration that "She is honest, and mindes hur own bisanis She is about fifty-five or sixty years of Age and we believe She will do no harm by being purmited to remain in the Republic."[35]

Other petitions of the same nature, since lost, reached Congress at this time. One such memorial from the citizens of San Augustine county for the relief of a number of free blacks which was presented by Sam Houston has not been found,[36] another from the citizens of Red River county has not been located.[37]

The Ashworth Act which resulted from the foregoing petitions, in combination with the law of February 5, 1840, had the effect of mitigating the harshness of the law by dividing the free blacks into three chronological groups. Black immigration subsequent to the passage of the 1840 law was prohibited. The first group, who continued to enter in violation of the immigration provision, sought the right to remain in contravention to it. The second body of blacks who immigrated subsequent to the declaration of independence and previous to February 5, 1840, and were permitted to remain two years, endeavored to have their time limit extended indefinitely. The third group, blacks who were residing in Texas on the date of the declaration of independence, were permitted to remain permanently. These favored persons immediately pursued further privileges, chiefly to be secured in their property rights.

This classification was logical and as just as any grouping could be. It respected the residence rights of those who had immigrated to Texas under the assurances of the Mexican government, it allowed blacks who had settled without governmental consent a reasonable time to dispose of their belongings and quit the country, and it forbade future entry. But it did not conform to the preconceived notion of southerners in general and Texans in particular that free blacks as a group, regardless of the chronology of their entrance, were an undesirable element in the population. They fully recognized that their own washerwoman, cook, barber and neighboring farmer were good blacks, peaceably earning their livelihood in a manner which benefited the community. They were not concerned whether a black entered the country in January or March, whether in 1839 or 1841. With the individualism of the frontier, they wished to deal with a black as a person, and if he performed useful labor and conducted himself in a manner which they conceived becoming to his race and his station in life, he was a welcome addition to the community and was assured protection as a black who merited exception from the law. Harboring such views, as most Texans did, the chronological classification soon broke down.

Despite the law prohibiting immigration, free blacks entered Texas and remained with impunity. A mulatto barber took passage in the early part of 1840, subsequent to the passage of the law, from New Orleans to Galveston. During the voyage by claiming his own berth he narrowly missed having his throat slashed by two respectable gentlemen emigrating to Texas.[38] Arrived at Galveston he had no further difficulties although under the law he should have received ten days' notice to quit the country and the ship captain should have been heavily fined for bringing him to Texas. David, a manumitted slave from Tennessee, immigrated to the Republic in 1843, and was so little aware of the law that he did not petition the state legislature for permission to remain until 1853.[39] Mary Madison came to Galveston sometime between 1841 and 1843, and remained unmolested. She was "a valuable citizen in many ways especially in the capacity of a nurse in case of sickness and many citizens and strangers afflicted with disease have experienced her kindness, attention and watchfulness."[40]

These three blacks, doubtless, proved themselves useful and peaceable and remained upon the sufferance of their local communities which refused to prosecute them. Several additional cases came to the notice of Congress. Lovinia Mansell with her three children immigrated to Texas in 1843, without a knowledge of the law, and could not leave "without great expense and inconvenience."[41] A bill was introduced in the eighth Congress to allow Lovinia and her three children to remain permanently.[42] On its second reading it was referred to a select committee of five which reported it back with an amendment requiring Lovinia to post bond of one thousand dollars for herself and children "conditioned for their good behavior, so long as they remain citizens," and recommended passage. The names of John Day, Free Tom of Gonzales and Silas of Bowie, evidently new arrivals, were added to the bill.[43] The disposition of the House to annul general laws of the land through private acts was sufficiently irksome to one member to cause him to propose a further unconstitutional amendment "that all free persons of colour in the Republic be recognized as citizens," which was lost by a vote of 2 to 23. The term citizen had frequently been used loosely to refer to any inhabitant of the country but to satisfy its fastidious member the bill was amended by striking out citizens and inserting residents. A motion to suspend the rules and read the bill a third time was lost by two votes, 22 to 14, and a few days later enough representatives changed their vote to defeat the bill 18 to 12.[44]

Lovinia admitted that she had entered the country in violation of the immigration law, Congress refused to exempt her from it, yet Lovinia was neither forced to leave nor did she suffer the penalty of sale into slavery. This refusal resulted only in the submission of a second bill to the ninth Congress which received the favorable recommendation of the committee on the state of the Republic.[45] On the floor, an amendment was offered and adopted providing for "bond with approved security" to be entered in such amount as the Chief Justice of her county should direct. An additional amendment "that she remain under the protection and direction of some white family" was adopted, and a third amendment to restrict her residence to the "county where she now resides" was rejected. Two days later the bill was laid on the table and never taken up, but Lovinia continued her residence unmolested.[46]

The mere existence of the law may have discouraged some blacks from coming to Texas and others may have been refused passage on ships bound for Texan ports but no direct evidence of such effects has been discovered. Those who did come, as far as is known without exception, were permitted to remain without molestation. So it was, that with a stringent law on the statute books effectively designed to rid Texas of its free black population within two years of its enactment, their numbers were actually increased through immigration.

The second group of blacks, those who immigrated subsequent to March 2, 1836, and previous to February 5, 1840, under the law were forced to emigrate before February 5, 1842. They sought to extend their residence privilege indefinitely. A beginning in this direction had been made by the Ashworth act which specifically exempted David and Aaron Ashworth, both of whom emigrated in 1838, from the provisions of the law applying to this group; and on November 10, 1840, the House committee on the state of the Republic in considering the petition of Henry Tucker, who arrived in 1838, had rendered the opinion that all petitions in favor of a black's residence signed by as many as forty respectable citizens who testified to his good character should receive the sanction of Congress.

Two additional petitions were received from Henry Lynch and Andrew Bell, both of whom immigrated subsequent to the declaration of independence. Henry Lynch, a resident of Austin, sent in an unendorsed petition in which he claimed that he "emigrated two years since, at the time when there was no law prohibiting the settlement of free persons of colour in Texas. He has a wife in the country as well as many other ties which endear the country to him," and on these grounds he asked for permission to remain.[47] Andrew Bell came to Texas in 1837; he was a "good brick mason and his services valuable to the improvement of the country." Six endorsers including Thomas J. Rusk believed that "No injury and much benefit" would result from granting Bell permission to remain in Texas.[48]

The committee on the state of the Republic, in reporting on these petitions, deemed it "inexpedient to allow any free persons of colour to remain in this republic," although evidently referring only to late arrivals, as this same committee reported favorably on all petitions of blacks who had immigrated previous to the declaration of independence.[49] The decision of the fifth Congress in accepting the committee's report, was that all free blacks who had immigrated subsequent to the declaration of independence must remove from the Republic before February 5, 1842.

With the convening of the sixth Congress on November 1, 1841, members of this group made their final pleas to the legislature for permission to remain. Pleasant Bious related that he had emigrated to Texas "without a knowledge of the law prohibiting free persons of colour to remain and abide in the country." He testified that he had lived in Texas about three years and had a wife and children who were slaves and therefore could not leave with him "to any other Government." He prayed Congress "that he may be permitted to Remain and abide within the Republic protected by the Laws of the Country from the many wrongs and abuses which he has heretofore suffered, from those who is disposed to use the power of the Law or abuse your petitioner because he is Black and of the African Race (Though free) your petitioner doth further Show that he has Service in the army in defence of this Republic and Begs to be permitted to live in the Country which he has defended and is at all times willing to defend."[50] A bill was introduced to permit Pleasant Bious to remain, and an amendment adopted to restrict his residence to Houston county, but the bill was lost.[51]

In her first petition in 1840, Zelia Husk, Houston washerwoman, alleged that she had immigrated in 1835, and after the passage of the Ashworth act her petition was endorsed "provided for by an act already passed." To her dismay, Zelia soon discovered that she had arrived subsequent to the declaration of independence and consequently that she did not share in the benefits of the Ashworth act. In the year intervening between her two petitions the number of her endorsers and presumably of her washings increased from forty-one to fifty, and she no longer complained that she lacked the means of transportation, but now the "law requiring removal [reads the petition] would bear heavily upon herself and daughter Emily . . . inasmuch as she would not know where to go if driven hence." Endorsers declared that they had known the woman for the last two or three years, that she "Conducts herself well and earns her living by Honest Industry in the capacity of Washerwoman," and that they were perfectly willing for her to continue.[52]

The first unendorsed petition sent in by Henry Lynch had been ignored by the fifth Congress, so Lynch collected the signatures of his employers to a second. Thirteen citizens of Austin who frequently hired him declared that they had "always found him [an] honest, sober, well disposed, and humble fellow, and would be pleased to see Congress give him the liberty to remain."[53] When the petition was presented in the Senate, Francis Moore moved for rejection, but the motion was lost by a seven to three vote and referred to the judiciary committee.[54]

Sixty-seven citizens of Red River county brought to the attention of Congress that Chance [Charles] Grubbs was "notorious for his good reputation and is strictly and perfectly honest truthfull and not in any way evil disposed and withal a good mechanic and of industrious habits and all those who are acquainted with the said Grubbs are perfectly willing for him to remain in the country" together with his five children.[55]

John Hemphill wrote his own unendorsed memorial in which he claimed that at the time of his immigration from Alabama in 1838, he "believed it was not contrary to law, at least it was the custom so to do." If he could not be granted the right to remain permanently he prayed Congress for time to collect money due him for his labor, as "from the extreme scarcity of money and hardness of the times, he could not raise the means now of returning" to Alabama. Evidently he could raise bond as he was willing to post a forfeit for his good behavior if permitted to remain for a year. By granting his prayer Congress would prevent him "from being driven a peniles and a houseless wanderer on the face of the earth."[56]

On January 5, 1842, the House committee on the state of the Republic recommended the indefinite postponement of the petitions of Zylpha Husk, Nelson Kavenaugh, Silas Porter, Charles Grubbs and Henry Lynch.[57] Evidently it was the will of the sixth Congress as of its predecessors that all free blacks who had come to Texas subsequent to the declaration of independence should either emigrate or suffer the consequence of being sold into slavery.

One last appeal was made and it was heard. On February 5, 1842, the day on which the 1840 law became effective, when Congress adjourned without exempting these blacks from the provisions of that law, Sam Houston, by presidential proclamation remitted the penalties of the act for one year, evidently anticipating future legislation. He declared, "It has been represented to me that there are a number of honest and industrious persons of that description, who have been citizens of this country for a number of years, and have always heretofore conducted themselves so as to obtain the confidence and good opinion of all acquainted with them, and are now anxious to be permitted to remain in the Republic for the next twelve months," and he therefore exempted these blacks from the law under certain conditions. All persons who wished to obtain the benefits of this remission were required to make satisfactory proof of their good conduct and post a bond of five hundred dollars with the Chief Justice of their county to guarantee good behavior during the year provided in the proclamation.[58]

This year of grace afforded blacks the opportunity of making one more appeal to Congress for permission to remain. For this purpose Henry Tucker prepared his third petition. Ignoring the provisions of the Constitution which forbade permanent residence to free blacks without the consent of Congress, Tucker had the temerity to say that he had immigrated to Texas in 1838, "with an assurance under the then existing laws that he should be entitled to a residence and protection as a citizen of said Republic," and added that "during residence in the country he has faithfully observed the Laws." As a further plea he stated that "he expended what little means he brought with him . . . in procuring himself a home that should he now be forced to leave the country he would be totally ruined which would be a peculiar hardship as he made a great sacrifice in migrating to the country." Nine endorsers including Thomas

M. League, Francis Moore, Jr., A. Brigham and Memucan Hunt "Most willingly and cheerfully testify that we have for many years known Henry Tucker . . . and during our acquaintance with him he has conducted himself with great decorum and propriety . . . and believing him, if any of his colour is entitled to . . . relief," they prayed Congress to grant him consideration.[59] The committee on the state of the Republic reported a bill for Tucker's relief which was amended to include the names of Pleasant Bious, Rutha Simmons and Henry Lynch, and then laid on the table.

Other blacks who would be affected by the resumption of the law and their supporters again appealed directly to the President. On December 21, 1842, a day before the committee reported on the Tucker petition, Sam Houston issued a second proclamation remitting the penalties of the law for an additional two years to February 5, 1845, under the same conditions outlined in his previous edict.[60]

Few efforts were made to gain the favor of the last two Congresses of the Republic to a further extension of residence. William Gladden and Charles Grubbs, both of whom arrived previous to February 5, 1840, were refused permission to remain permanently.[61] Other blacks in this group, discouraged by repeated rejection of their pleas, came to depend upon continued executive clemency, but without avail. No presidential proclamation remedied the failure of the last Congress to revise the act of February 5, 1840; the section directed against blacks who arrived before its enactment and subsequent to the declaration of independence went into effect on February 5, 1845, and in the eyes of the law the status of these blacks was reduced to that of the first group of illegal immigrants, semi-outlaws living upon the sufferance of their white neighbors. There is, nevertheless, no evidence of any exodus of free blacks and no evidence of any arraignment. As long as they gave no offence, local authorities refrained from prosecuting them. As time passed, all blacks who remained unmolested, by virtue of that fact, were presumed to have resided in Texas on the day of the declaration of independence and this legal fiction was later confirmed by judicial decision.[62] The statute, however, gave the white man a whip hand, since by its provisions, upon proof that a black had entered the country subsequent to March 2, 1836, he could at any time be given ten days' notice to quit the country. Although by general reputation the African is by nature light-hearted, living today without much care for the morrow, the quick protests of the blacks to the unfavorable legislation in 1840, is evidence of the fact that many of them looked with some concern at least two years into the future. The fear of summary banishment, doubtless, gave them a feeling of impermanence and insecurity which hindered an economic and social progress among them that might have taken place under more favorable circumstances.

The third group of blacks, those who immigrated previous to the declaration of independence, were protected in their residence by the Ashworth law, but they had no assurance that their land claims would be recognized or respected. A few blacks like Greenbury Logan and Samuel H. Hardin had completed their titles under the Mexican laws[63] and these titles were never brought directly into question. No land patents, however, had been granted by the Republic of Texas to blacks previous to 1840, chiefly on the grounds that they were permanently barred from citizenship and this disability was generally construed to preclude land ownership. In a committee report of the first Congress answering the petition of John and Henry Bird, a tacit opinion that the plea of blacks for land rights was unreasonable received the approval of the House of Representatives.[64] In the case of Samuel McCullough who neglected to apply for lands to which he was entitled under the laws of Mexico, and for which he sought remedy through congressional action, a committee report deemed it impossible to take any action.[65] A similar fate awaited the attempt of Lewis B. Jones to have patented a grant of half a league of land which he received from Austin in 1834,[66] and Jean Baptiste Maturin had no better success in his attempt to perfect title to a Mexican grant.[67] The solid opposition to black ownership of land broke down with the passage of a bill in the Senate authorizing William Goyens to apply to the land commissioner and secure a certificate for a league and labor of land to which he was entitled under the Mexican law. The bill was amended to give the same rights to John Bird, Henry Bird and Edward Smith, and passed the Senate but the House adjourned on the following day without hearing the bill.[68] The tendency to recognize a black's claim to land ownership in the case of William Goyens was reversed in that of Joseph Tate. He applied to the land commissioner for land to which his bounty certificate for four months of service in the army entitled him. Refused a patent by the commissioner, Tate appealed to Congress.[69] In the debates which ensued, the opinion was expressed and confirmed that no law authorized Africans to hold land within Texas, and in lieu of land Tate was granted a sum of money.[70]

Previous to the law of February 5, 1840, then, the opinion that blacks were not entitled to hold land had been upheld by the land commissioner and by Congress. Blacks, nevertheless, continued to occupy the land upon which they settled, and although the government considered it to be part of the public domain no official efforts were made to dislodge them. They could not convey a legal title to it and they were in constant fear that some white person would locate upon it and acquire a legal title. In order to avoid the consequences of an imperfect title, in 1841, John Bird and his son-in-law, Edward Smith, together with their families decided to make a second effort to acquire a patent to their land. They petitioned Congress for the "privilege of holding property both real and personal [the same] as other citizens." Fifty-nine citizens of San Augustine county certified that the Birds were "good citizens supporting in good moral caracter and some of them have served several campains in the army during our struggle for independence,"[71] but Congress ignored their plea.

On January 29, 1840, an act to provide for issuing patents to legal claimants had set up new machinery to facilitate perfection of land titles. Two boards of three travelling commissioners were authorized, one east of the Brazos and one west. These commissions were to visit the counties in their districts and in conjunction with three commissioners appointed for each county were to inspect claims. Upon the return of a survey and by authority of a certificate returned as legal by the travelling commissioners, the commissioner of the General Land Office was to issue a patent. Appeals from the decision of the board of land commissioners were to be taken to the district court and decided by jury verdict. Upon a favorable court decision, the Commissioner was required to issue a patent, the same as if the commissioners had approved it.[72]

The board of travelling commissioners set up for itself twenty-five faulty characteristics of claims on the basis of which they refused to recommend patents. Two of these directly concerned free blacks: first, "persons married to individuals of African descent and claiming land as heads of families"; and second, "free persons of African descent, claiming headrights as citizens," were refused patents.[73] On May 7, 1841, William Goyens sued the board for rejecting his claim, but the jury found "a true verdict in behalf of the Republic," and Goyens received a bill for "all costs of this proceeding."[74] The court refused to overrule the commissioners.

The travelling commissioners likewise refused to recommend for patent the certificates which the Bird and Ashworth families received from the local board of Jefferson county "for their head right to the lands they would have been entitled to, under the Mexican government at the time they emigrated!"[75] The commissioners were convinced of the justice of their claims and believed that they should be allowed, yet a doubt existed in their minds whether the constitution permitted them to recommend patents to black claimants since they were excluded from citizenship. So much impressed were they with the injustice of the ruling which they believed the law required that they resorted to the strange device of appealing to Congress to reverse their decision. If Congress could not lawfully vest title in land to a black, the board suggested two alternatives, first, that blacks be considered aliens capable of holding land "by titles emanating directly from the government" as provided in section 10 of the general provisions of the Constitution, or second, that they be granted long term leases on the land within their claims. In this plea, the three travelling commissioners for the district east of the Brazos were joined by the three members of the local board and seventy-odd citizens of Jefferson county.

> [These] good and worthy members of the Community, labor by reason of their being people of colour under great and embarrassing inconveniences. For that notwithstanding the said individuals have uniformly discharged the duty of good and patriotic Citizens of [the Republic of Texas], both during the Contest with Mexico for our independence (as the records of the War office will show) and since that time as industrious and orderly Citizens yet a doubt exists that the Constitution and laws of the Republick prevent their attaining the Ownership in Law of the homesteads and headrights for the sake of which they emigrated originally to the State of "Coahuila and Texas" and in the Continuation of which hope they sustained to the best of their pecuniary and personal abilities the Cause of our independence. Your Memorialists represent to your "Honorable Body" that they view with strong feelings of sympathy the situation of these worthy families, and prays your "Honorable Body" That if they may not be received as Citizens under the Constitution, that the Declaration of the Genl Consultation in favour of those who should aid in establishing the liberties of the Republick may be remembered in their particular case either by means of a right or patent emanating from the Government to them and their Heirs considered as Aliens or by lease for a long term of years of the Headright that that [sic] would have accrued to them had there been no taint of blood in their veins. And your Memorialists further represent to your Honorable Body the Justice and propriety of the enactment of a law which should operate to prevent the location of claims which they possess by virtue [of] supposed Headright claims as well as those lands owned by them in virtue of their respective Military Bounty Certificates.[76]

"With these views and placing undoubting confidence in the Wisdom, Justice and Magnanimity of your Honorable Body," the commissioners forwarded the memorial to Congress. The report of the House committee on the state of the Republic on December 15, 1842, confirmed the facts outlined in the petition, and "without avowing any partiality for this description of population," it recommended the passage of a bill requiring the Land Office to issue patents on the certificates granted by the local board of Jefferson county to William, Abner and Aaron Ashworth, John and Henry Bird, and Aaron Nelson.[77] The bill passed both Houses without recorded opposition and was presented to the President for his signature on January 10, 1843, becoming law eight days later.[78]

No further petitions praying for recognition of land rights were received during the Republic and it is reasonable to suppose that in the remaining two and a half years no further cases appeared in which the black's legal right to own real property was questioned on a basis of color.

The basic rights of residence and ownership guaranteed to the white man by the constitution and essential to the fundamental rights of protection to life and property were inadequately guarded to the black by statute. A continuous discussion of proposed changes by successive legislatures kept the free black under a veil of uncertainty. Despite this basic handicap and others corollary to it still to be considered, free blacks, aided and encouraged by white friends, were able to acquire important additional extralegal compensations which did not silence their mild protests against political inequality. Their appreciation and use of concessions made to them, however, fully justified the increasing faith of their white protagonists.

NOTES

1. This petition has not been found.

2. G. A. Pattillo to M. B. Lamar, February 24, 1840. Lamar Papers, MS. No. 1729, Texas State Library.

3. The name of Jessee is lost in subsequent petitions. The rapid fluctuation in the given names of the Ashworth brothers, as well as of other Blacks, is probably accounted for by a number of names under which some of them were known rather than by continuous migrations. On September 19, 1840, the names of the four Ashworth brothers are given as Joshua, Aaron, David and William. It is supplemented by another of the same date in which two of these brothers are called Abner and William (Memorial No. 19, File 49, September 19, 1840). In the latter part of 1842, the names of the "heirs of Moses Ashworth," their father, are given as William, Abner, Aaron, Elisha, Lamas, Elija and Thomas (Memorial No. 11, File A, no date). On January 6, 1843, three brothers are named William, Abner and Aaron (Bill No. 2706, File No. 29, January 6, 1843, Seventh Congress). The names of the four brothers are assumed to have been William, Abner, Aaron and David.

4. Memorial No. 21, File 21, December 3, 1840. This petition for the relief of Allen Dimery and his family, old residents, was sent to Congress in order "that all apprehension may be set at rest."

5. Gammel, *The Laws of Texas*, II, 326.

6. Memorial No. 19, File 49, September 19, 1840.

7. Memorial No. 19, File 49, September 19, 1840.

8. Memorial No. 18, File 49, September 18, 1840.

9. *House Journal*, Fifth Congress, 27.

10. Committee Report No. 2582, File 28, Sixth Congress. This undated report belongs in the papers of the Fifth Congress. *House Journal*, Fifth Congress, 33.

11. *House Journal,* Fifth Congress, 33.

12. The law was self-contradictory on the date of its effectiveness. Section 8 allowed free blacks to remain until February 5, but Section 10 required the president to issue a proclamation commanding all free blacks to remove before January 1. Gammel, *The Laws of Texas,* II, 326. President Houston disregarded Section 10, interpreting the intent of the law to be February 5.

13. Memorial No. 16. File T, no date; *House Journal,* Fifth Congress, 32.

14. Committee Report No. 2200, File 23, Fifth Congress. *House Journal,* Fifth Congress, 63.

15. *House Journal,* Fifth Congress, 34.

16. *House Journal,* Fifth Congress, 35.

17. Committee Reports No. 1677, File 19; No. 1527, File 17, Fifth Congress.

18. *House Journal,* Fifth Congress, 40.

19. Memorial No. 23, File 75, October 19, 1840.

20. Memorial No. 18, File FE no date. This petition received a favorable committee report on November 19, 1840. Committee Report, No. 2200, File 23, Fifth Congress.

21. *House Journal,* Fifth Congress, 40.

22. *House Journal,* Fifth Congress, 52.

23. *House Journal,* Fifth Congress, 54.

24. Congressional Papers, Fifth Congress. *Senate Journal,* Fifth Congress, 38.

25. Bill No. 1610, File 18, Fifth Congress. Endorsed, "Substitute of Senate read and adopted."

26. Gammel, *The Laws of Texas,* II, 549. The same act erroneously appears again as a separate act with the Ashworth name spelled "Ainsworth" in Gammel, *The Laws of Texas,* II, 648.

27. Gammel, *The Laws of Texas*, II, 468. The bill was amended twice before passage. A wholly unnecessary provision to the effect that the present bill was not intended to exempt the McCulloughs from the provisions of any future act in relation to free persons of color, was struck out. The bill was further amended to include the descendants of the McCulloughs (Bills No. 1677, File 19; No. 1527, File 17, Fifth Congress), but is without significance since the Ashworth Act by including the families of its beneficiaries was construed to mean their descendants.

28. Memorial No. 13, File 32, September, 1840.

29. The petition reads, "they are the children of David and Sophia Gowns, the last named a free person of colour."

30. Memorial No. 13, File 32, October 18, 1840.

31. Memorial No. 16, File 65, October 30, 1840.

32. Memorial No. 5, File T, December 13, 1840.

33. Memorial No. 380, File 45, December 14, 1840; *House Journal*, Fifth Congress, 244. In the following year, Zelia was to discover that she arrived in 1836 instead of 1835, necessitating a second petition to be discussed presently. Memorial No. 122, File 40, December 11, 1841.

34. Memorial No. 16, File 54, December 14, 1840.

35. *House Journal*, Fifth Congress, 504; Memorial No. 144, File 74, December 31, 1840. This petition is ambiguously endorsed "Inexpedient and unnecessary." If Patsey immigrated previous to the declaration of independence the petition was unnecessary; if she came subsequently to that time Congress may have deemed action inexpedient, but both terms were not applicable.

36. *House Journal*, Fifth Congress, 146. This petition was probably for the relief of John Bird and his family, old residents in San Augustine County.

37. This petition was for the relief of Wiley. *House Journal*, Fifth Congress, 188.

38. Autobiography of James N. Smith, 3, 7, 8, 9. University of Texas transcripts.

39. Memorial No. 88, File 95, November 28, 1853.

40. Memorial No. 251, File 64, no date. This petition is signed by eighty-two "of the most respectable ladies and gentlemen of the city of Galveston." Bill No. 39, File 53, Fourth Legislature.

41. Memorial No. 51, File 60, February 25, 1846.

42. Bill No. 2816, File 30, Eighth Congress.

43. The name of William Goy[e]n[s] was also added. Goyens already had legal permission to remain under the Ashworth law. Further amendments were made to include William Gladman [Gladden] and Chance [Charles] Grub[b]s. These two blacks immigrated previous to February 5, 1840, and are considered later. *House Journal,* Eighth Congress, 246, 248, 266, 288; Bill No. 2816, File 30, Eighth Congress.

44. *House Journal,* Eighth Congress, 266, 288.

45. *House Journal,* Ninth Congress, 66, 83.

46. *House Journal,* Ninth Congress, 109, 112; Bill No. 2915, File 32, Ninth Congress; Memorial No. 51, File 60, February 25, 1846.

47. Memorial No. 54, File 17, December 15, 1840. Endorsed "Inexpedient and unfavorable."

48. Memorial No. 46, File 5, December 4, 1840.

49. Committee Report, No. 2202, File 24, Fifth Congress; *House Journal,* Fifth Congress, 375.

50. Memorial No. 45, File 5, November 5, 1841.

51. Memorial No. 2228, File 25, Sixth Congress.

52. Memorial No. 122, File 40, December 11, 1841.

53. Memorial No. 28, File 54, December 15, 1841.

54. *Senate Journal*, Sixth Congress, 76.

55. Memorial No. 217, File 36, December 18, [1841].

56. Memorial No. 28, File 54, no date.

57. Committee Reports, Sixth Congress. The petitions of Silas Porter and Nelson Kavenaugh have not been found.

58. *Austin City Gazette*, February 9, 1842.

59. Memorial No. 16, File T, December 3, 1842.

60. Gammel, *The Laws of Texas*, II, 879.

61. *House Journal*, Eighth Congress, 266, 288.

62. Carter v. Marks, 17 *Texas* 539.

63. Spanish Titles, IV, 1022; VIII, 581.

64. *House Journal*, First Congress, 219–220.

65. *House Journal*, First Congress, Adjourned Session, 105.

66. Memorial No. 49, File 5, October 8, 1837; Austin's Colonists, II, 91.

67. Memorial No. 13, File M, April 21, 1838.

68. Bill No. 999, File 11, Second Congress, Adjourned Session.

69. Memorial No. 1, File T, no date; *Senate Journal*, Fourth Congress, 32.

70. *House Journal*, Fourth Congress, 47, 63, 69, 150; *Reports and Relief Laws*, 216–217.

71. Memorial No. 33, File 80, January 3, 1841.

72. Gammel, *The Laws of Texas*, II, 313–317. Section 8, applying to appeals, was repealed on February 5, 1840 (Gammel, *The Laws of Texas*, II, 317), but without affecting recourse to the courts by rejected claimants.

73. *House Journal Appendix,* Fifth Congress, 302.

74. Nacogdoches District Court, Minute Book C, 10. University of Texas photostats.

75. *House Journal,* Seventh Congress, 63.

76. Memorial No. 11, File A, no date. The names of some of the endorsers of this petition have been deleted by autograph hunters.

77. *House Journal,* Seventh Congress, 63; Memorial No. 11, File A, no date; Bill No. 2706, File 29, Seventh Congress. The name of Aaron Nelson was inserted in the petition at a time after its original writing. Nothing is known of Nelson except that he was "of mixed blood though nearly white." An unsuccessful attempt was made in December, 1843, to repeal the law resulting from this petition in so far as it applied to Nelson but the cause is not revealed. Bill No. 2772, File 30, Eighth Congress; *House Journal,* Eighth Congress, 54.

78. *House Journal,* Seventh Congress, 73, 80, 198; Gammel, *The Laws of Texas,* II, 875, contains only an abstract. A bill to grant the free black children of Nimrod Doyle the right to hold property "and other rights of free persons," was introduced on January 9, 1843, engrossed, but failed to pass. Bill No. 2719, File 29, Seventh Congress.

6

THE EXTENT OF DISCRIMINATION
AND ITS EFFECTS

Harold R. Schoen

The Mexican government in Texas offered to free blacks liberty, equality and the full rights of citizenship. It engaged to encourage their immigration by offering them land and tools for cultivation, and protection in order that they might pursue their work peacefully. Arrived in Texas, they were accepted as colonists by the leading empresarios side by side with white men. Some of them emigrated to Texas for the purpose of enjoying this greater liberty; others who found themselves in Texas for diverse causes readily accepted the boon and became easily accustomed to it.

In the revolution against the Mexican government, free blacks contributed of their property and their personal services to retain their rights, only to find that in victory they had lost them. As an ironic reward for their patriotism, the constitution permanently excluded them from citizenship and reserved the right to pass individually upon their continued residence, seriously circumscribing their rights in the state without in any way limiting their obligation to it.[1] In setting up the machinery of government the free black population was not counted in the apportionment of representation.[2] Since their numbers were always small,[3] their omission had no practical effect in determining election districts. Aside from the moral effect of branding them as unfit to participate in government, this loss of the franchise was not serious.

All the practical value of representation was retained through the right of petition.[4] The privilege of free blacks to petition Congress, at least in matters pertaining to residence, was tacitly recognized in the provision giving Congress the power to grant them the right of permanent residence in the Republic.[5] Most black petitions were endorsed by white men whose intercessions, doubtless, added strength to the pleas, but were not at all a legal necessity.[6] Two unsuccessful attempts were made to interfere with the petition process. At the beginning of the fourth Congress which convened close upon the failure of the city of Houston to rid itself of free blacks by judicial procedure and adjourned with the passage of the law of February 5, 1840, which made such procedure effective, Beden Stroud introduced a bill, part of which prevented the Senate from receiving or entertaining petitions from free blacks.[7] The bill was at first tabled, later referred to the judiciary committee[8] and finally emerged as the law of February 5, 1840, which denied them the right to remain in the country but did not disturb the privilege of petition for exemption from the law. The second attempt was made by Francis Moore, Jr., in the sixth Congress by moving to reject the petition of Henry Lynch. This motion was not for a denial of the prayer but for an expulsion of the petition itself as an intruder into the Senate. The proposal was defeated by a seven to three vote and the petition referred to the judiciary committee for consideration, thus affirming the right of the free black to be heard.[9]

In addition to the formal procedure of petition, free blacks presented their grievances personally or by private letter to members of Congress.[10] They had come to know some of these public men as their frontier neighbors and others as their officers in the Revolutionary army. These Congressmen needed no prompting to protect the rights of their black friends. Although the Congressional Journals show that they were not always familiar with the privileges already granted to particular blacks, they were sure to add the names of their own favorites to bills which granted any black special privileges. Certainly every petition and as far as we know every grievance presented was brought to the attention of Congress and received parliamentary consideration.

A frequent complaint of free blacks continually brought to the attention of Congress was the exclusion from citizenship. Because the term citizen was commonly used loosely as a synonym for resident, it is not always easy to know whether a black was asking solely for resident privileges or for all the rights of citizenship. Certainly many of them asked for more than the right to remain, most frequently joining resident rights with the privilege of holding real property the same as other citizens.[11] Two petitions went still further. Memucan Hunt, James Reily, Robert Wilson and others believed that Nelson Kavanaugh "should be allowed most of the privileges of a white man, such as holding real estate, suing and being sued and the right to swear in court."[12] The traveling board of land commissioners, as one method of granting land to the Ashworths and Birds thought that they might "be received as Citizens under the Constitution," despite their black blood.[13] The eighth Congress overstepped its bounds by bringing the question of citizenship for blacks to a vote when a constitutional amendment would have been required to settle the question. Other circumstances throw doubt upon the sincerity of the two members of the House who voted in favor of the measure.[14] At no time was there the slightest possibility of black citizenship being seriously proposed.

Apart from the question of the legal right of blacks to retain real property granted to them by the Mexican government or secured by purchase,[15] was their right to share in the undivided public domain. The constitution and a series of laws generously distributed headrights to white immigrants, adult residents and young men coming of age, but blacks received nothing.[16] This exclusion from land donations was logical since the well-established policy of the Republic at first discouraged and later prevented free black immigration. These disqualifying acts threw considerable doubt upon the right of blacks to own land under any circumstances, even by purchase; increased their immediate difficulty of establishing themselves upon farms; and may have prevented some of them from laying the bases for family fortune.

Despite insecurity of titles, blacks continued to improve the land upon which they had settled and increased the acreage of their farms by purchase, while some landless ones entered the propertied class. Jean Baptiste Maturin, made "valuable improvements" on his *sitio* which enabled him to support "himself, his family and his stock of cattle" for at least ten years, although his one-fourth black blood forced him to live in constant fear that he would lose both land and improvements.[17] Tomas Morgan, an "industrious and useful negress" who was brought to Texas as a slave in 1832, "and purchased her freedom with the proceeds of her own labor sometime during the year 1834," continued to display her industry after that date and "acquired a considerable amount of Real Estate in the Country." She was married to an equally industrious black, Emanuel J. Hardin, who, starting with nothing "Acquired a considerable amount of property in the Country."[18] Samuel H. Hardin, possibly a relative, who had the original advantage of a grant of half a league in Waller county from Stephen F. Austin, in 1843 owned one hundred acres of improved land in Brazoria county valued at $500, and six town lots in Brazoria and Velasco worth $1,100.[19] Allen Dimery sold two thousand acres to Major John Durst in the early 'forties, apparently to improve the remainder of his league.[20] William Goyens "accumulated considerable property in land."[21] In 1839, he bought a "portion of a Mexican grant" adjacent to

his own league and labor.[22] By the terms of a complicated agreement
two years later, typical of the time, and by the varying amounts of land
which he owned from year to year,[23] he appears to have made a business
of buying, improving and then selling virgin land. For seven thousand
dollars Henry Baguet was to choose one thousand acres of land in a
certain tract owned by Goyens "including Mills, Dwellings and all the
improvements on Said Land," Baguet to pay Goyens fifty-five hundred
dollars in land at the rate of one dollar an acre to be chosen by Goyens in
three disjoined tracts out of Baguet's five leagues, each tract "to be as near
equal in quality of the whole league as possible." For the balance of fifteen
hundred dollars due Goyens, Baguet assumed a debt of twelve hundred
dollars which Goyens owed David Towns, and agreed to pay him three
hundred dollars in cash at a time to be determined by future events.
If Goyens lost a Supreme Court appeal from a district court judgment
against him, Baguet was to pay him the three hundred dollars at the
time of the adverse decision, but if Goyens won the case Baguet was not
to pay him until "such time as they can agree on." Baguet was to take
possession of the mills on December 15, 1841, and of the entire premises
seven weeks later.[24] The twelve hundred dollar debt, itself, was due to
David Towns in payment of a quarter league of land which "goins and
Debad" bought from Towns.[25] Goyens was evidently a shrewd trader.
In 1841, he owned 4,160 acres of improved land valued at $20,600, two
town lots, fifty head of cattle and two work horses in addition to other
property for which he was assessed $128.50 in taxes.[26]

In addition to securing land by purchase, it was also possible for blacks
to lease land for farming purposes. Abner Ashworth, in 1838, leased a
league of land on Tailor's Bayou for the term of one year for twenty
dollars. According to the terms of the lease, Ashworth was not to "Cut
any Wood or Timber on Sd Primescis Except Dead Timber. [He was] To
Use Sd Land in Cultivation in a Husband like Manners, to render Piusful
Possession [and] at the Expiration of Sd term . . . forwarn any person
Against Trespassing on Sd Primiacis afore Sd."[27] The Ashworth brothers
are perhaps the prime example of Black frugality, industry and success

in farming. In 1837, the first available report, they owned 1,113 acres of titled land, 934 head of cattle, 52 horses and five slaves. Eight years later they had increased their property to 14,296 acres, 2,240 head of cattle, 84 horses and ten slaves,[28] which constituted a considerable investment and a large scale enterprise for the time.

The ownership of slaves by colored freemen was not unique in the case of the Ashworths. Hendrick Arnold held his daughter as a slave, and later sold her with the provision that her new owner manumit her within five years.[29] Aside from blacks holding members of their families as slaves as a means of giving them actual freedom, other free blacks like the Ashworths owned slaves for purely productive purposes. Among them were William Goyens who engaged in lively slave trades under the Mexican regime[30] and continued to own as many as nine slaves during the Republic;[31] and Samuel H. Hardin, who in 1844, owned four blacks.[32]

Apart from their legal right to hold personal property, which was never disputed, and real property, which was partially recognized in 1843, the distinction between slaves and colored freemen was slight. In all respects save that of the relationship between slave and master, the disposition of the Republic was to place free blacks on a footing of equality with slaves. They were governed by the same criminal code, forbidden to bear witness except against other blacks and confused with slaves in other legislation, proposed and accepted, designed primarily for the protection of the peculiar institution of slavery without consideration for the encroachment upon the free status of some blacks.[33] Unsuccessful attempts were made to include free blacks in an act to prohibit the sale of spirituous liquors to slaves; to prohibit them from keeping arms without license; to make it a criminal offense for a black "to lift a hand" in opposition to any white person; and to bar them from exercising "the functions of a minister of the Gospel."[34] In addition, efforts were made to restrict their movements to the county in which they resided.[35] Attempts were also made, beginning in 1842, to inaugurate a slave patrol to "visit in black quarters and places suspected of containing unlawful assemblies

of slaves and other disorderly persons." The broad powers extended to
the patrol authorized them to force open the doors of free blacks when
access was denied. The opposition of non-slaveholders to uncompensated
service patrolling their rich neighbors' slaves, and differences among the
slaveholders themselves, made impossible the framing of a bill which
would satisfy all factions and the several attempts met with no success
until after annexation.[36]

The criminal code when completed discriminated against the free black
by prescribing special offences and more severe punishment for common
crimes.[37] In accordance with the constitutional declaration against cruel
and unusual punishment, the penalties for blacks while more severe in
degree did not vary in kind. Whipping, branding, imprisonment, fines and
hanging were usual punishments for black and white alike. Additional
offences and increased punishment did not actually work a hardship on
blacks, since they were peaceable residents, and their offences few.[38]

In social matters, legislation definitely impressed blacks with their
own inferior status. By arbitrary ethnological definition persons were
prohibited from "obeying the divine precepts and laws of morality" since
they could not legally marry those whom they took "in the fervour and
integrity" of their desires if those persons happened to be on the opposite
side of an unscientific color line.[39] The principle was morally justified by
the notion that amalgamation of the races would inevitably lead to disease,
decline and death. The existence of the mulatto was living evidence
that the ostensible design of the law to prevent miscegenation failed. By
illegitimating offspring, persons with African blood were prevented from
coming into inheritances. The white parents' release from all responsibility prevented, in some cases, the formation of emotional ties and thus
preserved the cleavage between the races. The same irresponsibility,
doubtless, increased the mixture of white blood into the black race.

Previous to the enactment of the statute penalizing mixed marriages,
free blacks of the highest social standing showed a preference for white
wives. William Goyens, in 1832, was living "happily together with a

white woman from Georgia." The couple were "considered as very respectable," and the marriage was approved by two brothers of Mrs. Goyens who "appeared well satisfied with their coloured brother-in-law."[40] Hendrick Arnold, immediately after the Revolution, married his captain's daughter by his Mexican wife,[41] and Arnold's daughter by a previous black wife followed her father's example in hybridizing by taking a Mexican husband.[42]

Although David L. Wood was indicted under the law for marrying a black woman,[43] the passage of the statute did not result in rigid prosecution. Samuel McCullough, Jr., on August 11, 1837, two months after the law was enacted, married Mary Lorena Vess, the white daughter of "Jonathan Vess, one of Austin's old colonists," and she remained married to him with impunity from the law long enough to bear him at least three children, and until her death in 1847.[44] Other cases of white men marrying free black women are not lacking. Andrew Bell's sister, Louiza, married David Towns;[45] Eliza and Louisa Gowns, like their mother, married white men.[46] These unions had the effect of diminishing the already inadequate supply of eligible free black women for men of the same status.

Deprived of women of their own class, many free black men remained bachelors, but others contented themselves with slave wives. The obvious disadvantages of such an arrangement were somewhat offset by the fact that the husband was not only relieved of the responsibility of supporting his family, but also he might secure work or engage the protection of his wife's master in time of need. Pleasant Bious, for example, "who had a wife and children who are slaves and therefore cannot go with me to any other Gover[n]ment" made this his plea for permission to remain, and although his wife's master is unknown, his name is doubtless among the endorsers of the petition.[47]

For the most part free black marriages to slaves were dictated by the paucity of free black women rather than by a desire to avoid responsibility, and such marriages did not preclude true affection. Richard R. Barkeson was a free black who on occasion worked for Mirabeau Lamar. When his wife and child were offered for sale for $1,400, he pleaded with the General to purchase them and offered to bind himself "by any papers to you you may think proper" because "in serving you I should be well aware to have a Master who would protect them under his care."[48]

In addition to national legislation, blacks were subject to special regulations by city ordinances which interfered with their freedom of person and may have hindered them in their business as well as in social life. A Galveston ordinance, for example, prohibited free blacks as well as slaves from being "found abroad at unseasonable hours of the night." No free black was allowed on the streets after the untimely hour of eight o'clock unless he had a permit from some responsible person, and in no case was he to be out-of-doors after ten o'clock.[49]

Many of the personal indignities which free blacks suffered were the result of ingrained prejudice and could not have been remedied by law. When in appreciation of her many kindnesses white women visited "Puss," the black wife of John Webber, they did not meet her as an equal. "At such times she flew around and set out the best meal which her larder afforded; but neither herself or her children offered to sit down and eat with her guests, and when she returned the visit she was set down in the kitchen to eat alone."[50] Pleasant Bious complained of more serious discrimination. He asked to be "protected by the Laws of the Country from the many wrongs and abuses which he has heretofore suffered, from those who is disposed to use the power of the Law or abuse your petitioner because he is Black and of the African race (though Free)."[51] Even if the law were violated in the abuse of blacks; the exclusion of black testimony made it necessary for ill treatment to be witnessed by white men willing to testify, an obvious difficulty, and even then it might be prudent for the black to suffer the abuse silently rather than attempt to prosecute a white man.

The courts did protect free blacks from flagrant abuses when given an opportunity. Jesse Benton committed assault and battery upon Eli

Williams, a free black, and Williams sued Benton for damages in the district court of Harris county on January 15, 1840. In answer to Williams' petition, Benton filed a plea, first of justification, and second, that Williams was of African descent and "not entitled by law to maintain his action, except by his guardian or next friend." Williams demurred to the second plea and was sustained by the court, and the trial proceeded on the first plea of justification. The jury found Benton's attack unwarranted and returned a judgment in favor of Williams. Benton appealed the case to the Supreme Court on the ground that the lower court erred in sustaining Williams' demurrer to his plea that free blacks could not sue in court.

The Supreme Court, reviewing the case in 1843, was unable to find any authority to sustain the principle that free blacks could not sue white men. The only possible ground, the Court decided, upon which such an argument could be based was their exclusion from citizenship. "But we cannot conclude that because they are not entitled to particular privileges, they are, while actually residing in our country, out of the pale of the protection of the law, and that injuries and aggressions may be wantonly committed on their persons and property, and that when they ask for a redress of such grievance, they are to be told that the courts of justice are closed against their complaints. We cannot, by sustaining the defendant's plea, establish a principle which we regard against law, contrary to the spirit of institutions, and in violation of the dictates of common humanity."[52]

The right of free blacks to sue, affirmed by the Supreme Court in this case, was not brought to question again and seems to have been taken as a natural right in litigation previous and subsequent to Benton's objection. In 1837, James and Sylvia, free people of color, sued for the freedom of their child held by Radford Berry and his wife as a slave. In the first trial the jury disagreed, in May, 1841, the case was continued by agreement, and a year later the jury decided that Sylvia's child was a slave. The right of a black to sue, however, was never questioned.[53] Similarly, in 1839, William Goyens sued Patricio De Torres for debt, and two years later he sued the board of land commissioners for title. The government raised no objection to the suit of a black against its white officers.[54]

The aid which white men offered free blacks was by no means confined to modification of the law. The large segment of this population which depended upon employment for their livelihood relied upon the good will and satisfaction of their white employers. These employers in turn showed themselves well disposed toward free black workers and often were helpful in finding use for them. Samuel A. Roberts of Mobile, Alabama, advised Thomas McAllister, a free man of color, to go to Texas "to better his fortune," sending him with a letter of introduction to Mirabeau Lamar. In this letter McAllister was described as "remarkable for his intelligence industry & strict honesty." "I have particularly advised him to go *first* to you," wrote Roberts to Lamar "thinking you might need some one to take charge of your household affairs—one who could get up and attend to your dinners (particularly when you have company) and keep everything about in order. If you need such a man I am confident you can find no one more competent to the task—He has been head waiter in several large Hotels in mobile & for the last four years Steward on board of the best packet Steam boats on the Alabama at a salary of $75. per month—and in any situation given entire satisfaction—Should you not want him you may safely recommend him to any of your friends . . ." Roberts intended to follow McAllister to Texas, and requested of Lamar that "Should Thomas want any pecuniary aid before my arrival if not inconvenient to you I hope you will assist him. I will repay any sum not more than four or five hundred dollars you may advance him. I shall take out with me means of his to something like this amount."[55]

Although blacks, doubtless, gained employment because they worked for less than their white competitors, continued service is ample evidence that they performed their work well. Menial workers like washerwomen were kept busy if not prosperous and were able to acquire "a little property,"[56] while skilled workers like Andrew Bell, a brick mason, found his services were valuable for the improvement of the country, and had no difficulty in securing work.[57] Likewise, Mary Madison, although she illegally entered the Republic, was permitted to remain unmolested and without formal exception from the law because she was a good nurse and the "services she has rendered . . . to the sick" were of "immense value to the community."[58]

Free black orphans seemed to have little difficulty in securing homes and parental care during their minorities. Albert Mitchell was taken into the home of John M. Clifton with a legislative order to regain full freedom when he reached the age of twenty-one,[59] and Marthan Moore, a fourteen-year-old orphan daughter of Violet Hamblet, a free woman of color, by her own consent and court decree was placed in the home of Mrs. Jane Harris to remain until she was twenty-one, meanwhile compensating Mrs. Harris with her labor.[60]

Adolphus Sterne hired white and black draymen without distinction for which he paid them "One fourth the Produce (Corn, Potatoes, etc.) the Hawl," and in the process of hiring William Smith, a free black, gained enough confidence in him to sell him a house and a piece of land "for $400 payable half in 12 months and the other half in 24 months," putting him in immediate possession of the place.[61]

Sometimes blacks were aided by white men in establishing enter-prises in direct competition with other white men. Joseph Hutchinson complained that William Ashworth "is trying to Establish a ferry at Beaumont whair my Wifes ferry is and Frederick W. byden & others are assisting him But Ogden is the principal & A part of my Gardon was on them Lotts But Ogden stated the other day that He ogden had Bought them Lotts from the Grigsbays, and ordered A Man to Teare Down the fence and Erect a Cowpen for the purpose of Swimming cattle and which pen by Ogden Said Win Ashworth should have the use of from him." Hutchinson wanted to buy the lots on reasonable terms if they were not already sold to Ogden for the use of Ashworth. "Theire reason for wanting the Lotts on the bank of the river in Beaumont is to own Land on Both sides of the River and by that Means Breakup my Wifs Ferry."[62]

The success of the free black in business depended upon white patronage and from the number and variety of enterprises in which they engaged neither seemed to show any aversion to dealing with the other. Carey, after buying his freedom from Thomas F. McKinney, engaged in the livery business in Galveston, renting out horses and buggies.[63] James Richardson in his inn midway between Velasco and San Luis was patronized sufficiently to make a satisfactory living and at the same time enjoy a black bent for oystering and boating which he no doubt learned in Philadelphia. He was guaranteed a monopoly of the business since his inn was located at a place where a white man equally serviceable could not be expected to survive.[64]

Several blacks showed remarkable business acumen. Peter, the manumitted slave of Wyly Martin, with his horse and wagon and by trading in farm products "accumulated a fortune of perhaps $16,000."[65] William Goyens's wealth was based upon his blacksmith shop, the actual labor in which he relegated to slaves and hired white men while he himself engaged in land deals, amateur detective work, racing horses, and litigation in connection with his variegated business and social activities.[66]

As might be expected, not all black businesses were continually successful. Greenbury Logan previous to the Revolution was a blacksmith. In storming Bexar he received a wound in his shoulder through which he "almost entirely lost the use of his right arm," incapacitating him for his trade. He and his wife, Caroline, in the following years displayed considerable versatility without achieving permanent success. They opened a boarding house, tavern and retail store in Brazoria sometime in 1836 or 1837, and apparently got along well for a time. In 1839, they owned four lots in Brazoria valued at $3,100, a year later they owned but three, and in 1841, Logan, impoverished and in debt, was forced to ask the government for a pension in the form of a remission of taxes in order that he might not lose the little property he had left. Two years later he tried his hand at farming, at the time owning nine work horses and twenty-eight cattle, but apparently had little success, as in 1845, he owned no taxable property.[67]

Throughout the South, blacks showed a great proclivity for the barber trade, and in Texas more were engaged in that business than in any single occupation except farming. Nelson Kavanaugh dignified his agility with the razor as a profession.[68] Thomas Cevallos was "by trade a barber, but by inclination a soldier, and between expeditions found time to practice his trade in Bexar.[69] Henry Tucker acted "in the capacity of a Barber, and as such gives entire satisfaction to a respectable and numerous patronage" including George W. Hockley, sometime acting secretary of war; Ashbel Smith, George Fisher, Henry Foote, J. B. Ransom, and A. C. Allen, founder of Houston.[70] Ingles Oliver to gain a livelihood made a rare combination following "his vocation of Baking and Barbering."[71] In the first capacity he competed with John Bird's wife, Charity, who supported herself "by baking cakes and vending them." She sold her cakes in quantities sufficient to defray the expense of a vacation spent with old friends in the United States.[72]

The inability of blacks to collect debts in the courts at a time when most business was done on credit constituted a considerable deterrent to increased business activity. Although they had the right to sue, they could not bear witness against their white debtors but were forced to hire the services of a white man. Oftentimes, doubtless, it was more advisable to suffer the loss than attempt a lawsuit, and the general tendency was to delay action in the hope that debts would be amiably settled. Andrew Bell delayed until 1848, his attempts to collect two old debts contracted during the Republic. One was a six months' note for twenty-eight dollars for a rifle gun sold to Stephen Richards, overdue since October, 1845; the other a revolutionary war claim of seventy-five dollars "against the government of Texas for a horse, saddle and bridle for which I took a Receit from John S. Roberts, acting quartermaster . . . that I have lost." Bell sent his claims with his instructions to Dr. James H. Starr who apparently was in the habit of accepting such business. "If you can possible collect . . .

you will plas after paying your self out of it gave the balance to my sister—Louiza Towns—." Bell complained, "I have nothing to say in state business being a poor black man therefore I am compelled to get some person to act for me and my choice is you above all other in that place."[73] Starr evidently informed Bell that Richards had died, and that he had little chance of collecting his claim against the State, probably because he had lost his receipt. Bell took his losses philosophically. "As far as regards my claim against the State of Texas I have no idea that I shall be able to get eny thing for it and that has always bin my opinion . . . you will pleas to commit the note [of Stephen Richards] to the flames if [you] cant collect it and that ends the matter."[74]

Henry Lynch, a barber, evidently ran accounts for his customers. In petitioning Congress he prayed that if he could not remain permanently he might be given time "to collect money due him for his labor," as he could not otherwise "raise the means now of returning" to Alabama.

The full effect of the unequal rights in the courts might best be judged by the use of them made by one free black in the course of his business. In the ten-year period previous to the establishment of the Republic, William Goyens had been a party to some thirty suits, in half of them as plaintiff; appeared as a witness in two others; and at least on one occasion acted as attorney.[75] In addition he was accustomed to serving as arbitrator in the courts according to Mexican usage.[76] Under the Texas Republic he was not even permitted to present his own testimony.

In the way of intellectual attainment, William Goyens was perhaps the outstanding character. His frequent legal disputes had made him familiar with Mexican law, and he seemed to be in his element bearing witness, making depositions, filing pleas and coming to ponderous judicial decisions in the capacity of arbitrator. He wrote reasonably well and with equal fluency in English and Spanish, and could speak several Indian languages including Cherokee, a fact which frequently caused him to be called upon by his country to negotiate Indian treaties. Other blacks were described as remarkable for their intelligence, and a number of them, as we have seen, were able to write letters. The Republic maintained no schools, precluding official discrimination against the black. Apparently no objection to the formal education of blacks was raised, perhaps because it was not attempted.

The difficulty attending an investigation of intelligence in a group for the most part inarticulate is equally great in discovering religious qualities. Early church records contain the names of numerous slave members, but no free blacks. Services for white persons and blacks were generally held separately, and often the slaves of a single plantation constituted a congregation.[77] That they were welcomed in neither group and were nowhere numerous enough to have their own services probably explains the absence of any record of their attendance or membership. Edmund J. Carter, who came to Texas in 1837, held to "the doctrine of Election and the final perseverince of all Saintes through grace to glory and Baptism by immersion and that believers are the only subjects," brought with him an honorable dismissal from the "baptist Church of Christ at new hope," Arkansas, which was to become effective as soon as he was "Joined to another Church of the Same faith and order" in Texas.[78] Brother Carter, doubtless, could find no organization in Texas willing to accept a free black communicant.

Occasionally Texans expressed fear of a slave revolt led by free blacks and abetted by abolitionists, designed to overthrow the government and destroy slavery.[79] In order to allay this want of confidence in his patriotism and to demonstrate his unqualified adherence to the government, Nelson Kavanaugh in his plea to remain in Texas declared that he was "no friend of the abolitionists who he is well aware more than even the ill conduct of some of his colour and condition have drawn down upon us the ban of the Republic."[80]

At no time did the Republic officially doubt the loyalty and courage of black soldiers and sailors who were regularly enlisted and fully armed and equipped. Immediately after San Jacinto a number of them remained in the standing army and when danger of Mexican invasions or Indian raids threatened the country free blacks were generally among the volunteers.[81]

At all times free blacks were in more or less obvious danger of losing their liberty. Those who gained their freedom by flight, protected by no statute of limitations, were subject to recovery by their owners after long periods of enjoying freedom. In 1841, A. Briscoe inquired of E. L. R. Wheelock about "a reputed free black 'Jarret Young' . . . [who] obtained land as a colonist in the Nashville Colony in 1834 or '35." Briscoe had reason to believe Jarret belonged to his father and was intent upon recovering him despite his six years emancipation and obvious success as a freeman.[82] Runaway blacks, doubtless, lived their whole lives fearing they might meet their former masters at every turn.

Not only were escaped slaves liable to recapture but those legally free might be seized on fraudulent claims and enslaved by law. Free papers were by no means conclusive evidence that blacks were entitled to their freedom. Henry Forbes admitted on the gallows that his had been forged by a white man,[83] and runaway slaves able to write were in no need of white men's collusion. When Ben, a dark mulatto slave, ran away his master gave notice that "He will no doubt pass for a free man,"[84] and James Doswell advertised that two blacks who ran away from his plantation in Mississippi might be heading for Texas and "passing as Free men."[85] In the process of recovering slaves alleging themselves to be free, blacks actually free might have been enslaved. An advertisement in 1838, illustrates a situation where a fraudulent claim to ownership could easily have been recognized and enforced. Robert Stevenson, the sheriff of Washington county, arrested Palmer Jackson, who "says . . . he was brought out to Texas in September last in a small whale boat by Mr. Robert Bushare [of Attakapas, Louisiana], that he has been living in Houston ever since he arrived in Texas and that he is a free man." The distrust in which the sheriff held this black and the ease with which Palmer Jackson might be fraudulently claimed as a slave, is indicated by the fact that the sheriff added to his notice, "The owner can have him by applying to me and paying expenses."[86]

In addition to the possibility of being reduced to slavery by law, free blacks faced the danger of being seized without legal pretense and sold into slavery. One story that surfaced follows:

> There lived in Yocum's neighborhood an old Frenchman who had a black woman for a wife, by whom he had a large family of mulatto children, among them several grown daughters. The Yocum's, associated with Earpe Wingate and Col. Gravenor—who had at one time been a soldier at Fort Jessup, planned the killing of the old man, and taking his wife and children to western Texas, and selling them into slavery. Accordingly they approached the old man one night and murdered him, and burnt him in a log heap. Then they drove his family across the Sabine into Texas, and secreted them in the Palogacho bottom, about half a mile north of the main road leading from San Augustine to the Sabine, and placed them under a strong guard, while the others secured horses to carry them to West Texas where they were to be sold into slavery. But a few nights before they were ready to go they got drunk and one of the young women affected her escape, and made her way to the neighboring house and made known their dreadful situation. I think it was the house of David Renfro, as brave and honest a man as ever trod the soil of Texas. This brave man at once rallied his friends, and drove these villains out of the country, and helped the women and children to return to their homes in Louisiana."[87]

Generally, abductions were done so furtively that they seldom attained record unless they failed. One successful attempt between 1835 and 1840 was uncovered by Joseph Hamilton, special British agent, who collected satisfactory evidence that Edward Hicks, a free black residing in Texas, was kidnaped and carried into the United States to be sold into slavery.[88]

The wealth and position of a free black did not deter seizures but on the contrary acted as an incentive. Bele (probably Bailey), an American, threatened to enslave William Goyens unless he paid him one thousand pesos. In order to raise the money, Goyens bought a black woman from a Mr. Llorca (probably York), giving in exchange a note for five hundred pesos payable in property. He then turned the black woman over to Bailey for his ransom and began to look up Santiago Leone to purchase on credit a piece of land to pay off the note. While thus engaged Goyens was recaptured and further ransom forced from him upon threat of taking him to New Orleans and selling him into slavery.[89]

Free blacks were also deprived of their liberty by the old device of indenture which continued to be used during the Republic to enslave them. Again, we can only know of the efforts which failed, as complete success would necessarily leave no historical trace. In the latter part of January, 1840, the British sloop of war, *Pilot,* arrived at Velasco bringing Commander Joseph Hamilton of the Royal Navy to demand the recovery of eight British Black citizens of the Windward Islands said to have been inveigled into Texas by John Taylor of the Barbadoes and sold for slaves.[90]

Lacking diplomatic channels, letters addressed to the "President or Officer Administrating the Government of Texas" were handed to the collector of the port for delivery to Mirabeau Lamar. Upon receipt of the communication of E. Murray McGregor, Governor of the Windward Islands, explaining Hamilton's mission, David G. Burnet, acting Secretary of State, replied to Hamilton that the government "has no knowledge of any person of the character described being within its jurisdiction," but admitted that the extensive seacoast and the imperfect organization of government conspired to expose some remote points to access by illicit traders. Burnet indicated the willingness of the Texas Government to surrender any blacks that Hamilton could positively identify as free men, and invited him to confer with President Lamar in Austin.[91]

Early in February, Hamilton conferred with Abner S. Lipscomb, Secretary of State,[92] and Lamar issued a proclamation calling upon Texas citizens to aid Hamilton in his search for the free blacks allegedly held as slaves.[93] Two months later Hamilton actually recovered five of the blacks, accounted for the other three and collected evidence which was to convict John Taylor for selling free blacks into slavery.[94]

Three of the blacks, Samuel Redman, Henry Small and William Thomas, were found in the possession of Joseph Grigsby; April Sashly and Edward Whittaker were recovered from Judge A. B. Hardin and William Moore, respectively. Edward Hicks, who was originally in the possession of Moore, had been kidnaped and carried into the United States; William Gunsil had been accidentally drowned, and another black man, unnamed, who was originally left with David Garner, had been sold in Louisiana.[95]

Although most free blacks were never actually disturbed in their residence, the fear of summary banishment hung heavily over their heads. The rights of even the most favored group were fixed by statute rather than by the constitution. Their status, therefore, was subject to change according to the capricious action of a single Congress. Until June 5, 1837, these blacks lived upon the sufferance of the white population. On that day they were given the right to remain permanently, only to see themselves deprived of all their rights on February 5, 1840, when they received two years notice to quit the country. On December 12, of the same year, their residence rights were restored, to be retained for the duration of the Republic. These blacks, nevertheless, were at the mercy of some incident which might move Congress again to deprive them of the right to live in Texas. On February 5, 1840, blacks who had immigrated between the declaration of independence and that day were given two years to leave the country. At the expiration of that time by presidential proclamation they were permitted to remain an additional year, and during that year by the same process they were allowed an additional two years. After February 5, 1845, they were at all times subject to ten days' notice to leave the State. Blacks who came to Texas after February 5, 1840, as illegal residents were always subject to the same ten days' notice to take themselves out of the Republic upon penalty of sale into slavery. Until January 10, 1843, no black person had any guarantee that his property rights would be respected, and after that date by private act only a few were given security in their holdings. That so many of them were able to achieve social respectability and economic independence becomes more remarkable in the light of this continual uncertainty which permeated their whole life and constituted perhaps their chief handicap.

The study of the free black in the Republic of Texas leaves us with two opposing pictures. One is drawn from generalizations of contemporaries depicting a theoretical attitude toward the group in which the black is described as irresponsible, disreputable and worse than useless because vicious and dangerous. The other sketch is inductively drawn from particularizations of contemporaries describing practical attitudes toward individual blacks in which they are uniformly portrayed as responsible, reputable and useful because industrious and peaceful.

These anomalous attitudes reflect the two current opinions on free blacks which Texans were never able to reconcile. Their interest and inclination as private citizens was invariably to look with favor upon those whose labor they might use to advantage. As public citizens, however, these same men were apprehensive lest the contact of free blacks would lead slaves to dissatisfaction, insubordination and finally to insurrection.

The attitude toward the class resulted from impersonal encounters and was embodied in the general laws; that toward the individuals grew out of personal contacts and was enacted into numerous private laws or more often, expressed itself in an unwillingness to enforce the general laws.

In whatever connection the problem of the free black was brought under consideration, these two diverging views were certain to be presented. To defend restrictions on manumissions we are told that freedom was a greater curse to the slaves themselves than the bondage in which they were held. In utter dispute of this assertion we are assured that the slaves were rendered discontent by witnessing the freedom of their colored brethren. At one time we are made certain that prejudice against color is implanted in our nature, at another that laws to prevent frequent mixed marriages are necessary to preserve that prejudice.

On the one hand the white man censured the indolence and viciousness of the free black class, on the other he praised the thrift and sobriety of the individuals. At once the black is accused of ignorance and at the same time of possessing talents to execute the most complicated and deep-laid plots. While he is suspected of attempts to subvert the peculiar institution of slavery and destroy the State, he is honored for his courage and patriotism in defense of it. The class is charged with addiction to vice and petty crimes, the individuals esteemed for their virtuous and orderly lives. In a general condition described as one of poverty, degradation and misery brought upon themselves by an aversion to labor, we find blacks engaged in productive work and often achieving economic independence.

To be at the same time disloyal and patriotic, indolent and thrifty, ignorant and talented, vicious and virtuous, obnoxious and harmless, wicked and worthy, destitute and prosperous is a paradoxical situation not infrequently met in human relationships because of the seeming necessity of men to be consistent with their principles. In the South and in Texas this necessity arose largely in defense of slavery. Every free black practically seemed to deny the principle that slavery was a boon for blacks, and every thriving one seemed to disprove the argument that if the black were set free he would starve rather than support himself. As one Texas Senator expressed himself, these facts swept away the strongest ground of slaveholders used in refuting the abolitionists. The disparaging generalities, doubtless, were designed to sweep away the facts and preserve the argument.

The inability of the Republic to draw a more intelligent distinction between master and servant than one based on color alone precluded disinterested consideration of the question. As a sovereign slave-holding State, Texas demonstrated an inability to solve a problem confined to an insignificant portion of her population, never exceeding three hundred persons. Aid and protection based upon the whims and interests of white persons to particular blacks in a class barred from equality was the solution offered by the Republic and bequeathed to the State.

Notes

1. General Provisions, Section 10. Gammel, *The Laws of Texas*, I, 1079.

2. Article 1, Section 7. Gammel, *The Laws of Texas*, I, 1069.

3. No census was ever taken in the Republic. The first state census of 1847, counted 304 free persons of color *(Texas State Gazette,* August 25, 1849), and it is reasonable to suppose that their number never exceeded 300 during the days of the Republic.

4. The bill of rights did not mention the right of petition, but the constitution provided that Congress should introduce by statute the common law of England. Section 13, Article 4. Gammel, *The Laws of Texas,* I, 1073. The statute was adopted on December 20, 1836. Gammel, *The Laws of Texas,* I, 1217.

5. General Provisions, Section 9. Gammel, *The Laws* of *Texas,* I, 1079.

6. Pleasant Bious, Henry Lynch and John Hemphill presented unendorsed petitions which were received and considered. Memorials No. 45, File 5, November 5, 1841; No. 54, File 17, December 15, 1840; No. 28, File 54, no date.

7. *Austin City Gazette,* November 27, 1839. A later issue reported that such a "gag" resolution was adopted by the Senate on November 29, 1839 *(Austin City Gazette,* January 8, 1840), but this report was erroneous. No mention of it was made in the journal and the Senate received and considered numerous black petitions subsequent to that date.

8. *Senate Journal,* Fourth Congress, 37.

9. *Senate Journal,* Sixth Congress, 76.

10. Greenbury Logan to R. M. Forbes, November 22, 1841. Document No. 2582, File 28, Sixth Congress. Logan's letter gives a rare glimpse into some of the grievances, presently to be discussed, as they appeared to a black. He wrote, "I hope you will excuse me for taking the liberty of riting to you. I knew not of you being in the county until the night before you left for

Austin. it was my wish to see you from the time you was elected but in consiquence of your absence I co[u]ld not. I presume it is unecessary to give you eny informasion abought my coming to Texas. I cam[e] here in 1831 invited by Col. Austin. it was not my intention to stay until I had saw Col. Austin who was then in Mexico. after se[e]ing him on his return and conversing with him relitive to my situation I got letters of sittizen ship. having no famoly with me I got one quarter League of land insted of a third. but I love the country and did stay because I felt myself mower a freeman then in the states. it is well known that Logan was the man that lifted his rifle in behalf of Texas as of fremans righted. it is also known that Logan was in everry fite with the Maxacans durinr the camppain of 35 until Bexhar was taken in which event I was the 3rd man that fell. my discharge will show the man[n]er in which I discharged my duty as a free man and a sol[d]ier but now look at my situation. every previleg dear to a freman is taken a way and logan liable to be imposed upon by eny that chose to doo it. no chance to collect a debt with out witness, no vote or say in eny way, yet liable for Taxes [as] eny other [person]. the goverment has giv [e] me a Donation and Premium [land] and now in short I must loose it for its taxes is well known. it is out of my pour to either settle on my land or to sell them or to labour for money to pay expenses on them. I am on examination found perment injurd and can nom[o]re than support by myself now as everry thing that is deare to a freman is taken from me. the congress will not refuse to exempt my lands from tax or otherwise restoure what it has taken from me in the constitution. to leave I am two poor and imbarrased and cannot leav honerable as I came. I am tow old and cr[i]ppled to go on the world with my famaly reeked. if my debts was payd I wo[u]ld be willing to leav the land though my blood has nearely all been shed for its rights—now my dear friend you are the first man I hay ever spoken to for eny assistance. I hombely hope you as a gentleman whose eze is single towards individuel is well noted al good will look into this errur and try if you cannot effect —something for my relief. I know I have friends in the house if a thing of the kind was brought up wo[u]ld be willing to git me sum relife. as to my caracter it is well known and if enything is wanted of that kind I am prepared

—please euse your best exertions and what ever obligations it may leav me unde[r], I am yours to acer the same. yours with respe[c]t, G. Logan." In accordance with Logan's wish, Forbes introduced a bill to release Logan's lands "from State and County Tax now due or hereafter falling due," but the bill was lost. Bill No. 2349, File 25, Sixth Congress.

11. Memorials No. 33, File 80, January 3, 1841; No. 101, File 67, no date; No. 15, File 5, September 20, 1836; No. 52, File 1, April 25, 1838.

12. Memorial No. 1, File 52, April 25, 1838. The "right to swear in court" was deleted, probably by the committee considering the petition. Free blacks always had the right to sue and the liability of being sued which will be discussed presently.

13. Memorial No. 11, File A, no date.

14. *House Journal,* Eighth Congress, 266, 26S. See Chapter V, *Southwestern Historical Quarterly,* XL, 278–279.

15. See Chapters IV and V, *Southwestern Historical Quarterly,* XL, 169–199; 267–299.

16. Gammel, *The Laws of Texas,* I, 1079–1080, 1324; II, 35, 554-555, 777–778.

17. Memorial No. 13, File M, April 21, 1838. Maturin was granted a league of land by Governor Viesca in 1828, at the place he selected, subject to the regulations of the colony in which he located. Spanish Titles, Vol. 68. Maturin never perfected title under Mexican laws and was barred from receiving title by the laws of Texas.

18. Memorial No. 18, File H, no date.

19. Brazoria County Tax Roll, 1843. State Controller's Office, Austin.

20. W. D. Wood, "History of Leon County," in *Southwestern Historical Quarterly,* IV, 211–212. Allen Dimery was accepted as a colonist by David G. Burnet on February 11, 1835, and was granted a league of land on April 23, 1835. Spanish Titles, Vol. 18, 219–220.

21. Memorial No. 13, File 32, September, 1840.

22. Deed from James Smith to William Goyens, May 30, 1839. Henry Baguet Papers, University of Texas Archives.

23. Nacogdoches County Tax Rolls, 1837–1845.

24. Agreement between William Go[y]ens and Henry Baguet, December 13, 1841. Henry Baguet Papers.

25. Bennenow Towns to Colonel Casneau, no date. Starr Papers.

26. Nacogdoches County Tax Roll, 1841.

27. [William B.] Burton's Lease to Ashworth, November 12, 1838. Benjamin C. Franklin Papers. University of Texas Archives.

28. Jefferson County Tax Rolls, 1837, 1845.

29. See Chapter III, 95-98, *Southwestern Historical Quarterly,* XL, 95-98.

30. Sale of the black Jerry, John Durst to William Goyen[s], January 3, 1829. Nacogdoches County Court Records. D, 39. University of Texas transcripts. Indenture, October 25, 1826, Nacogdoches Archives, XXX, 256. Sale of the black Peter, William English to William Goyens, January 20, 1826. Nacogdoches Archives, XXVIII, 219.

31. Nacogdoches County Tax Roll, 1841.

32. Brazoria County Tax Roll, 1844.

33. Texans generally had no qualms over the violation of democratic principles so far as they applied to blacks, but were rather touchy when the same violations seemed to threaten any class of white men. When opposition developed in the constitutional convention of 1845, to the provision making clergymen ineligible for seats in the legislature, Mr. J. S. Mayfield drew the analogy. He declared: "I shall first notice the argument that this provision is an infringement of the declaration that all men are free and equal, and entitled to equal rights. Now, sir, we have made no such declaration, and if we had made it, it would not be true in fact. We have simply declared that all freemen when they form a social compact, have equal rights, and

shall be entitled to equal privileges. Now I will ask, gentlemen, if a free black in this country, declared so by the laws of Texas, and a party to the compact, is not as much a freeman, as any who occupies a place upon this floor, or any minister of the gospel? And yet in sections long anterior to this, these gentlemen voted without any compunction of conscience, and without fears that in what they were doing, they were violating republican principles, or the rights of the dear people, to exclude the African and the man of mixed blood from any participation whatever in the legislation of the country. Their fears and alarms were not raised then, though the free black is as much a freeman according to that declaration as any man here. If gentlemen would be consistent with themselves, why not come forward and vindicate the rights of the free blacks, and admit him to a seat and companionship with themselves in our deliberative assemblies? They may show that the political situation of the country may render it necessary that such a qualification should be introduced into the Constitution itself to limit all these general principles. If then from the peculiar nature of the case and the circumstances by which we are surrounded, they see proper in that case to adopt a qualification seemingly incompatable with a declaration formerly made, is there anything inconsistent in this? . . . In what respect is a restriction of this kind an injury to the people? If it is the intention to give them unlimited power and control, if no restriction whatever of a political character is to be placed upon the exercise of their judgment and their will, why not throw the subject broad cast, and allow them to elect representatives from freemen of African blood?" Wm. F. Weeks (Reporter), *Debates of the Texas Convention*, 192–193.

34. Bill No. 2497, File 27, Fifth Congress.

35. *House Journal*, Ninth Congress, 109, 112.

36. Bills No. 2497, File 27, Sixth Congress; No. 2668, File 29, Seventh Congress; No. 2632, File 29, Seventh Congress; *Senate Journal*, Ninth Congress, 129, 139; *House Journals*, Eighth Congress, 171; Ninth Congress, 194. The slave patrol was finally created on May 9, 1846. Gammel, *The Laws of Texas*, II, 345.

37. See Chapter IV, *Southwestern Historical Quarterly*, XL, 187, note.

38. For the character of offences previous to February 5, 1840, see Chapter IV, *Southwestern Historical Quarterly*, XL, 188-189. In the remaining five years, offences were few and continued to be reported in a humorous vein, indicating that they were not a serious menace. Henry Tucker was arrested for assault and battery upon another barber, Price, "a mongrel, a cross of the Chinese and Maltee." Tucker endeavored to *"lather"* Price, who, he accused, "had *shaved* him out of . . . [some] pictures." Tucker employed a lawyer who frequently honored his client by referring to him as Mr. Tucker. "But the Marshall and Recorder were determined that if there was any *shaving* done, they would handle the *brush* and razor, so the Recorder fined Tucker $10 and costs." The barbers of Houston "put shaving up to four bitts," which the editor considered "barberous." *The Weekly Times* (Houston), April 9, 1840. One black man claiming to be free was sentenced at Galveston on October 21, 1840, to be hung on November 13, for burglary. He confessed on the gallows that he was a slave in the United States and that a white man in Texas forged free papers for him. *Daily Picayune*, October 28; November 18, 140. Perry, a free man of color, was indicted for larceny but given a verdict of not guilty, indicating that an accusation against a free black was not tantamount to conviction. Harrisburg County District Court Records, D, 351. Harris County Court House, Houston.

39. Memorial No. 33, File 94, November 11, 1841. Gammel, *The Laws of Texas*, I, 1294–1295.

40. *Life of Lundy*, 116.

41. Memorial No. 4, File 1, January 4, 1836; Proceedings of the General Council, Gammel, *The Laws of Texas*, I, 750–751; Arnold v. Martin.

42. George M. Martin to Col. Thomas W. Chambers, September 10, 1851. Chambers Papers.

43. See Chapter IV, *Southwestern Historical Quarterly*, XL, 170.

44. W. P. Zuber to Z. T. Fulmore, November 10, 1899. Fulmore Papers, University of Texas Archives.

45. Andrew Bell to Dr. James H. Starr, May 8, 1848. Starr Papers, University of Texas Archives.

46. Memorial No. 13, File 32, October 18, 1840.

47. Memorial No. 45, File November 5, 1841.

48. Richard R. Barkeson to Gen[era]l Lamar, August 5, 1838. *Lamar Papers,* 11, 190.

49. *Civilian and Galveston City Gazette,* September 14, 1842.

50. Smithwick, *Evolution of a State,* 225–226.

51. Memorial No. 45, File 5, November 5, 1841.

52. Benton v. Williams; J. W. Dallam (compiler), A *Digest of the Laws of Texas: containing a full and complete compilation of the land laws: together with the opinions of the Supreme Court,* 496-497; Supreme Court Docket, Austin Sessions, 1842–1845, Cause No. 17.

53. Nacogdoches District Court Minute Book, A, 17; B, 199; C, 189; Complete Records, 25–26. University of Texas photostats.

54. Nacogdoches District Court Minute Book, A, 22, 98; B, 14, 183; C, 10.

55. Samuel A. Roberts to Mirabeau Lamar, February 8, 1838. *Lamar Papers,* V, 172–173.

56. Memorials No. 380, File 45, December 14, 1840; No. 18, File 54, December 14, 1840; Nos. 16, File 65, October 30, 1840.

57. Memorial No. 46, File 5, December 4, 1840; Andrew Bell to Dr. James H. Starr, May 8, 1848. Starr Papers.

58. Bill No. 39, File 53, Fourth Legislature; Gammel, *The Laws of Texas,* III, 1042.

59. *Reports and Relief Laws,* 249.

60. Harrisburg County Probate Court Records, A, 332. Harris County Court House, Houston.

61. Harriet Smither (editor), "Diary of Adolphus Sterne," in *Southwestern Historical Quarterly,* XXXII, 255; XXXIV, 347; XXXVI, 315.

62. John Hutchinson to G. T. Smith, March 30, 1845. G. W. Smyth Papers, University of Texas Archives.

63. Mrs. [M. C.] Houstoun, *Texas and the Gulf Coast or Yachting in the New World,* I, 291–295.

64. Memorial No. 23, File 75, October 19, 1840.

65. *Senate Journal,* Fourth Congress, 63.

66. This statement is based upon more documents that can be conveniently cited. Materials for an extended biographical sketch of William Goyens may be found in the Nacogdoches Archives (State Library), the Congressional Papers and Journals, the Nacogdoches County Tax Rolls, and in the records in the Nacogdoches County Court House.

67. Brazoria County Tax Rolls, 1837–1845; Logan to Forbes, November 22, 1841, Document No. 2582, File 28, Sixth Congress.

68. Memorial No. 1, File 52, April 25, 1838.

69. Cevallos came to Texas in a company of Mississippi volunteers to participate in the Revolution but arrived after the battle of San Jacinto. He took part in several expeditions against the Indians and Mexicans and was severely wounded at Salado in 1842. He later fought with the Kentucky volunteers in the Mexican War under General Taylor. Memorials No. 7, File S, December 15, [1840], No. 91, File 81, November 7, 1851; *Daily Picayune,* August 8, 1852.

70. Memorial No, 16, File T, November 15, 1839.

71. Memorial No. 5, File 71, no date.

72. Memorial No. 33, File 80, September 25, 1839.

73. Andrew Bell to Dr. James H. Starr, May 8, 1848. Starr Papers.

74. Andrew Bell to Dr. James H. Starr, July 29, 1848. Starr Papers.

75. Nacogdoches District Court Records; Nacogdoches Archives. Demanda de Henry Linley contra Juan Walker, January 11, 1831. Records in the Nacogdoches County Court House, University of Texas transcripts. Goyens acted as attorney for John Walker.

76. Ciprian de el toro v. Juan Jose y barba, no date; T. S. Pierson v. Wille Tomas, July 30, 1829; Marcogne Indians v. Guero Gueg, April 3, 1833; Plummer v. Mensack; Nacogdoches Archives Vol. 28, p. 119, Vol. 40, p. 184, 344–345, Vol. 32, p. 202.

77. "The Records of an Early Texas Baptist Church," in the *Quarterly* of the Texas State Historical Association, XI, 92; Numerical Statistics for the Methodist Episcopal Church in Texas, December 28, 1841; Class Paper for 1844. O. M. Addison Papers, University of Texas Archives.

78. Memorial No. 6, File C, March 17, 1838.

79. See, for example, the speech of Senator Barnett. *Senate Journal,* Fourth Congress, 64.

80. Memorial No. 1, File 52, April 25, 1838.

81. Joseph Tate served in the army from March 26 to July 26, 1836, Memorial No. 1, File T, November 15, 1839; Elijah Thomas from July to October, 1836; Gibson Perkins from July 7 to October 7, 1836; Edward Smith from July 4 to September 4, 1837; Henry Bird from June 4 to September 4, 1838; Controllers Military Service Records. Pleasant Bious had "Service in the army in defence of the Republic" some time between 1838 and 1841, Memorial No. 45, File 5, November 5, 1841; Joseph Taylor was permanently disabled in an engagement with the Indians before 1846, House Bill No. 100, File 45, Third Legislature; Thomas Cevallos was severely wounded in the battle of Salado in 1842, *Daily Picayune,* August 8, 1852. Thomas Beale, a seaman on the *Brutus,* had the only dishonorable record among blacks, but under extenuating circumstances. Two weeks previous to his desertion, S. Rhoads Fisher, secretary of the navy, described conditions aboard the *Brutus* as "miserable" and reported that

rations would not last more than two weeks. Beale's disappearance with the exhaustion of the food supply may have been more than a coincidence. At any rate, desertions were frequent. In the one available payroll report of the *Brutus,* nine desertions are recorded between August 30 and October 16, 1837. *Telegraph and Texas Register,* May 2, 1837; S. Rhoads Fisher to Colonel A. S. Thuston, Commissary General, April 15, 1837, Schooner *Brutus,* Payroll No. 3, Navy Papers, Texas State Library.

82. A. Briscoe to E. L. R. Wheelock, February 4, 1841. Wheelock Papers, University of Texas Archives. Jarret Young was accepted as a colonist by Robert Leftwich and as a married man received a league of land on February 25, 1835. Spanish Titles, Vol. 14, pp. 137–139.

83. Daily *Picayune,* November 18, 1840.

84. *Telegraph and Texas Register,* September 9, 1837.

85. Nacogdoches Archives, Vol. 89, p. 1.

86. *Telegraph and Texas Register,* March 24, 1838. The law provided that a notice of runaway slaves held in jail should be published weekly for one month, and if not claimed in six months, upon thirty days' notice the blacks were to be sold to the highest bidder at public auction. Gammel, *The Laws of Texas, II,* 649.

87. [A. Horton], "History of San Augustine, Reminiscences of an Old Time Resident," 20–21. University of Texas transcripts.

88. Joseph Hamilton to Abner S. Lipscomb, April 21, 1840. *House Journal Appendix,* Fifth Congress, 23.

89. Nacogdoches Archives, Vol. 30, pp. 59–62.

90. *The Morning Star,* January 28, 1840.

91. David G. Burnet to Commander Hamilton, January 29, 1840. *House Journal Appendix,* Fifth Congress.

92. Abner S. Lipscomb to Commander Hamilton, March 31, 1840. *House Journal Appendix,* Fifth Congress, 24–25.

93. Abner S. Lipscomb to Commander Hamilton, February 14, 1840. *House Journal Appendix*, Fifth Congress, 23–24.

94. Joseph Hamilton to Abner S. Lipscomb, April 21, 1840. *House Journal. Appendix*, Fifth Congress, 23. The chief evidence upon which Taylor was convicted, in addition to the testimony of the blacks themselves, was the deposition of Joseph Grigsby that since the adoption of the constitution he had regarded the blacks in his care as slaves. Before the trial Taylor asked Lamar to conduct an investigation to determine if any of these blacks had been held *de jure* or *de facto* as slaves. On the grounds that an inquiry would be attended with some trouble and expense and that it was not essential to Taylor's vindication, Lamar contented himself with a declaration that no person who was not a slave previous to his immigration could be subjected to "absolute" slavery. A month after Taylor's conviction, Lamar complied with Taylor's four month old request for an inquiry which was confined to depositions made by those involved in the transactions. In these depositions, Grigsby, for one, contradicted the testimony first given to Hamilton. Apparently the new evidence did not, in the eyes of British justice, warrant a new trial, and here the matter was dropped. George P. Garrison (editor), *Diplomatic Correspondence of the Republic of Texas*, II, 901–905, 911–914; *House Journal Appendix*, Fifth Congress, 19-25; *The Morning Star*, January 28, 1840; *Telegraph and Texas Register*, October 21, 1840, February 24, 1841.

95. Hamilton to Lipscomb, April 21, 1840, *House Journal Appendix*, Fifth Congress, 23; Taylor to Lamar, July 28, 1840; depositions of Joseph Grigsby and A. B. Hardin; contract between William Moore and John Taylor, May 28, 1836, George P. Garrison (editor), *Diplomatic Correspondence of the Republic of Texas*, 911–914. Daniel O'Donnell, the British abolitionist, claimed that an additional twelve British subjects were detained in slavery in Texas, and he proposed that a British legion of twelve hundred men be sent to ally with Mexico and wage war, but nothing seems to have come of the charge. *Telegraph and Texas Register*, February 24, 1841.

CHAPTERS SEVEN THROUGH TEN

STATEHOOD TEXAS

7

Free Blacks in Harris County

Andrew Forest Muir

Viewed as competition by white labor, patronized by white benefactors, and forbidden to associate with their kinspeople, still slaves, free blacks in the South dragged out a miserable existence.[1] So unsatisfactory was their freedom that they often voluntarily chose masters and placed themselves in servitude, in accordance with the legal provisions of most if not all southern states. Despite their social and economic privation, they nevertheless enjoyed a relative security. To be sure, their legal position was humble, resembling that of metics in a Greek city, resident strangers. They could neither hold office, vote, sit on juries, nor give testimony against any except slaves and other free blacks. Their offenses against property and persons were penalized as though committed by slaves, more severely than the same offenses committed by whites. Despite these restrictions, they were able to live undisturbed by legal agencies, to receive justice at the criminal bar, and to assert their freedom against illegal seizure. Cases drawn from the records of Harris County, doubtless typical of the South despite its late settlement, furnish proof of these conditions.

Even when it permitted free blacks, Texas strictly regulated their position. A black, it first ruled, was one who had as much as one-fourth black blood,[2] but later he became one with as little as one-eighth.[3] Blacks were punished alike, whether slave or free. While whites were punished with death, imprisonment in the penitentiary and county jail, forfeiture and suspension of civil and political rights, and pecuniary fines,[4] blacks were punished with death, branding, imprisonment in the penitentiary, whipping, standing in the pillory, and labor upon public works.[5] "Insurrection or any attempt to excite it," by free blacks, "poisoning or attempting to poison, committing a rape or attempting it on any free white female, assaulting a free white person, with intent to kill, or with a weapon likely to produce death, or maiming a free white person, arson, murder, burglary" all were punished with death.[6] A free black who was convicted of using insulting, abusive, or threatening language to a white person should receive between twenty-five and one hundred lashes.[7] He could not play cards or other games of chance with whites, for the law provided punishment for whites who so played with their inferiors.[8] A free black could not "preach the gospel or . . . exhort at any religious or other meeting" unless at least two slaveholders were present.[9] An act approved on May 11, 1846, forbade a free black to hire slaves,[10] though no statute prevented his owning them.

On the other hand, the State insured against the sale of free persons into slavery, although the intention of the law was more likely the protection of whites than of blacks.

> Every person who shall unlawfully sell any free person for a slave, or hold any free person as a slave against his will, knowing the person so sold or held to be free, shall be punished by confinement to hard labor in the Penitentiary not less than one year nor more than ten years, or by fine not exceeding one thousand dollars, and imprisonment in the county jail not exceeding one year.[11]

While it is doubtful that any convictions were had under this law, weakened by the clause "knowing the person so sold or held to be free," it nevertheless provided a theoretical safeguard against illegal seizure.

Numerically, free blacks were scarce, though there are no satisfactory figures giving the exact number in Harris County at any time. The Houston *Morning Star,* in 1839, guessed that there were twenty or thirty in Houston, perhaps an over-estimate.[12] The only official statements are those of the censuses of 1850 and 1860, but the accuracy of these is doubtful.[13] The 1850 census, the first taken by the United States in Texas, named seven free blacks in Harris County: Dick Ellett, aged 50 years;[14] Emily Routh, 23, Mary J. Routh, 3 months;[15] Abby Townsend, 14, Stama Townsend, 40, William Townsend, 1;[16] and Charlotte Vince, 38.[17] By 1860, the number had increased imperceptibly to eight: Fanny McFarland, 58;[18] Emily Mimms, 30, Ida Mimms, 6, Rose Mimms, 3, Sam Mimms, 4 months;[19] G. Phillips, 60;[20] Fanny Sneed, 90;[21] and Sally Vince, 50.[22] What became of those listed in 1850 but not in 1860? Perhaps they died, or moved away, or were not counted, or were counted as slaves. Whence came those enumerated in 1860 but not in 1850? Perhaps they moved in, or were emancipated during the decade, or were not counted in 1850, or were counted as slaves.

All free blacks in the South were either manumitted slaves or descendants of manumitted slaves. There were, then, but two ways for free blacks to get to Harris County or to any other American locality. Either as free blacks they moved there or they were there emancipated. Legislation in the Republic and State of Texas, as elsewhere, was concerned first with free blacks within its jurisdiction at its passage and secondly with further immigration and emancipation, both by deed and will. As shall be seen, with but rare exceptions, free blacks were legislatively forbidden to remain in Texas. Law, however, does not enforce itself, and for the social historian it is not the statute that is the more significant but the manner in and the degree to which the machinery of administration and adjudication applied the statutory law in specific instances.

Quite logically the status of free blacks already resident in Texas was handled legislatively first. Though not returned by Governor Henry Smith, the ordinance of the General Council of the Provisional Government, passed January 5, 1836, seems to have had the force of law.[23] It recognized as citizens those free blacks then in Texas. The Constitution of 1836 altered this by requiring free negroes to secure Congress' permission to remain.[24] President Houston, never a racial bigot, on June 5, 1837, eased this constitutional prohibition by granting to those free blacks living in Texas on March 2, 1836, "the privilege of remaining in any part of the republic so long as they choose; on the condition of performing all the duties required of them by law."[25] On February 5, 1840, President Lamar, more race-conscious than Houston, approved an act, which repealed all laws contrary to its meaning and spirit and commanded all free blacks to remove from the Republic before January 1, 1842.[26] In May he issued a proclamation, in pursuance of the act, instructing sheriffs and constables to carry it into effect.[27] Considering that a number of free blacks had fought in the Texas Army during the Revolution, President Houston, who succeeded Lamar, on December 21, 1842, remitted for a time the penalty of the act of February 5, 1840, "provided those who wish to obtain the benefit of this proclamation, apply to the Chief Justice of the County in which they reside, and make satisfactory proof of their good character, and also enter into bond and security, in the penal sum of five hundred dollars, payable to the President during the term specified in this proclamation."[28] This remission remained in effect until February 5, 1845. After that date, it would appear illegal for any free black to remain within Texas, unless the Legislature provided specific relief. No Harris County black was so relieved.

Despite all this legislative thundering and executive evasion, those free blacks already in Texas quietly went their way and disregarded both Congress and President. Some few, no doubt, found other places more inviting than Texas. Emily D. West, who had come out from New York with Colonel James Morgan, in September, 1835, requested a passport that she might return to her native state,[29] but she was exceptional. For the most part, free blacks remained despite the disapproval of the law. Local executives and magistrates, generally, were not only too busy with more pressing problems, but they were positively disinclined to interfere. Chief Justice Isaac N. Moreland signed every one of the five petitions submitted to Congress by Harris County free blacks.[30] Some bear the signatures of practically every man who held political office in Harris County during the Republic, as well as of several members of the cabinet and the highest ranking officers of the Army.[31] Occasionally, however, some attempt was made to enforce the law. On February 28, 1842, the Houston City Council resolved "That the City Marshall and all other City and County officers be and are hereby requested and required forthwith to enforce the laws of the Republic against Free Negroes upon all Free Negroes now living within this corporation."[32] Considering this as the rank impertinence of a body who had no control over them, the Harris County constabulary certainly disregarded it, and there is no evidence that the city marshal did otherwise. But one free black took advantage of President Houston's remission of penalty. On March 3, 1843, Ann Tucker went before Chief Justice Moreland, fulfilled all of the provisions of the proclamation, and was discharged until February 5, 1845.[33] Ann, who had been in Houston as early as March 5, 1840, when she purchased a lot from the notorious Pamelia Mann,[34] remained in Houston until her death, January 1, 1846.[35] Four other free blacks remained without hindrance, though they apparently did not comply with the law. Fanny McFarland, who was emancipated by William McFarland in Texas in 1835,[36] lived in Houston at least from 1838 to 1866,[37] although she was in Brownsville at the taking of the 1850 census.[38] She engaged in a number of real estate transfers and managed to make a profit on her investment. Despite the refusal of Congress to grant her permission to remain, she stayed until the United States Government made her and all blacks citizens. Dick Ellett first came to Texas in about 1820, but he left before the Revolution. On March 17, 1836, he returned on the schooner *William Francis* which landed at Copano. When he misplaced his emancipation papers, William B. Reeves and George Hunter Bringhurst, both of whom held public offices, made affidavits to his good character, but there is no evidence that he entered into bond.[39] Sally Vince, who maintained her freedom at law, as will be later pointed out, remained undisturbed, getting into no public records other than the decennial censuses. Diana Leonard, a washerwoman in Houston, had come to Texas in 1835, possibly with Emily D. West, and had spent one year in Colonel James Morgan's service.[40] Congress refused to act on her petition to remain, and it is possible that after some time she returned to the United States.

The numerous legislative bodies of Texas also took precautions against an increase in the free black population by making provisions against immigration and emancipation. The General Council's ordinance of January 5, 1836, which recognized as citizens free blacks then in Texas, prohibited the immigration of additional free blacks.[41] The congressional act of February 5, 1840, also made illegal their immigration and provided for the selling into slavery those who violated it.[42] These laws were likewise disregarded, and free negroes not only came to Texas, but, fearing the loss of their credentials more than the operation of the law, they boldly filed their emancipation papers with the county clerk.

Nelson Kavanaugh, who had been emancipated in Richmond, Kentucky, and had lived as a free man for some time in Clinton, Mississippi, moved to Texas in the spring of 1837 and plied his trade as barber in Houston.[43] Congress declined acting on his petition to remain, and he soon dropped from sight, probably returning to the United States.

In September, 1837, Robert Bushare, of Attakapas, Louisiana, brought an ex-slave of his, Palmer Jackson, to Texas in a whale boat. Jackson lived unmolested in Houston for several months, and it was not until March, 1838, that he found his freedom hampered, and that due only to his leaving Houston and going to Washington County.[44] So long as a free black remained in a place in which he was known by whites he was secure, but when he went beyond the limits of his acquaintance, he was more than likely to find himself jailed as a runaway slave.

In the spring of 1838, Thomas McAllister presented to Mirabeau B. Lamar, in Houston, a letter from Samuel A. Roberts, of Mobile, in which Roberts stated McAllister had been head waiter in Mobile hotels and steward on the best packet steamboats on the Alabama River. Roberts heartily recommended that Lamar hire McAllister as his factotum.[45] While Lamar did not do this, neither did he turn McAllister over to the sheriff.

In July of the same year, Henry Tucker immigrated to Houston and established a barber shop.[46] If the men who signed his petition to Congress patronized his service, his clientele was most distinguished, for the names on the petition read as a register of the cabinet and the military command. Tucker disappeared, but it is possible that Ann Tucker, who made bond, was his widow.

One master accompanied his manumitted slaves to Texas and personally appeared before the county clerk to declare on oath that he had set them free. Eldred Barker, of Natchitoches, Louisiana, on March 6, 1839, acknowledged before County Clerk DeWitt Clinton Harris that on November 8, 1837, Rose and her four children, Henry, Edmon, Clisaan, and Mary had made the last payment on their freedom; whereupon he had emancipated them.[47]

In 1839, Zilpha Husk, a native of Richmond County, Georgia,[48] who had established her freedom in the circuit court of Autauga County, Alabama, in November, 1837, was in Houston, receiving from George B. McLeskey, of Washington County, the revocation of the apprenticeship of her daughter, Emily, made in Montgomery, Alabama, November 13, 1837.[49] Emily probably was as well fitted to take care of herself as the majority of white women, for there is no reason to assume that McLeskey had not lived up to his contract and taught Emily to read and to write and instructed her in "the art of carding spinning weaving and sewing."[50] Zilpha's three petitions to Congress failed to secure for her permission to remain in Texas,[51] but she remained nevertheless.

But one prosecution clouded this disregard and contempt for the law. In April, 1839, a number of free blacks, variously estimated from eight to twenty, was haled before the city recorder. According to the editor of the *Morning Star,* these arrests were the first attempts to enforce the ordinance of January 5, 1836.[52] If we may trust the lack of evidence to the contrary, they were also the last. Counsel for the defense denied the competency of the court and argued "that so far from the free Negroes being prohibited from residing in the Republic, or the 9th Art. of the Constitution in the slightest degree strengthening the previous acts of the Convention in this particular, it was susceptible of being construed *into an invitation held out to free Negroes to emigrate to the Republic!* —For," he asked, "how can they petition Congress for permission to remain, unless they first emigrate to the country ?"[53] The recorder, humbly viewed the jurisdiction of his office and dismissed the defendants. On the following day, the city council enacted an ordinance under which the marshal should arrest, at the end of thirty days, all free blacks and carry them before the district judge.[54] Two months later the grand jury addressed the district judge on the evils of having free blacks at large.

> As a population, they are much worse than useless: in general, they neither perform any productive labor, nor exercise reputable callings. With scarcely an exception, they are addicted to vice and the commission of petty crime. They are often irresponsible instruments in the hands of white men. But it is chiefly the mischievous influence which the free Negroes exert over our slaves, to which the Grand Jurors would invite especial attention. . . A family of free Negroes commonly presents the impersonation of indolence, ignorance and dishonesty. Such a family, unless strictly and perpetually watched, and kept at a distance, will render the slaves of the plantations near which they are situated, dissatisfied, disobedient, restless, thievish and corrupt. In the towns where the facilities for dishonesty by slaves are much greater than in the country, the presence of free negroes is felt as a very great evil. In addition to their other vices and petty crimes, the free Negroes being addicted to Gambling, initiate the slaves, who supply the means of pursuing it by stealing from their masters. The Grand Jurors . . . would likewise mention, that they have been informed on undoubted authority, that one free Negro at

least is in correspondence with the abolitionists of the north, if not an emissary of theirs.[55]

All of this was a serious charge, but it appears to have been not entirely true. The law continued to be inoperative, but no one seems to have suffered unduly, as one would expect if the accusations were correct.

In 1846, Peter Allen, a barber, moved to Houston. He did not petition for permission to remain in Texas until 1863, after he had served as a body servant to an officer of Terry's Regiment during the battles of Woodsonville and Shiloh.[56] The Legislature refused his request.

As late as 1847, free blacks continued to immigrate. On March 31st, of that year, George William, vaguely described as "aged about twenty years height five feet five inches, complexion Black, Hair Black & wooley scars none by profession a Mariner Born in Boston Massachusetts," filed with the county clerk an instrument signed on May 7, 1845, by Adam P. Pentz, a notary public in New York City, stating William was "a freeman and citizen of the United States of America and entitled to be respected accordingly in person & property at all times and places both by sea and land in the due prosecution of his lawful concerns."[57] This was unmitigated abolitionist sentiment, but it seems to have passed unnoticed.

The Constitution of 1836 provided that no slaveholder should emancipate slaves without the consent of Congress, unless he sent them out of the Republic.[58] This was laid open for modification but not modified by the Constitution of 1845, which granted to the Legislature the power to pass laws by which masters could emancipate their blacks;[59] the Legislature did not provide any such laws. The 1861 or Confederate Constitution of Texas absolutely forbade emancipation.

> No citizen, or other person residing in this State shall have power by deed or will, to take effect in this state or out of it, in any manner whatsoever, directly or indirectly, to emancipate his slave or slaves.[60]

Two slaveholders emancipated their blacks by deed, but both before secession. On January 4, 1847, the writer's great-grandmother, Cynthia Annie (Meriwether) Ewing, sold to William Gammell, Thomas M. Bagby, and Archibald Wynns, for $400, a black woman named Lyle. Gammell, Bagby, and Wynns were to use their efforts to induce the Legislature to authorize them to emancipate Lyle; in addition to which they agreed "to permit Said negro Lyle to go hence free and to use her time as her own on condition of her proper behavior."[61] Bagby filed the deed in the county clerk's office at Austin and petitioned the Legislature for permission to emancipate the black woman.[62] This the Legislature refused to grant.

On January 24, 1859, Nathaniel Bailey sold freedom to his forty-year-old female slave, Keziah, and appointed the same Thomas M. Bagby "to have and take charge of said Negro woman and to allow her to enjoy the fruits and revenues of her labor & to exercise just so much control over her as will be for her own good & in accordance with the laws of the State."[63] Here we have a clearer statement of what Bagby was doing. Since the Legislature only reluctantly gave its permission for manumission, so far as official curiosity was concerned, Lyle and Keziah were Bagby's slaves, but in actuality they were free blacks.

Four Harris County residents emancipated their blacks in their wills. On January 25, 1837, James Routh, an old and well-to-do settler on Galveston Bay, made his will, which is remarkable for its great length if for nothing else. The first intimation of a philanthropic impulse is a bequest of three hundred and twenty acres "to my negro woman Sylvia & her six children, to wit: Sally Ann, Mary Jane, Emily, Jackson, Isabella and Margaret."[64] Since chattel could not hold title to property, one is mystified until somewhat later in the lengthy document, at which point Mr. Routh got to the nub of his intentions.

> I hereby will and bequeath full freedom to my negro woman, Sylvia & her six children and her further increase . . . nevertheless upon the following conditions: Sally Ann and Mary Jane to be bound to live, as servents with Ophelia [Mrs. James] Morgan untill they

arrive at the age of twenty one years—the balance of the children to live with their Mother, Sylvia, to be supported and protected by her, untill their Guardian may think proper to bind them out, which is to be done, untill they shall arrive at the age of twenty one years, to have their freedom to all intents and purposes, as far forth as the laws of the country will allow.

To Sylvia, I will her full freedom at my death provided she takes care & protects her children as here tofore stated . . . and I wish my executors to endevor to have Sylvias children before named, educated, so far as to read and write, & to pay for the same out of my Estate and hereby authorize them to appropriate three hundred Dollars for that purpose.

I will and bequeath to negro man Jim, at my death full freedom for his meritorous services, & requeast my executors to see that he obtain it. . . .

And I hereby constitute & appoint my friends Dr. George M. Patrick and Col. James Morgan my only executors to this my last Will and testament and constitute them Guardians to Sylvia & her six children, before named as well as to Jim, whom I have set free by these presents.[65]

Routh died on July 19, 1837.[66] Unfortunately the record does not reveal what happened between his death and April 14, 1838. On that date, Colonel Morgan applied to Andrew Briscoe, Chief Justice of the county, "for commitment of negro slave Silvie belonging to the estate of said Routh, who he alleged has become unruly and refused to submit to his authority."[67] Well might Sylvia have become insubordinate, if Morgan viewed her as a slave. Briscoe, a slaveholder himself, committed Sylvia to the county jail "subject to the order and at the expense" of Morgan.[68] Two days later, Morgan applied for the commitment of Jim who likewise had become unruly; he too was packed off to jail.[69] At this point Jim disappears forever from the record, but five years later Sylvia reappears. On November 27, 1843, she petitioned the probate court for letters of guardianship of Sally Ann, Mary Jane, Emily, Jackson, Isabella, and

Margaret.[70] Her request was granted, and title to the three hundred and twenty acres on Clear Creek passed to her and her children.

On August 24, 1844, William Smallwood, in his will, emancipated his slave, June, and bequeathed her his entire estate. He directed his executor to give June "all aid in asserting her rights under this will."[71] Some years later, on September 27, 1852, Sarah Noble willed her slave, Becky, to her son, Edwin B., on condition that he emancipate her at the testator's death.[72]

There was no want of justice meted to free blacks charged with criminal offenses. In fact, it appears that not one of them was convicted in the Harris County District Court and but few in the City Recorder's Court. In 1838 the grand jury indicted Richard Green for retailing goods without a license[73] but was unable to find a true bill against William White for the more serious offense of petit larceny.[74] On December 28, 1838, the District Attorney dismissed the charge against Green.[75] As indicated previously, the free blacks arraigned before the City Recorder in April, 1839, were discharged for want of jurisdiction. City Recorder D. W. Babcock, on April 3, 1840, fined Henry Tucker ten dollars and costs for fighting with a Chinese barber named Price over ownership of some pictures.[76] On May 18, 1849, the grand jury indicted Edmund Mitchell, a white man, and Zilpha Husk for fornication.[77] When a petit jury found Mitchell not guilty,[78] the district attorney dismissed the case against the black woman.[79]

No evidence of the just treatment of the free black is more compelling than his ability to maintain, before slaveholding judges and juries, cases against whites for illegally holding him in slavery. The Harris County District Court heard two civil suits in which blacks charged whites with holding them in illegal servitude, and in both the blacks were victorious.

At the fall term of court, 1838, Sally Vince filed suit against Allen Vince (who, with Wilson Strickland, was the chief character in the recent prodigious litigation in the Montgomery County District Court and the United States District Court at Houston over title to the Conroe oil field), charging him with holding her, a free woman, in slavery. She based her freedom on a deed executed by William Vince, September 7, 1834, granting her freedom at his death. Allen Vince's ownership of Sally was devious. On April 3, 1838, Allen, administrator of William, in his inventory of the estate, contended that William had owned but a third interest in Sally.

> Allen Vince Administrator of the estate of William Vince, deceased being duly sworn upon his oath deposeth and says, that the Bill of Sale of the above named negro Sally has by time & accident been lost or estrayed, but that he is impressed with the belief that the Bill of Sale was made to his (Allen's) son to wit, William Vince, Junior but he is now informed that the said negro belongs jointly to William Vince, deceased, to himself and to Susan Vince, Now Susan Summer.[80]

When William Vince's property was sold, Allen himself purchased Sally for five hundred dollars; whether two-thirds or all of her, it is impossible to determine.[81] There is no indication that Susan Summer was defendant, for the cause is styled "Sally Vince *versus* Allen Vince." On January 7, 1839, the case went to the jury. Allen Vince's attorneys, Archibald Wynns and Henry W. Fontaine, moved the court to instruct the jury "that admitting the deed of manumation for William Vince to Sally Vince to be true that under the constitution it affords to the plaintiff no right of freedom."[82] Judge Benjamin C. Franklin reserved the question for deliberation, and the jury returned an alternative verdict: if the court gave the instruction prayed for by the defendant, they found for the defendant; if not, they found for the plaintiff. Whereupon, Judge Franklin delivered his opinion.

> The only question presented for the consideration of the Court is as to the effect of a deed of manumation did the deed become operative from the moment of its execution and delivery, so as to vest any right in Sally? —the words of the Deed are "have this seventh day of September Anna Domini eighteen hundred and thirty four Liberated Manumited and after my death set free a certain

female slave named Sally, at this time aged about twenty three years—I the said William Vince having the entire order control, management and command over the *services* of the said female slave for certain considerations me hereunto moving do hereby bind myself my heirs executors administrators & assigns that after my death for faithful services and obedient and submissive conduct *have* her the aforesaid Negro slave named Sally free from all obligation to any . . . other person whomsoever"—This same rule of construction must be applied to the deed of manumation,— that would be applied to any other Deed, by these rule we find that the *freedom* of the negro Sally —is a remainder limited to a person in being & appertained upon a particular estate (the life estate reserved by Wm Vince) the termination of which is absolute and certain, and which does not depend upon any contingency.

So that the execution of the Deed of Manumation, vested the right of liberty in the negro Sally but postponed only the enjoyment and not the right Suppose that ten days after the execution of the deed of manumation when the master was at liberty to manumit his slave, William Vince had died, would not the negro girl to all intents and purposes [be] free? Certainly and she would have derived her *right to liberty* from the deed, and taken possession of [and] entered upon the enjoyment of the previously acquired *right* as the necessary effect of the deed upon the death of Vince. What a man has once conveyed by deed he cannot affect by any subsequent conveyance and in the present case had Vince sold the negroe Sally after executing the deed of manumation the sale would have had no force for he could not divest by any act of his a vested right to freedom.

The manumation having taken effect before the adoption of this constitution, the plaintiff was not at that time holden as a slave bona fide the property of William Vince.

Wm. Vince having departed this life the only obstacle entervining between the right of Liberty & the enjoyment has been removed and the court is of opinion that she is free . . . and that Allen Vince the defendant has no right or property to the said Negro Sally —and it is ordered that she go hence free and liberated from all custody or control by the said Allen Vince and recover of him all costs in this behalf expended.[83]

Some years later a similar case with identical results was tried in the same court. On May 4, 1847, the law firm of Peter W. Gray and Abner Cooke, Jr., filed a petition in which Emeline stated that she was a free woman of color and a citizen of Tennessee. She represented to the court that her mother, Rhoda, was free at the time of her (Emeline's) birth and was yet free, but that on or about December 20, 1846, in Houston, Jesse P. Bowles "with force and arms assaulted your petition[er] and then and there took, imposed and restrained her and her children [James and William] of their liberty, and held her & them in servitude from said day to the commencement of this suit against the laws of the land and the will of petitioner."[84] Five weeks later Emeline amended her petition. "And your petitioner further shows that living under the charge & custody of the said Bolls she is very much restricted in her movements and has not an opportunity to consult with her Lawyers & take their advice as to the means necessary to protect her rights and has therefore left that matter to her Sister Lucy Thompson [of New Orleans] who is aiding her to establish her freedom and came to Texas for that purpose." Judge C. W. Buckley, on the same day, enjoined Bowles and those acting under his direction, counsel, or authority from removing the plaintiffs outside the jurisdiction of the court, upon Emeline's making bond of two hundred dollars. In his answer to the petition, Bowles stated that his late mother, Elizabeth, whose administrator he was, had bought Emeline and held her as a slave until her (his mother's) death.

In July both parties became active in gathering evidence. Bowles' attorney applied to the court for a commission to take the testimony of Philip M. Cuney, of Austin County. The interrogatories inquired whether Cuney had seen Emeline in James B. Beckham's possession and whether she had acquiesced in this possession. Gray and Cooke propounded a series of cross-interrogatories, asking whether Emeline were in the possession of a Mrs. Seip, of Rapides Parish, Louisiana, and whether Mrs. Seip sent her off with Beckham when Rhoda established her freedom in Tennessee.

> Have you not been a negroe proprietor for many years? Are you not well acquainted with the way negroes are managed by their masters & overseers?—And have they not the means to make their negroes *acquiesce* in being sold whether they will or not? . . . Was it not just such conduct as might have been looked for from a negroe woman like Emmeline, under the power of an overseer, without friends at hand and ignorant of her rights[?]

The record contains neither a commission for the interrogatories nor Cuney's answers, but this is not conclusive that the one was not granted nor the other returned.

Toward the latter part of the next month, Gray and Cooke propounded interrogatories to a number of people in Alexandria, seat of Rapides Parish. Of James T. Flint, husband of Mrs. Seip's sister, Susan, John Curtis, and Coleman W. Calvit, they asked about Mrs. Seip's parents, about Emeline's age, color, and husband, and about the circumstances of Emeline's leaving the Seips. The last question Mr. Flint refused to answer, stating that he was the Seips' attorney who had been consulted professionally in the matter. He stated, however, that Mrs. Seip was the daughter of Thomas and Martha Martin, of Nashville, Tennessee. Emeline, he added, was a "likely" mulattress. She had two children, and he had heard that a slave belonging to Mrs. S. K. Johnston passed for her husband. Curtis affirmed Flint's evidence and stated that Emeline was about twenty-two years old. To the third question he replied that Beckham took Emeline to Texas in the fall or winter. Calvit did not make a deposition, or if he did the record has not survived.

Of Mrs. Flint, attorneys Gray and Cooke inquired in what manner Mrs. Seip got Emeline and the name of Emeline's mother. Mrs. Flint answered that Emeline belonged to her father, and that from his estate Mrs. Seip received Emeline, whom she took to Louisiana in 1839. She added that

Emeline was the daughter of Rhoda who belonged to her father from her earliest recollection to her father's death.

Gray and Cooke also interrogated Dr. and Mrs. Seip, asking especially whether they sent Emeline off with Beckham, whether they gave him a bill of sale, whether he sold her, and whether he gave them any of the money he received for her. Either the Seips did not answer or the record has been misplaced.

In December the case was continued to the spring term of court.[85] Bowles' attorneys propounded interrogatories to Robert Chappell, of Washington County, after whom the town of Chapel Hill was named. He answered that he had seen Emeline in Houston in November and December, 1846, and that she had told him "she was willing to be sold" and "that Beckham had come honestly by her."

Bowles' attorneys requested the plaintiff to produce the original bill of sale for Rhoda executed by Donelson Caffery to Thomas Martin subsequent to her return from Pennsylvania, or they would prove its content by parol. In May the case was continued until fall.[86]

On November 24, 1848, the case at last went to trial. J. J. Cain, John F. Crawford, John Dickinson, William J. Hutchins, and E. B. Noble were summoned as witnesses. Since there is no transcript of the oral evidence, one cannot even surmise to what they testified. In addition to this verbal testimony and the answers to the interrogatories, there were depositions from Washington Jackson and Mrs. Ellen Kirkman, but these are not now with the papers of the case. One knows they were offered as evidence, for the defense attorneys objected to their introduction on the technical point that Jackson and Mrs. Kirkman "were sworn by the Commissioner who took their deposition to testify in a cause pending between Emeline a free woman of color Plff [Plaintiff] and Isaac P. Bowles defendant—and that said witnesses were not sworn to testify in the aforesaid suit in which Emeline a free woman of color is Plff and Jesse P. Bowles defendant." Judge Buckley overruled the objection and permitted the testimony to go to the jury. The next day, Gray and Cooke prayed the court to charge the Jury that if they believe from the testimoney that Rhoda the mother of plff was sent by her master to the state of Pennsylvania after the year 1788 *with the intent & purpose that she should thereby be come free,* and was so carried with the consent of her master to that State, that the said Rhoda by that act became free.

That if they believe from the evidence that Rhoda the mother of plff was carried voluntarily & with her master's consent to Pennsylvania after the year 1788 and remained in that state six months or more, that the said Rhoda became free

That if the Jury believe from the evidence that the plaintiff is the daughter of a woman who was free at the time of her birth then the plaintiff was born free: and can assert her claim to freedom in the Courts of this state

The defense excepted to this charge.

The jury, many of them slaveholders, among whom was Andrew Briscoe, retired and returned the same day with the verdict: "We the Jury find for the Plaintiff Emeline that she and her children are free as claimed by her, and assess her damages at one dollar." Whereupon, the Court adjudged Emeline and her children free persons of color and charged them to "go hence free from the service of defendant & all others." Emeline went forth free and so disappears from the record.

From the depositions that are available, one is at a loss to determine precisely on what grounds the jury found for Emeline, when the evidence seems more to indicate that she was a slave. If there were additional evidence, now lost, it must have been potent to have counteracted in the minds of the slave-holding jury the testimony of the Flints and others. That the jurors could objectively consider this unknown evidence is a refutation of the abolitionist's insistence that a black could not secure justice in a Southern court. In this case, certainly, a negro received not only justice but also what appears to be mercy as well.

Though Washington Jackson's deposition is not available in the present papers of the case, it is extant in the attic of the Davidson County Courthouse at Nashville, Tennessee (in which the writer, innocent of daylight-saving-time, was locked one September afternoon in 1940), one of the papers in the case of Rhoda, George, Margaret, and Matilda *versus* Mrs. Patsy Martin.[87] Jackson deposed:

> I owned her [Rhoda] several years; I lived in Philadelphia & Natchez during that period; the said woman was employed on a plantation in Attakapas Louisiana, owned by me and in which Mr Donelson Caffrey [Caffery] had a nominal interest; Caffrey had several children by this woman Rhoda and [Caffery] being about to marry, I relinquished my interest in her and her children to him for the sole purpose and distinct understanding of having her and them emancipated: and according to said agreement, I took Rhoda and her children three in number, named according to the best of my recollection William, James, & Lucy to Philadelphia Pennsylvania, with me by sea, from New Orleans, Louisiana, for the purpose of their emancipation. With a view to this emancipation I took for the woman and her said three children a nominal price; perhaps one third of their value. I arrived in Philadelphia from two to three weeks after leaving New Orleans. I think that this was early in the year *1816*. I have little doubt that we reached Philadelphia before the 1st of May of that year. Afterwards in that year I often saw the woman at the *house* of my sister Mrs. Ellen Kirkman in Philadelphia. After Rhoda had been in Philadelphia, sometime, not being able to support herself, free of expense, she was sent by Caffrey's request, to his friend Thomas Martin who lived near Nashville Tennessee for the purpose of having the boys bound to trades, and that the mother should live with him [Martin] and work for her own and their support. Martin was a particular friend of Caffrey and knew the relation which had existed between him and Rhoda, and Caffrey relied upon his taking care of her and her children and doing justice to them. They had lived neighbors in Attakapas on adjoining plantations.

This evidence, buttressed by Mrs. Kirkman's, probably to the same effect, was conclusive enough to cause two Southern juries, in widely separated Nashville and Houston, to return freedom to seven free blacks held in duress. One may speculate whether Mrs. Kirkman was an abolitionist, but Washington Jackson was certainly not one. He had been a slaveholder in two large plantation areas, Natchez and Attakapas. In the latter place he raised sugar; seven years' work on such a plantation, according to abolitionists, killed even the stoutest blacks. At the time of the deposition, he was living in New Orleans, in which there were more than enough free blacks to prove one way or another the quality of this anomalous class. In the light of Jackson's deposition, the decision of the court seems no more than just.

Shortly before the outbreak of the Civil War the Texas Legislature, following those of other Southern States, reversed the tradition of English law and provided means for free blacks voluntarily to enter permanent and irrevocable slavery. On January 28, 1858, Governor Hardin Richard Runnels signed an act allowing free blacks over fourteen years of age to petition the district courts for permission to be bound in slavery to masters of their own choosing. The district court was instructed to examine separately the free black applicant, the master whom he had chosen, and the two who had witnessed the free black's petition. The district attorney should represent the petitioner at the court hearing. Upon finding no evidence of coercion or fraud and determining the good character of the selected master, the court should adjudge the petitioner a slave. The person thus enslaved should not be subject to any liens made or judgments rendered prior to his enslavement, thus making more secure the relation between voluntary slave and selected master.[88] Free blacks all over Texas took the opportunity of exchanging the dubious and unsatisfactory liberty of free people of color for the restriction and security of slavery. On May 3, 1861, the Harris County District Court heard the petition of Bob Allen, who had selected as master William Thomas Neil. Upon examination of Allen, Neil, and the two witnesses, Robert Page Boyce and William Ferguson, the Court adjudged Allen a slave.[89]

The Civil War brought another class of free blacks, blacks in the United States Army and Navy captured by the Confederates. A number of such prisoners of war, who had been captured at the Confederates' taking of Galveston, January 1, 1863, were brought to Houston, together with other prisoners.[90] These blacks were the source of some trepidation on the part of the city fathers. On June 8, 1864, Mayor William Anders complained to General J. B. Magruder, commanding the District of Texas:

> The board of aldermen of city of Houston, by resolutions passed at their last regular meeting, have instructed me to communicate to you the fact that the negroes and persons of color, some thirty in number, captured by the forces under your command from the enemy and considered as prisoners of war are now going at large within the city of Houston, mixing and associating with our slave population, contrary to the laws of the State of Texas and to the laws of the Confederate States; and they further instructed me to request you that these persons be ordered by you to be removed from our midst to work on the fortifications, or that they be turned over to the civil authorities and to be sent to the penitentiary under the State law. In complying with the wishes of the board of aldermen, I beg leave to remark that the same matter was laid before you by me in the beginning of this year, that an order was promptly issued from your headquarters ordering the negroes spoken of to be confined. Subsequently, however, that order was modified and partially revoked, and the "Yankee negroes" are now freely ambulating within our city. Numerous complaints of our best citizens have been made to the authorities, and it seems that the whole community is alarmed. The most evil influence is exerted by those negroes, who, most of them, are intelligent, shrewd, and capable to read and write, and try to obtain a mastery over our slave population. It is true a portion of those negroes are employed by the city and are guarded, but they are not under the exclusive control of the city. They are frequently sent for by officers to do special work, and so the city cannot be responsible for their conduct. Most of them, however, are employed as body servants to different officers, and thus enjoy the very best opportunity to obtain information and communicating the same to our negroes.

General, the matter laid before you is of the greatest importance to the welfare not only of this city, but to the country at large, and I deem it my solemn duty to request you to give it your immediate attention. The board of aldermen do not desire anything else but that the negroes alluded to be restrained from associating with our home negroes. Whether they are made to work on the fortifications or be sent to the penitentiary does not concern them. They desire them placed in such position as the law provides and where they can exert no influence injurious to the best interests of this community.[91]

Busily engaged in the prosecution of a war, General Magruder did not personally answer, but on June 10th, his Assistant Adjutant-General, E. P. Turner, replied tartly to the city's interference.

I have the honor to reply to your communication of 8th instant in reference to the captured negroes now in Houston, and by direction of Maj. Gen. J. B. Magruder, commanding, &c., to say that they are prisoners of war. Some, whose conduct has not been conspicuously correct, are under strict guard, others are in charge of officers under surveillance, but of these latter none are to have any privileges except those who have behaved well. Some have been confined closely by the commanding general within a few days. He will give the subject his early attention and make such arrangements as will prevent any injury to the slaves of this city. It is entirely beyond the power of the city and State authorities to say how, where, or on what work these negroes shall be employed, or in what manner the commanding general may treat prisoners of war so long as he does not violate the laws of the city or State. It is, in the estimation of the commanding general, gratuitous on the part of the city authorities to request him to put prisoners of war to work on the fortifications, and whether they do anything for officers or not, since there is no State or municipal law on the subject, and does not come properly within the province of the city authorities to comment upon, he is the sole judge of such service.[92]

A year and nine days later, General Gordon Granger, U. S. A., in command of the army of occupation, arrived in Galveston and issued his famous General Order No. 3, which emancipated all blacks in Texas.[93]

The mass of evidence here adduced indicates that though legislative enactments relative to the free blacks and emancipation were harsh, judges and administrative officials were liberal to the point of dereliction. Free blacks immigrated and were emancipated, sued and were sued, and went about in their subservient and humble condition without jeopardizing their own freedom or inciting slaves to rebellion.

Notes

1. For a more extended but less intensive treatment of the free black, see Harold Schoen's "The Free Negro in the Republic of Texas," in the *Southwestern Historical Quarterly,* XXXIX, 292–308; XL, 26–34, 85–113, 169–199, 267–289; XLI, 83–108. The principal defects of this work are its limitation to the Republic and its failure to utilize county archives. It is undoubtedly a mistake to view admission of Texas into the United States as a legitimate terminus for any other than purely political and diplomatic studies. County archives, collections of prosaic legal documents, portray the free black in a more normal and domestic light than that indicated in the proceedings of Congress.

2. *The Penal Code of the State of Texas. Adopted by the Sixth Legislature* (Galveston: Printed at the News Office, 1857), p. 7.

3. H. P. N. Gammel (ed.), *The Laws of Texas, 1822–1897* (Austin: Gammel Book Co., 1898), IV, 1115. A supplement to the penal code prohibited the marriage of a white with one descended from negro ancestry to the third generation, that is one-eighth negro. *Ibid.,* pp. 1036–37.

4. *Penal Code,* p. 12.

5. *Ibid.,* p. 164.

6. Gammel, *Laws,* I, 1385.

7. *Ibid.,* p. 1386.

8. *Ibid.,* IV, 1459.

9. *Ibid.,* p. 1463. On March 1, 1841, the Houston City Council forbade slaves and free blacks to assemble for "balls," unless the mayor specifically granted his permission. *Morning Star* (Houston), March 4, 1841, p. 3, col. 1.

10. Gammel, *Laws,* II, 1501–02.

11. *Ibid.,* III, 1503.

12. *Morning Star,* August 13, 1839, p. 2, col. 1.

13. Census takers had varying notions as to whom were free blacks. Cases could be multiplied, but one will do. According to the printed summaries of the 1850 census, there were nine free blacks in Calhoun County. J. D. B. DeBow, *Statistical View of the United States . . .* (Washington: Beverley Tucker, Senate Printer, 1854), p. 308. When one examines the original schedules, one finds that though the nine were listed as free blacks, they actually were Mexicans. 1850 Census, Texas, Schedule 1, Calhoun County (Microfilm in Archives, University of Texas Library), Families 43, 167, 176, 181, 182. While some free blacks were no doubt born in Mexico, when one finds a situation in which every person born in Mexico is regarded and listed as a free black, the fallacy is apparent.

14. 1850 Census, Texas, Schedule 1, Harris County, Family 577.

15. *Ibid.,* Family 305.

16. *Ibid.,* Family 304.

17. *Ibid.,* Family 313.

18. 1860 Census, Texas, Schedule 1, Harris County (Microfilm in Archives, University of Texas Library), Family 641.

19. *Ibid.,* Family 985.

20. *Ibid.,* Family 208.

21. *Ibid.,* Family 641.

22. *Ibid.,* Family 760.

23. Gammel, *Laws,* I, 1024–25.

24. *Ibid.,* p. 1079.

25. *Ibid.,* p. 1292.

26. *Ibid.*, II, 325–27.

27. *Brazos Courier* (Brazoria), August 4, 1840, p. 1, col. 2.

28. Gammel, *Laws*, II, 879.

29. Passports, 1836-44; Letter Book of the Department of State (MSS. in Archives, Texas State Library, Austin), II, 47–48.

30. Memorials and Petitions (MSS. in Archives, Texas State Library), Petitions of Zilpha Husk, Nelson Kavanaugh, Diana Leonard, Fanny McFarland, and Henry Tucker.

31. The signers of these petitions were what Aristotle called political fractions. Some few were of the first importance in the Republic: Augustus Chapman Allen, Robert Barr, Hamilton P. Bee, Asa Brigham, William G. Cooke, Lorenzo de Zavala, Jr., Alexander Ewing, George Washington Hockley, Memucan Hunt, Felix Huston, Albert Sidney Johnston, William Miller Shepherd, and Ashbel Smith. Seventy-three of the remaining 227 signers held, without counting reelection and reappointment, 142 offices in Harris County, Houston, and Harrisburg, during the period of the Republic, that is within two or three years of the dates of the petitions.

32. Minutes of the Houston City Council (MSS. in Assistant City Secretary's Office, Houston), A, 148.

33. Deed Records of Harris County (MSS. in County Clerk's Office, Houston), I (letter of alphabet), 60. The dates given are correct, although the original transcription contains two obvious errors. As a rule, county clerks numbered their volumes from A through Z, inclusive, and then numerically beginning at one. The chief justice heard testimony relative to another free black, but the black did not make bond. On August 4, 1842, District Judge Benjamin C. Franklin made an affidavit before Chief Justice Algernon P. Thompson that Richard Robertson, a free man, came to Texas on the brig *Henry,* in April, 1835, under the protection of David B. Macomb. Thompson added to the affidavit the statement that Robertson plied "his trade of Engineer" in Houston. *Ibid.*, H, 197–98.

34. *Ibid.,* F, 160. On April 7, 1840, Tandy K. Brown, the last husband of Pamelia Mann, was charged with stabbing Ann Tucker, but as all of the witnesses were blacks, the Recorder discharged Brown. *Weekly Times* (Houston), April 9, 1840, p. 2, col. 4.

35. Probate Records of Harris County (MSS. in County Clerk's Office, Houston), G, 290.

36. Memorials and Petitions, Petition of Fanny McFarland, October 30, 1840.

37. Deed Records of Harris County, A, 456; F, 533; N, 585; P, 41, 227, 621; Q, 151; I (numeral), 132; II, 68, 337.

38. 1850 Census, Texas, Schedule I, Cameron, Starr, and Webb Counties, Family 207.

39. Deed Records of Harris County, X (letter of alphabet), 419–20.

40. Memorials and Petitions, Petition of Diana Leonard, December 14, 1840.

41. Gammel, *Laws,* I, 1024–25.

42. *Ibid.,* II, 325–27.

43. Memorials and Petitions, Petitions of Nelson Kavanaugh, April 21 and 25, 1838, and two without dates.

44. *Telegraph and Texas Register* (Houston), March 24, 1838, p. 3, col. 3.

45. Harriet Smither (ed.), *The Papers of Mirabeau Buonaparte Lamar* (Austin: Texas State Library, 1927), V, 172.

46. Memorials and Petitions, Petitions of Henry Tucker, November 6, 1840, and two without dates. On September 13, 1842, Tucker announced that he had "again opened a BARBER-SHOP." *Morning Star* (Houston), January 3, 1843, p. 1, col. 1.

47. Deed Records of Harris County, C (letter of alphabet), 449.

48. Memorials and Petitions, Petition of Zilpha Husk, December 16, 1841.

49. Deed Records of Harris County, J, 65–67.

50. *Ibid.,* p. 66. Binding free black children as apprentices apparently was common. On January 19, 1839, Nelly Norris bound her son, Thomas, about nine years old, to Stephen S. Tomkins. *Ibid.,* E, 43. Again on July 29, 1840, Nelly bound Thomas to Benjamin F. Tankersley. *Ibid.,* F, 393-94.

51. Memorials and Petitions, Petitions of Zilpha Husk, December 16, 1841, and two undated.

52. *Morning Star* (Houston), April 10, 1839, p. 2, cols. 2–3.

53. *Ibid.,* col. 3.

54. *Ibid.,* p. 3, col. 2.

55. Minutes of the 11th District Court (MSS. in District Clerk's Office, Houston), B, 172–73. The punctuation and capitalization follow the copy in the *Morning Star,* June 3, 1839, p. 2, cols. 2–3.

56. Memorials and Petitions. Petition of Peter Allen, undated.

57. Deed Records of Harris County, L (letter of alphabet), 528. In 1843 someone interested in a free woman named Martha, daughter of Violet Hamlet, filed the will of Merrit M. Coates, dated October 2, 1823, in which Coates emancipated Violet and her son Carter. Samuel May Williams stated that Coates had kept Violet as his wife. *Ibid.,* H, 515. On January 3, 1838, Chief Justice Briscoe appointed his mother-in-law, Mrs. Jane Harris, guardian of Martha, the fourteen-year-old daughter of the deceased Violet. Probate Records of Harris County, A, 332. On January 10, 1844, John W. Moore made an affidavit that Martha, then the wife of Peter Towns, had been considered a free black since 1827, when Coates apparently died. Deed Records, I (letter of the alphabet), 204. Lucille, a free woman, on May 6, 1851, filed a deed of emancipation from R. C. Ballard, of Natchez, Mississippi, dated March 3, 1847. *Ibid.,* 0, 586. On February 4, 1854, Maria filed the emancipation deed from Isaac D. Hamilton, of Crawford County, Arkansas, dated February 26, 1841. *Ibid.,* R, 44–45.

58. Gammel, *Laws,* I, 1079.

59. *Ibid.,* II, 1296.

60. *Ibid.,* V, 22-23.

61. Deed Records of Harris County, L, 330. Since this article was set in type, the writer has found another case of manumission by deed. On August 6, 1847, James Cocke emancipated his slave Tom Jefferson, who was born in Washington County, Mississippi, in about 1838. *Ibid.,* M (letter of alphabet), 217–18.

62. Deed Records of Travis County (MSS. in County Clerk's Office, Austin), E, 144–45. Petition of Citizens of Houston, undated. Memorials and Petitions.

63. Deed Records of Harris County, U, 680.

64. Probate Records of Harris County, A, 199.

65. *Ibid.,* pp. 201-02.

66. *Telegraph and Texas Register,* July 29, 1837, p. 3, col. 2.

67. Record of Board [of] Commissioners and Election Returns (MS. in County Clerk's Office, Houston), p. 92.

68. *Ibid.*

69. *Ibid.*

70. Probate Records of Harris County, F, 359.

71. *Ibid.,* G, 304.

72. *Ibid.,* L (letter of alphabet), 54–55. Another case of emancipation by will occurred on December 24, 1855, when John Sowell signed a will which granted freedom to Anderson or Henderson who served "in sickness and in health all of his life." The will was filed January 18, 1856. Deed Records, S, 237–38.

73. Minutes of the 11th District Court, A, 81.

74. *Ibid.,* p. 74.

75. *Ibid.,* B, 67.

76. *Weekly Times,* April 9, 1840, p. 1, col. 3.

77. Minutes of the 11th District Court, F, 17.

78. *Ibid.,* 45.

79. *Ibid.,* 47.

80. Probate Records of Harris County, A, 70.

81. *Ibid.,* p. 260.

82. Minutes of the 11th District Court, B, 72.

83. *Ibid.,* pp. 72–74. In 1842 the district court heard the petition of Stama or Tamer and Abby, her daughter, "to be released from the illegal detention by one Robert Walker." Judge A. B. Shelby adjudged them free people of color. Tamer, who came from New Orleans, was born in about 1792 and her daughter in about 1825. Deed Records of Harris County, N, 564. On February 11, 1850, Charles Shearn returned freedom to a free black held in duress, without the formality of a judicial hearing. He purchased Dick on March 2, 1847, at a sale of the effects of Samuel Childs, deceased. When he learned that Dick had been born free in Alexandria, Virginia, and had merely accompanied Childs to Texas, Shearn released his claim on Dick and started him on his way back to Virginia. *Ibid.,* p. 338.

84. Civil Docket of the Harris County District Court (MSS. in District Clerk's Office, Houston), File 1674. Unless otherwise indicated, the information presented and the documents quoted are from original documents in this file.

85. Minutes of the 11th District Court, E, 332.

86. *Ibid.,* p. 388.

87. Records of the Davidson County Circuit Court (MSS. in Circuit Clerk's Office, Nashville), unnumbered file. In April, 1844, Rhoda and three of her children charged that on January 1, 1844, Mrs. Martin "with force and arms, assaulted the plaintiffs, and them then and there took and imprisoned, and

restrained them of their liberty, and held them in servitude from said day to the commencement of this suit, against the law of the land, and the will of the plaintiffs." On September 21, 1846, a jury found that Rhoda and her three children were not slaves but free persons of color. See also Minutes of the Davidson County Circuit Court (MSS. in Circuit Clerk's Office, Nashville), 0, 363; P, 40, 137, 307, 471, 476, 478, 483.

88. Gammel, *Laws,* IV, 947-49.

89. Minutes of the 11th District Court, J, 467.

90. *Houston Tri-Weekly Telegraph,* January 5, 1863, p. 4, col. 1.

91. *The War of the Rebellion: A Compilation of the Official Records of the Union and Confederate Armies* (Washington: Government Printing Office, 1899), Series II, Volume VII, 214–15.

92. *Ibid.,* 222–23. The loss by fire of the minutes of the Board of Aldermen for this period obscures the board's reaction to this letter.

93. *Tri-Weekly Telegraph,* June 21, 1865, p. 4, col. 4.

8

FREE BLACKS IN FORT BEND COUNTY, TEXAS

Andrew Forest Muir

During the periods both of the republic and of the state, Texas had a fairly uniform policy toward free blacks. In general, no free black could immigrate; no free black could remain without the approval of the Congress or of the Legislature; and no slave owner could emancipate any slave without permission of the Congress or of the Legislature. Despite the official severity toward free blacks, there were, nevertheless, few attempts to enforce the laws relating to them. Free blacks continued to immigrate and to remain in Texas, and slave owners continued to emancipate their slaves, both by will and by deed. On the other hand, some slaveholders, fearing this administrative indifference would not always obtain, went to some trouble to secure legislative permission for the emancipations they wished to make.[1]

In Fort Bend County, west and southwest of the City of Houston, an extra-legal subterfuge was used as a means of providing free blacks with some degree of security. This subterfuge indicated that there were many whites in the area who were willing to countenance an evasion of the laws in order to provide for the welfare of free blacks whom they knew. The first chief justice of the county, who himself owned a slave he wished to emancipate, set by his first ruling on the subject a precedent that was followed by his successors, that of appointing a guardian for the person and property of the free black. Although there was no legal justification for the practice, it was never called into question. Statutes provided for guardians of minors and of the insane, but not of adult, sane free blacks. The guardianship proceedings in every case were irregular; with but one exception the guardian did not enter into bond for the faithful discharge of his duties and did not take an oath of office, and in no case did he present annual or final accountings of his stewardship. Having obtained a nominal supervision over his ward, he apparently considered his responsibility at end. The free black, in turn, completely disregarded the guardian; in his own name and upon his own authority, he bought and sold property without reference to court or to guardian.

On February 16, 1838, William H. Pool petitioned Chief Justice Wyly Martin for letters of guardianship upon Peter Nelson, a free black who had wandered in and requested his protection. Peter, he stated, was "reputed an honest and industrious man and as such entitled to be protected in his person and property." Ten days later Martin granted the petition.[2] In this case, Martin scrupulously observed the procedure regulating the appointment of guardians. He required Pool to enter into security for $5,000 and to take the oath of office as guardian.[3]

The most successful free black in the county was Peter Martin, born about 1810,[4] who, as a slave, had belonged to Wyly Martin. As early as 1833, Martin intended Peter to be free, for in his will, executed on September 3 of that year, he emancipated Peter, the emancipation to become effective at the testator's death.[5] Having provided for Peter's eventual manumission, Martin apparently permitted him to mind his own affairs. During the Texas Revolution, Peter rendered assistance to the revolutionary army by hauling, with his own team and at his own expense, military stores and provisions for the troops preparing to make an assault upon Bexar.[6] In 1838 Peter obtained a license to retail wine and spirits,[7] and in the following year, with Martin's consent, he purchased a lot and a house in Richmond.[8]

As Wyly approached the end of his life, seemingly he became more concerned about Peter's manumission. Perhaps he feared that his bequest would be inoperative, as later laws had prohibited emancipation. In any case, he deemed a special act of Congress the solution to his problem, and on November 5, 1839, he petitioned Congress for authority to emancipate Peter. He stated in the petition that he had owned Peter for nearly thirty years and, having no close kin, he wished to free him before he died.[9] Oliver Jones, senator from Austin, Colorado, and Fort Bend Counties, who had known Martin and Peter since 1823, introduced the petition into the Senate on November 21 and moved its reference to a special committee. The president of the Senate appointed a committee with Jones as chairman and this committee returned a favorable report with an attached bill, which was read for the first and second times. Upon Jones's motion for engrossing, an extended debate began. Stephen Hendrickson Everitt, a native of New York, representing Jasper and Jefferson Counties, regarded the matter as a dangerous precedent. He was willing to emancipate slaves only on condition they left the republic.

He thought "an evil of the deepest dye might be the result" of this action, and "he should take no hand in bringing destruction and bloodshed upon his country." He cited the law and the Constitution as forbidding a Free Negro's remaining within the Republic.

Jones replied that the Constitution made emancipation subject to the will of Congress. He himself was opposed to free blacks, but this was an exceptional case. Peter had rendered faithful, honest, and humble service to his master and had aided the country "during her hours of danger and invasion."

At this point, Everitt moved an indefinite postponement. George W. Barnett, representing Washington and Montgomery Counties, seconded the motion in order to provide time for deliberation. He too would never consent to the emancipation of a slave unless he removed from the country. He felt that Peter's industry and prosperity made him greatly more dangerous, for if he chose he could "exert an influence in co-operation with the abolitionists, that would strike at the very root of our most useful domestic institution, and at the peace and security of ourselves and families."

Dr. Francis Moore, Jr., a native of New York, editor of the *Telegraph and Texas Register,* representing Harris, Galveston, and Liberty Counties, thought that emotion had got the better of Jones's judgment. His laudation of Peter's industry and wealth swept from slaveholding nations, which "always insisted that slaves and free negroes are incapable of self government," their strongest ground in refutation of abolitionism. Free blacks in the midst of a slave population created "dissatisfaction, insubordination, and finally insurrection." Emancipate Peter, but let him take himself and his fortune to Africa or elsewhere. A motion to postpone action was lost by a vote of five to seven, and a motion to lay the bill on the table was carried by a vote of seven to six.[10]

The bill was ordered engrossed and on November 29 was passed by a vote of nine to three. It then went to the House, which read it and referred it to the Committee on the State of the Republic, which soon returned it with an amendment. On a motion for engrossment the vote was twenty-nine in favor and six opposed. Although the journal of the House fails to record the passage of the bill, it was passed with the amendment and then sent back to the Senate for approval. The Senate concurred in the amendment, and President Mirabeau Buonaparte Lamar approved it on January 3, 1840. This act permitted Wyly Martin to emancipate Peter but required him to make bond in the sum of one thousand dollars to guarantee Peter's never becoming a public charge.[11]

Martin, however, was in no hurry to complete the legal details. It was not until May 11, 1842, when he was at the point of death, that he executed the deed of manumission. Had he failed to have done so, the provision in his will would have become operative, as the act of Congress did not stipulate that manumission be accomplished in any specific manner. On the same day he executed a bond for one thousand dollars.[12]

After Martin's death, which occurred between May 11 and 20, 1842,[13] Peter continued for some time as he had during Martin's lifetime. On September 28, 1846, however, Mills M. Battle petitioned the County Court for appointment as guardian of Peter and his house, lot, and some eight or ten horses.[14] The court approved Battle's appointment, but it exacted of him neither bond nor oath.[15] Peter continued the even tenor of his way. In 1846, 1847, and 1849, he obtained licenses as a hawker and peddler,[16] and during the 1850's he purchased seven additional lots in Richmond.[17] Battle died, on January 15, 1856,[18] and references to Peter cease shortly afterwards; perhaps he too died.

Unlike Peter, Nathan Burnett had long been a free black man, in law as well as in practice. Described as a bright mulatto, born about 1800, five feet ten and three-eighths inches tall, with a scar on the left side of his head and a small black mole on the right side of the middle finger of his left hand, Burnett had lived as a free man in Fayetteville, North Carolina, as early as 1815. In 1819, "being desirous to travel to the Western Country," he obtained from thirteen citizens of Cumberland County, including six justices of the peace, a statement of his good character, honesty, and propriety. By 1822 he had reached Perry County, Mississippi. He then wandered to Copiah County, where he was dispossessed of his "free papers" by some white ruffians; after which he returned to Perry County, and in 1833 turned up in Hinds County.[19] There he apparently remained until January, 1835, when he removed to Texas. In the summer of 1842 he was in Fort Bend County and applied to William P. Morton to become his guardian. Morton petitioned the County Court for letters of guardianship,[20] and the court complied with his prayer, without requiring of him either oath or bond. With this action, references to Burnett cease.

On August 20, 1849, Oliver Brown, a mulatto, about twenty-one years old, some five feet eight inches tall, and heavily made, appeared before the County Court and proved to the satisfaction of the chief justice and his associates that he was free and that he had resided in Texas before March 2, 1836, the date of the Declaration of Independence. The court issued him a statement that he was "entitled to remain in Texas under the laws of the State now in force,"[21] but it did not require a guardian for him. Brown also disappeared from the records.

According to the printed abstract of the 1850 census, there were five free blacks in Fort Bend County,[22] but an examination of the manuscript* schedules reveals the fact that three of those listed as free blacks were actually Mexicans.[23] Indeed, the only free blacks listed were Peter Martin and Oliver Brown.[24]

It is apparent from the four cases herein discussed that free blacks were able to obtain fair treatment from whites in a slaveholding area, but it must be remembered that they had no political rights and were unable to associate either with whites or slaves.

Notes

1. For a discussion of the legal position of free blacks in Texas, see Andrew Forest Muir, "The Free Negro in Harris County, Texas" in *Southwestern Historical Quarterly*, XLVI (January, 1943).

2. Probate Case Papers of Fort Bend County (MSS.), file No. 10. Unless otherwise indicated all manuscripts cited are in the County Clerk's Office, Richmond, Texas.

3. Probate Records of Fort Bend County (MSS.), A, 20. Pool's surety was John V. Morton, sheriff of the county.

4. United States Census, 1850, Texas (Microfilm in Archives, University of Texas Library, Austin), Fort Bend County, Schedule 1, dwelling and family No. 192.

5. Probate Records, A, 293.

6. Report of Oliver Jones in Harriet Smither (ed.), *Journals of the Fourth Congress of the Republic of Texas* ... (Austin: Texas State Library and Historical Commission, n.d.), I, 58.

7. Marriage Records of Fort Bend County (MSS.), A, unnumbered page. The contemporary county clerk recorded all licenses in the Marriage Records.

8. Thomas Barnett to Peter Martin, August 17, 1839, in Deed Records of Fort Bend County (MSS.), A, 191.

9. Memorials and Petitions (MSS. in Texas State Library, Austin).

10. *Journals, 4th Cong.,* I, 63–65.

11. *Ibid.,* I, 74, 80, 143, 159, 186; II, 86, 91, 126, 142, 150, 156; III, 231–32. Copy of act, certified November 7, 1840, in Probate Records, A, 363.

12. Probate Records, A, 363. Mills M. Battle was surety in the bond.

13. On May 20, Randal and Henry Jones petitioned the County Court for letters testamentary on Wyly Martin's estate. Probate Case Papers, file no. 104. Elsewhere, in error, the date of Martin's death is given as April 2, 1842. Harold Schoen (comp.), *Monuments Erected by the State of Texas to Commemorate the Centenary of Texas Independence* (Austin: Commission of Control for Texas Centennial Celebrations, 1938), 165. Also, as April 26. Harriet Smither (ed.), *Journals of the Sixth Congress of the Republic of Texas* . . . (Austin: Texas State Library and Historical Commission, 1940), I, vii n. Elizabeth LeNoir Jennett (ed.), *Biographical Directory of the Texan Conventions and Congresses, 1832–1845* (n.p., n.d.), 134.

14. Probate Case Papers, file No. 122.

15. Probate Minutes of Fort Bend County (MSS.), A, 143–44.

16. Marriage Records, A, unnumbered pages.

17. J. Austin Jones to Peter Martin, May 5, 1851, in Deed Records, B, 656; Oliver Jones to Martin, June 2, 1852, ibid., 778; and William B. Branch to Martin, May 12, 1856, ibid., D, 81–82.

18. Tombstone in Morton Cemetery, Richmond.

19. Probate Records, A, 316–17.

20. Probate Case Papers, file No. 107.

21. Deed Records of Fort Bend County, B, 543. There is no record of this appearance in the Minutes of the County Court (MSS.), Probate Records, or Probate Minutes.

22. J. D. DeBow, *Statistical View of the United States* ... (Washington: Beverley Tucker, Senate Printer, 1854), 308, 314.

*Editors' note—Be wary of Muir's interpretation; as mentioned in the Introduction and in other studies, a number of free blacks lived in Texas with Spanish names. What is even more surprising than Muir's conjecture is that more free blacks were **not** listed in the Census.

23. United States Census, 1850, Texas, Fort Bend County, Schedule 1, dwellings and families Nos. 55, 87, and 102.

24. *Ibid.,* Nos. 192 and 195.

9

Free Blacks in Jefferson and Orange Counties, Texas

Andrew Forest Muir

Free blacks, unlike slaves, comprised but a small fraction of the population of the South, and in few places were there heavy concentrations of them. In Texas their number was never large,[1] but in one small area they constituted a fairly numerous minority, a minority, moreover, deprived of the rights of voting, holding office, and serving on juries. Nevertheless, they were able to own property and to acquire wealth. The area under survey is the extreme southeastern corner of Texas. During the period of the Republic and for some years afterwards, except for an abortive attempt to establish a judicial county, it was included within the limits of Jefferson County. In 1852, the eastern half of the county, the mesopotamian region between the Sabine and the Neches, in which lived the free black population, was created into Orange County. In this paper, therefore, most of the sources for the period previous to 1852 will be records of Jefferson County and after that date records of Orange County.[2]

The original Jefferson County was bounded on the east by Louisiana and on the south by the Gulf of Mexico and Lake Sabine. Into the lake flows the Sabine and Neches Rivers, both of which, at the time under survey, were navigable by light draught steamers. The lands along the waterways were then, as now, timbered with a variety of hard woods —oak, gum, beech, hickory, bay, maple, ash, magnolia, holly, and wild peach—and with cypress and pine.[3] One of the two principal industries of the area was, therefore, lumbering. In 1850 Jefferson County had a lumber mill with an annual output of 1,200,000 board feet and a shingle-making plant of 576,000 shingles.[4] Ten years later, Orange County had two steam sawmills and a shingle factory.[5] The lands between waterways and along the gulf were prairies, for the most part waterlogged, seldom utilized for agriculture but ideally adapted for stock raising, which was the second important industry. The principal market for cattle was New Orleans, to which city droves of beeves went overland from the area,[6] but, in addition, hides were locally tanned and made into Spanish saddles.[7]

The area was an illiterate, backwoods community, its population chiefly derived from other Southern states. In 1850, there were no newspapers or libraries in Jefferson County, only one church, which housed a Methodist congregation, and but six one-room common schools, with six teachers and ninety pupils.[8] Ten years later, the situation had only slightly improved in Orange County. There were then but a few common schools and three Methodist societies served by a local preacher and a circuit rider, but still there were no newspapers or libraries,[9] although Jefferson County, by this time, had two weeklies, the Beaumont *Banner* and the Sabine Pass *Times*.[10] By the outbreak of the Civil War, two railroads had penetrated the area. The Texas and New Orleans had been built from Houston to Orange, the county seat of Orange County, and the Eastern Texas from the neighborhood of Sabine Pass to a railhead slightly north of Beaumont.

Most of the free blacks in the area were members of one large family named Ashworth. The progenitors of the clan in southeast Texas were four men who appear to have been brothers. William moved to Lorenzo de Zavala's colony in East Texas in 1831, Aaron in 1833, Abner in 1834, and Moses in 1835.[11] They came from Calcasieu Parish, Louisiana,[12] but two and possibly three of them had been born in South Carolina.[13] Three obtained orders of survey from the Mexican government,[14] but before they were able to locate their lands, the Texas Revolution began and the Texan government closed the land offices. On March 2, 1836, the date Texas declared its independence from Mexico, three were heads of families and one was married but apparently had no children.[15] It would not seem that any of them went into the Texas Army, as did some free blacks, but two sent substitutes who served from July 7 to September 7, 1836, in Captain B. J. Harper's company of Beaumont Volunteers.[16] Like other property owners, the Ashworths were plundered by refugees fleeing before the Mexican Army in what is aptly termed the Runaway Scrape.[17]

The settlement of free blacks in the area was not without opposition, for as early as 1835 the revolutionary Committee of Public Safety at Beaumont warned the General Council of the dangers inherent in admitting this class, whereupon the Council passed an ordinance forbidding their immigration.[18] The ordinance did not operate against the Ashworths, who remained within the area, although at times during the Revolution they were mistaken as runaway slaves.[19] Within two years of the founding of the Republic of Texas they had established themselves a place in the community, for in 1838 William Ashworth obtained from the Jefferson County board of roads and revenues a franchise to operate a ferry across Lake Sabine and up the Neches River to Beaumont.[20] The esteem in which their neighbors held them placed them in good stead a short while later. In 1840, the Texas Congress ordered all free blacks within the Republic to remove themselves from the national limits within two years, upon pain of being sold into slavery.[21] The Ashworths' friends immediately came to their rescue.

One prominent man in the county, G. A. Pattillo, wrote to President Mirabeau B. Lamar enclosing and endorsing the memorial of Jesse Ashworth for permission to remain within the Republic until the next meeting of Congress, when, apparently, he proposed to petition for a relief act. In this letter Pattillo confessed having known Ashworth in the United States and Texas for fifteen years during which time he had always maintained a reputation for good character and for being "a quiet and unassuming good citizen." In addition, Ashworth was described as "a man of some property" and therefore "of some benefit to the government."[22]

At the ensuing session of Congress, three petitions were presented on behalf of Jefferson County free blacks. Each of the three was signed by virtually all of the prominent office holders and electors of the community. One petition represented that Abner and William Ashworth had lived in Texas for six years and had "contributed generously to the advancement of the Revolution."[23] A second showed that Aaron, David, Joshua, and William Ashworth, who were mistakenly identified as brothers, had resided within the county for two years and were "peaceable and Respectable Citizens."[24] The third described Elisha Thomas in similar language and identified him as having been a resident at the time of the Declaration of Independence.[25] All three petitions requested Congress to pass relief acts permitting the several free blacks to remain unmolested within Texas. Upon the many similar petitions presented to it, Congress acted favorably in only a few cases, but these included the free blacks in Jefferson County. The select committee of the House of Representatives to whom their petitions were submitted reported that free blacks as a general rule should not be encouraged but these were exceptions, for they had contributed both their substance and their personal service to the achievement of independence and, in addition, had "at all times conducted themselves well" and had proved themselves "men of good Credit wherever they are known [,] having been at all times punctual to their engagements [,] upright in their dealings and peaceable in their disposition."[26] The attached bill, exempting Aaron, Abner, David, and William Ashworth and Elisha Thomas, together with their families, from the operation of the law of February 5, 1840, passed both houses with hardly a dissent and was approved by the president on December 12, 1840.[27] By this act, the Ashworths and Thomas were permitted to remain in Texas, but a short while later they and others were obliged to seek further relief.

In 1842 a traveling land board charged with detecting fraudulent land certificates refused to certify for patents the headrights and bounty certificates which the board of land commissioners of Jefferson County had issued to Aaron, Moses, and William Ashworth, Henry and John Bird, Aaron Nelson, Elijah and Elisha Thomas, all free blacks, on the ground that the law did not cover persons of their color. Nevertheless, all three members of the traveling board, as well as three members of the Jefferson board and some seventy-odd citizens petitioned Congress that these "good and worthy members of the Community" labored "by reason of their being people of colour under great and embarrassing inconvenience" and requested Congress to direct issuance of the patents.[28] Again, with little disagreement, both houses passed, and the president signed, the suggested bill, instructing the commissioner of the General Land Office to issue the required patents "in the same manner, as though the same had been recommended by the Board of Commissioners to detect fraudulent Land Claims for patent."[29]

Except for the two decennial censuses of 1850 and 1860, there are no records showing the exact number of free blacks in Jefferson and Orange Counties at any given time. In 1850, there were sixty-three free blacks in Jefferson County, of whom thirty-eight were named Ashworth. Three of the original Ashworth brothers were then alive, each with a family:

Aaron Ashworth, 47 years, born in South Carolina

Mary Ashworth, 40 years, born in Kentucky

Samuel Ashworth, 13 years, born in Texas

Nancy Ashworth, 10 years, born in Texas

Sublett Ashworth, 9 years, born in Louisiana

William Ashworth, 7 years, born in Texas

Mary Ashworth, 4 years, born in Texas

Aaron Ashworth, Jr., 2 years, born in Louisiana

At this time Aaron was a farmer and estimated his real property at $3,764. He had the unique distinction in the county of having in his house a schoolmaster, a white man named John A. Woods, presumably employed to tutor his four children of school age, who certainly attended school during the year.[30]

Abner Ashworth, 41 years, born in Louisiana

Sidney Jane Ashworth, 5 years, born in Texas

Lydia Ann Ashworth, 2 years, born in Texas

Abner was a farmer with real estate valued at $400. His wife, Rosalia, aged thirty-six, a native of Louisiana, was white.[31]

William Ashworth, Sr., 57 years, born in South Carolina

Clark Ashworth, 18 years, born in Texas

Emily Ashworth, 14 years, born in Texas

Nancy Ashworth, 13 years, born in Texas

Melissa Ashworth, 9 years, born in Texas

Jane Ashworth, 7 years, born in Texas

Louisa Ashworth, 4 years, born in Texas

David Ashworth, 2 years, born in Texas

William's wife, Leide or Delaide, aged forty-six, a native of Louisiana, was white. William described himself as a farmer, with holdings to the value of $7,205, and Clark as a stock raiser.[32]

There were also five families of second generation Ashworths:

Aaron Ashworth, Jr., 29 years, born in Louisiana

Serena Ashworth, 22 years, born in Louisiana

Sarah Jane Ashworth, 3 years, born in Texas

Martha Ann Ashworth, 1 year, born in Texas

Jordan Ashworth, 20 years, born in Louisiana

Aaron, Jr. was a farmer and Jordan a stock raiser.[33]

David Ashworth, 29 years, born in Louisiana

Anna Ashworth, 18 years, born in Louisiana

Valentine Ashworth, 1 year, born in Texas

David was also a stock raiser.[34]

Henderson Ashworth, 23 years, born in Louisiana

Mary J. Ashworth, 1 year, born in Texas

Henderson's wife, Letitia, aged seventeen, a native of Texas, was white. Henderson was a stock raiser.[35]

Joshua Ashworth, 34 years, born in Louisiana

Sarah Ashworth, 20 years, born in Louisiana

Allen Ashworth, 3 years, born in Texas

Eli Ashworth, 1 year, born in Texas

Joshua was a farmer.[36]

Luke Ashworth, 26 years, born in Louisiana

Lucinda Ashworth, 27 years, born in Louisiana

Luke Ashworth, Jr., 4 years, born in Texas

Rebecca Ashworth, 3 years, born in Texas

Elijah Ashworth, 1 year, born in Texas

Luke was a stock raiser with property valued at $800.[37]

There were five other free black families in the county with surnames other than Ashworth. Sarah Burwick, aged sixteen, a native of Texas, was the wife of William Burwick, an illiterate white laborer, aged twenty-one, also a native of Texas. They had no children.[38]

Eliza Bunch, 38 years, born in Louisiana

Hiram Bunch, 14 years, born in Texas

Jackson Bunch, 12 years, born in Texas

Elijah Bunch, 7 years, born in Texas

Elisha Bunch, 5 years, born in Texas

Washington Bunch, 3 years, born in Texas

Ephraim Bunch, 3 years, born in Texas

Eliza was either a widow or the wife of a slave, free black, or white man who maintained his residence elsewhere.[39]

Elvina Carter, 25 years, born in Louisiana

Sidney J. Carter, 8 years, born in Louisiana

Virgil S. Carter, 6 years, born in Louisiana

Henry P. Carter, 4 years, born in Louisiana

Jonathan M. Carter, 2 years, born in Louisiana

Rebecca Ann Carter, 1 year, born in Louisiana

Elvina was the wife of a white farmer, J. M. Carter, aged thirty-four, a native of Illinois.[40]

Robert Nelson, 25 years, born in Louisiana

Mary Ann Nelson, 20 years, born in Louisiana

Uriah Nelson, 1 year, born in Texas

Josiah Nelson, 1 year, born in Texas

Easter Gains, 19 years, born in Louisiana

Robert was a farmer.[41]

William Nelson, 36 years, born in Louisiana

Ellen Nelson, 9 years, born in Louisiana

Elizabeth Nelson, 5 years, born in Louisiana

Cynthia Nelson, 2 years, born in Texas

Moses Nelson, 30 years, born in Louisiana

William's wife was an illiterate white woman, named Sarah, aged twenty-seven. William was a farmer and Moses a laborer.[42]

Not the least interesting content of these records is the evidence of miscegenation. Three black men had white wives, and two black women had white husbands. Of the ten adult males listed, one was a laborer, four were stock raisers, and five farmers.

Ten years later there were only two free blacks in Jefferson County[43] and but twenty-nine in Orange. The principal cause of this decrease will be hereinafter discussed. The elder Aaron and his wife were listed in 1860 with six children, four of whom—Sublett, William, Mary, and Aaron—had been listed the previous decade and two of whom had been born subsequent to the 1850 census: Harriet, aged ten, and Abner, aged six, both natives of Texas. The whereabouts of Samuel and Mary, listed in 1850, was not made evident. Five of the children had attended school within the year. Aaron was still listed as a farmer, with real and personal property valued at $4,870, and Sublett as a stock raiser.[44]

Abner apparently had died during the decade, but his widow and three children—Sidney, Lidda A., and Phillipa, aged five, a native of Texas—were listed. Rozella's [Aaron's wife] property was valued at $11,444.[45]

William and his wife had survived, and they were listed together with their children: Melissa, Jane, Louisa, David, and a second Louisa, aged two, a native of Texas. William was described as a laborer, with property valued at $4,000.[46]

Luke and Lucinda had seven children. In addition to the three listed in 1850 were Delilah, aged eight; Sarah, six; Melissa, five; and Clark, three, all born in Texas. Luke was also a laborer, with property valued at $1,160.[47]

Eliza Bunch had disappeared, but three of her sons—Hiram, Elijah, and Washington—were all listed as laborers.[48]

These data are not sufficiently numerous to serve as the basis for any generalizations, but it is interesting to note that during the decade 1850-1859 William's occupation changed from farmer to laborer and Luke's from stock raiser to laborer. During the same period, the value of William's real estate dropped from $7,205 to $4,000 and Luke's from $800 to $160. These reductions, however, were probably the result of sales rather than of depreciation.

That the free blacks in the area were no worse off than the bulk of their white neighbors and indeed better off than most is evident from their real estate holdings. Thirteen members of the family acquired land within Jefferson and Orange Counties,[49] which they utilized principally for grazing large herds of cattle. In 1850, six of them were listed in the agricultural census.[50] One of the two Aaron Ashworths there listed, probably the younger, was the largest cattle raiser in the entire county, with 2,570 head, 220 head more than the runner-up.

Not only did the free blacks own land and cattle, but they also owned slaves. This was more unusual in Texas than in Louisiana, where many free blacks had large slaveholdings. In 1839, William Ashworth sold Lucy, aged about twenty, and her child, Sarah, about two, for $1,200, probably Texas money,[51] and a short while later he purchased for $1,150 an eighteen or nineteen year-old slave, Thornton,[52] whom he sold three years later for $1,000.[53] In 1846, Abner Ashworth bought Moses, aged twenty-two,[54] and in 1863, Mary Ashworth bequeathed a slave Peter to one of her sons.[55] At least one slave held by the Ashworths interpreted his ownership by a black man to be loss of caste, as reported by a Northern traveler:

> At another house where we stopped . . . we heard some conversation upon a negro of the neighborhood, who had been sold to a free negro, and who refused to live with him, saying he wouldn't be a servant to a nigger. All agreed that he was right, although the man was well known to be kind to his negroes, and would always sell any of them who wished it. The slave had been sold because he wouldn't mind.[56]

Despite this attitude on the part of some slaves, in 1850, Aaron owned six blacks, Abner three, Joshua one, and William two.[57] Ten years later Aaron, the white widow of Abner, and the white wife of William each owned four.[58]

Free blacks in southeastern Texas, we have seen, acquired both land and slaves. Their equality was not, however, merely economic. As hereinbefore mentioned, some of them intermarried, at least by common law, with whites, and their social equality is nowhere better demonstrated than in the titles of respect given to both their men and women. As early as 1844 and as late as 1861, Ashworth men and the women, both white and black, they married were given the titles of Mr. and Miss by county clerks when filling out marriage licenses.[59]

Like a large number of their neighbors, many of the Ashworths and other free blacks were illiterate. Positive evidence indicates that eight of them could not sign their names.[60] On at least one occasion schemers took advantage of an Ashworth's ignorance. A white named Barns broadcast hearsay that at the funeral of one Elliot, Abner Ashworth had drunkenly fallen into the open grave. Ashworth challenged the statement with the oath that if a man originated it, he was, according to the prudish rendering of a nineteenth century jurist or court reporter, a "d---d liar," and, if a woman, she was a "d---d whorish liar." To this, Barns replied that it was his wife and threatened to sue Ashworth for slander. By use of this threat he extorted from Ashworth three promissory notes totaling two thousand dollars in compromise of his threatened suit. Somewhat later, the notes found their way into the hands of Christian Hillebrant, who offered them to Ashworth in payment for his herd of cattle. Ashworth declined to be a party to the bargain, whereupon Hillebrant sued him for collection of the notes. In the district court, Hillebrant was unsuccessful, and, when the case was taken on appeal, the Supreme Court affirmed the decision of the lower court. Justice Royall T. Wheeler stated in his opinion that he had no doubt the notes had been obtained "without any value or sufficient consideration, and by taking advantage of his [Ashworth's] ignorance, and practicing upon his fears."[61]

Although, in Texas, free blacks neither held public office nor served on juries, either grand or petit, and presumably, therefore, were unable to represent their own best interests, the Ashworths seldom got into difficulty with law enforcing agents. Indeed, but for a number of nuisance suits alleging irregular sexual relations, they were but infrequently before the bar of justice. In 1855 Samuel Ashworth was indicted for assault and battery, but the case was nol-prossed in the following year.[62] Both William and Henderson Ashworth were indicted in 1854 for playing cards; they pleaded guilty, and each was fined ten dollars and costs.[63] Clark Ashworth was indicted for larceny in 1852, and the case was still on the docket at the end of the Civil War.[64] Henderson Ashworth was indicted for the same offense in 1854, but the case was later dismissed.[65] Moses and William Ashworth were both indicted for theft in 1857, probably for the same alleged offense involving a beef, but no action had been taken in either case by the end of the War.[66]

In one respect the Ashworths were plagued by the grand jury, and that in the matter of irregular sexual relations. Most of the indictments for alleged fornication and adultery undoubtedly grew out of common law marriages or formal miscegenetic marriages, for only one Ashworth was charged with improper relations with more than one person. Some of the suits involved relations between two Ashworths, some between

Ashworth men and white women, and some between Ashworth women and white men. In all there were seventeen indictments against persons of the Ashworth name, of which two were for adultery and fifteen for fornication, involving a total of nine Ashworths. All of the suits except one were quashed, and no execution was ever entered in that one case. Henderson Ashworth was indicted three times, once for adultery and twice for fornication with Letitia Stewart, a white woman.[67] The couple apparently had been married in Louisiana, but the State of Texas declined to interpret a miscegenetic union as legal.[68] Certainly in 1850 they appear to have been living together as man and wife.[69] Henderson was convicted in one of the fornication suits, but he took it on appeal to the Supreme Court, and although he lost there,[70] the trial court seems not to have issued an execution.[71] Keziah Ashworth was also indicted three times, once for adultery and twice for fornication with Willis Goodman, a white man.[72] Nancy Ashworth was twice indicted for fornication with Jackson Stewart, a white man,[73] and Sarah and Clark Ashworth were indicted the same number of times for the same offense.[74] Five were each indicted once: Martha Ashworth for relations with Jacob P. Pender, a white man; Emily Ashworth for relations with Joseph Young, a white man;[75] Sarah Ashworth for relations with William Burwick, a white man;[76] and Samuel Ashworth for relations with Melissa Ann Ashworth.[77] Both Sarah and Martha seem to have borne children by the men with whom they were charged, for in her will their mother, Mary Ashworth, left property to grandchildren with the names of Pender and Burwick.[78] In one case involving two Ashworths, a suit was dismissed after the defendants were legally married. Samuel married Melissa Ann Ashworth on December 4, 1855,[79] thirteen days after an indictment for fornication[80] and a month after purchase of a marriage license.

Whites occasionally got into trouble with the law because of the Ashworths. Not only were a number indicted for irregular sexual relations with them, but also one was indicted for marrying a black and two for selling spirits to free blacks. On January 14, 1845, Sillasta Gallier, a white man, married Margarette Ashworth.[81] A few weeks later, on March 5, he was indicted, but the case was quashed on October 20, 1847.[82] On November 29, 1861, A. Pavele was indicted on two counts and R. G. Woodvill on one for selling spirits to free blacks. Pavele was fined ten dollars and costs in each case and Woodvill fifty dollars and costs.[83]

With the approach of the Civil War, racial tension increased everywhere in the South. In southeastern Texas the tension reached a dramatic crisis, which strangely enough has been completely forgot. In June and July, 1856, there occurred a sustained armed struggle between two fairly equally divided groups in Orange County. One group was made up of a number of whites and free blacks, with the sheriff of the county said to have been at their head, and was called Regulators or the black party. The other, comprised of whites only, was known as Moderators or the law and order party. Undoubtedly the difficulty was based upon long standing personal differences, likely the result of economic competition, in which the racial issue had been injected as an excuse rather than a cause. Both sides were probably to blame, and there is no reason for assuming that the one party was morally superior to the other. Each included desperate characters.

The immediate cause of the conflict was the apprehension by Samuel Deputy, whose name appropriately describes what appears to have been his official position of deputy sheriff, of Clark Ashworth in the act of butchering hogs that did not belong to him. It is not unlikely that they were razorbacks of indeterminate ownership which thrived off the abundant mast in the region. In any case, Deputy arrested Ashworth and incarcerated him for trial before a justice of the peace. He did not remain long in jail, for his brother Samuel went his bond. With a crowd of friends supporting him, Samuel Ashworth invited Deputy to fight, but Deputy declined and obtained a warrant for Samuel's arrest. At Clark's hearing, he was found guilty and ordered to be punished by thirty-nine lashes on the bare back. The sentence was not executed, however, for Clark escaped, with the aid, it was said, of the sheriff. Shortly thereafter Clark and a second free black, Jack Bunch, lay in a skiff on the Sabine in ambuscade for Deputy, who soon passed in a second skiff. While Bunch maneuvered the boat, Ashworth fired at Deputy until his ammunition was exhausted. Deputy was then seen clinging to his boat, and both Bunch and Ashworth battered him with the butts of their guns until Deputy died, probably of drowning. The assailants then took refuge with their friends, apparently in a neighboring county, but it was believed they did not propose to leave the area permanently until they should have murdered three others against whom they had some grudge.

Warrants were issued for Ashworth's and Bunch's arrest, but the sheriff was either unable or unwilling to find them and to take them into custody. At the county seat, then known as Madison but now Orange, a vigilante committee organized, but there was no secrecy in its deliberations, for they were betrayed to the Ashworths by four of its members. The committee ordered all free blacks within the county to leave instantly and not to remain within fifty miles of its boundaries. Thirty-three of them, in turn, organized at a residence some distance from the county seat and threatened to destroy the town. With both sides organized and armed, a conflict was inevitable, and it soon began with a personal encounter between one Cross, of the law and order party, and Burwell Alexander, of the black party, in which the latter was shot. Cross then shot and killed Dr. Andrew Mairs. On June 22, twenty-eight members of the vigilante committee set out from Madison and surrounded the dwelling in which the black party was congregated. The committeemen killed J. C. Moore and E. C. Glover and captured William Blake, Mart Stewart, and Henderson Ashworth, who were lodged in jail, and J. D. Brandon, who was ordered out of the country. Under Glover's bed the committee found what was described as the "celebrated Sabine Bogus Mint," which included dies for making $2.50, $5, $10, and $20 gold pieces, and a stack of spurious land certificates.[84] There is some suggestion that the governor called out the militia to quell the disturbance,[85] but following the abandonment of the county by most of the free blacks, the situation quickly calmed down. Many of the blacks appear to have removed temporarily into the adjoining Calcasieu Parish in Louisiana.

One of them, Abner Ashworth, later said that he was "compeled [*sic*] by the disturbance in [the] County in the Month of June and July A D 1856 to remove Myself & [my] Said Children beyond the limits of Said County."[86] An observer shortly afterwards stated that there then existed in the county a desire to forget the past and an awareness that there would have been less difficulty if the established rules of legal and administrative procedure had been followed in the beginning.[87]

Clark Ashworth appears to have made good his escape, for his name does not reappear in the record,[88] but his accomplice Bunch was apprehended in Colorado County.[89] On change of venue he was tried in November before the district court of Jefferson County for the murder of Deputy, found guilty, and sentenced to be hanged on November 21. At the trial a rumor circulated that a party from Orange County planned to rescue him, and consequently between the dates of sentence and execution, he was guarded not only by the sheriff and his deputies but also by a committee of fifteen to twenty armed men. He appeared indifferent to his fate and, because he laughed, joked, and blasphemed, was regarded as a case hardened sinner. On the day of execution, he bantered to the steps of the gallows, but, having mounted the ladder, he exhorted his listeners to avoid bad company and to obey the dictates of their consciences. A few moments later all was well with him.[90] Aside from the personal tragedies, the principal result of the disturbance was that during the decade 1850-1859 the free black population of the area dropped from sixty-three to twenty-nine. Nevertheless, that so large a number of them returned to the county clearly indicates they were not persecuted as a class for the misdoings of a group of their fellows.

From the mass of evidence accumulated in the foregoing pages, one is able to describe in considerable detail the position of a substantial free black minority in a backwoods Texas area. Its members enjoyed more than a modicum of legal, economic, and social equality, despite their electoral and office holding disabilities. Their persons were inviolate against illegal seizure. Although harassed at times by grand juries, they usually escaped the penalties of the laws they were charged with violating. In two instances they were parties to suits heard before the highest appellate court of the state, showing that they were able to seek redress in the Supreme Court and could afford the expenses of the appeals. In two other instances, they sought relief in the halls of Congress from the operation of oppressive laws, and in both they were successful; they were permitted to remain in Texas and to receive headright and bounty lands from the government. Economically, they fared as well as or better than most of their neighbors. They owned real estate and slaves, farmed their acres, and grazed large herds of cattle. At their deaths, their estates passed in regular order to their heirs. Socially, they were as often literate as their white neighbors. In one notable case, an Ashworth, by having a tutor, showed himself more concerned with the education of his children than any other parent in the county. These free blacks were accorded titles of respect by their white associates, and they intermarried, either formally or informally, with whites, with less friction than one would have expected. Even after a bloody feud between whites and free blacks, almost half of the free blacks were able to return to the community and to maintain the positions they had created for themselves. These positions might have depended upon the patronage of whites, but, if so, the patronage was extraordinarily liberal. In 1950 there are many areas in the United States where blacks are worse off, or at least no better off, than the Ashworths were before 1865.

Notes

1. According to the United States census, there were 397 free blacks in Texas in 1850 and 355 in 1860. J. D. B. DeBow, *The Seventh Census of the United States: 1850* . . . (Washington: Robert Armstrong, Public Printer, 1853), 503–04; Joseph C. G. Kennedy, *Population of the United States in 1860* . . . (Washington: Government Printing Office, 1864), 476–79. These figures can not be accepted as reliable, for Mexicans were frequently listed as free blacks.

2. In 1850, the population of Jefferson County was composed of 1,504 whites, 63 free blacks, and 269 slaves, a total of 1,836. Ten years later it was composed of 1,684 whites, 2 free blacks, and 309 slaves, a total of 1,995. The population of Orange County at that time was composed of 1,495 whites, 29 free blacks, and 392 slaves, a total of 1,916. DeBow, *Seventh Census,* 503; Kennedy, *Population,* 485.

3. Statement of George A. Pattillo, assistant United States marshal, Eastern District of Texas, in U. S. Census, 1860, Schedule 6, Social Statistics (the originals of all of the 1850 and 1860 schedules except 1 and 2 are in Archives, Texas State Library, Austin), Orange and Jefferson County.

4. *Ibid.,* 1850, Schedule 5, Products of Industry, Jefferson County.

5. *Ibid.,* 1860, Schedule 5, Orange County.

6. The writer's examination of antebellum newspapers has revealed but two markets for Texas cattle during the period, Chicago and New Orleans.

7. U. S. Census, 1850, Schedule 5, Jefferson County; 1860, Schedule 5, Orange County.

8. *Ibid.,* 1850, Schedule 6, Jefferson County.

9. *Ibid.,* 1860, Schedule 6, Orange County, and Pattillo's statement.

10. *Ibid.,* 1860, Schedule 6, Jefferson County.

11. Record of Applications of Jefferson County (MS. in County Clerk's Office, Beaumont), 94, 95, 96, 145. In 1850, there were eighteen free blacks by the name of Ashworth in Angelina County, Texas, comprising the households of James, James, Jr., Jesse, and William. U. S. Census, 1850, Schedule 1, Free Inhabitants (microfilms of schedules 1 and 2 of the 1850 and 1860 censuses are in Archives, University of Texas Library, Austin), Angelina County, dwellings and families Nos. 101, 102, 103, and 104. James, born in South Carolina, was probably a brother of Aaron, Abner, Moses, and William.

12. James, Jesse, Moses, and one Taply Ashworth lived in Calcasieu, then a part of St. Landry Parish, in 1830. Carter G. Woodson, *Free Negro Heads of Families in the United States in 1830 . . .* (Washington: The Association for the Study of Negro Life and History, c. 1925), 38.

13. William was born in South Carolina about 1793 and Aaron about 1803. Abner was born in Louisiana about 1809. Moses died long before the first U. S. census in Texas, and the date and place of his birth are not ascertainable. U. S. Census, 1850, Schedule 1, Jefferson County, dwellings and families Nos. 3, 107, 119.

14. Aaron, Abner, and William had each obtained an order from George Antonio Nixon. Record of Applications of Jefferson County, 94, 95, 96.

15. Aaron, Abner, and William were heads of families, and Moses was married. *Ibid.,* 94, 95, 96, 145.

16. Comptrollers Military Service Records (MSS. in Archives, Texas State Library), files Abner and William Ashworth. Abner sent Elijah Thomas, a free black, and William sent Gipson Perkins. Under the terms of an act approved July 28, 1876, granting pensions to veterans of the Texas Revolution and their widows, Delaide, widow of William, and Mary, widow of Aaron, received pensions. Pension Papers (MSS. in Archives, Texas State Library), files Delaide and Mary Ashworth.

17. A. C. Gray (ed.), *From Virginia to Texas, 1835, Diary of Col. Wm. F. Gray . . .* (Houston: Gray, Dillaye & Co., 1909), 239.

18. H. P. N. Gammel (comp.), *The Laws of Texas, 1822–1897* (Austin: Gammel Book Co., 1898), I, 720–22, 1024–25.

19. Gray (ed.), *From Virginia to Texas,* 238.

20. W. P. A., *Inventory of the County Archives of Texas, No. 181, Orange County* . . . (San Antonio: Texas Historical Records Survey, 1941), 37.

21. Gammel (comp.), *Laws,* II, 325–27.

22. Pattillo to Lamar, Pattillo's Postoffiee, February 24, 1840, in Mirabeau Buonaparte Lamar Papers (MSS. in Archives, Texas State Library), No. 1729.

23. Isaac Applewhite and seventy-one others to Congress, September, 1840, in Memorials and Petitions (MSS. in Archives, Texas State Library), file Citizens of Jefferson County.

24. William Stephenson and fifty-six others to Congress, September 19, 1840, *ibid.*

25. Isaac Applewhite and sixty-one others to Congress, September 18, 1840, *ibid.*

26. Report of Joseph Grigsby, chairman of committee on petition of free men of color in Congressional Papers (MSS. in Archives, Texas State Library).

27. *Journals of the House of Representatives of the Republic of Texas: Fifth Congress—First Session, 1840-1841* (Austin: Cruger and Wing, Public Printers, 1841), 27, 33, 46, 52; *Journals of the Senate of the Republic of Texas, Fifth Congress—First Session* . . . (Houston: Printed at the Telegraph Office, 1841), 16, 17-18, 29, 30, 33, 37, 146, 150, 172-73; two drafts of the act in Congressional Papers, 5th Cong., unnumbered file; Gammel (comp.), *Laws,* II, 549–50, 648.

28. Nathan Holbert and seventy-six others (an additional two to four signatures have been clipped off, probably by an autograph collector) to Congress in Memorials and Petitions, Restored Documents, file William Ashworth. John Bird, a son of Dorcas Bird and grandson of one General Bird of Virginia, and his son Henry lived for some time in Russellville, Kentucky,

and then near Courtland, Alabama. They arrived in Texas about January 15, 1836, and Henry served from June 4 to September 4, 1836, in Captain Reed's company of the Texas Army. John and Henry Bird to Congress, September 20, 1836; affidavit of Robert W. Micklon and Willie Connor, justices of the peace of Lawrence County, Alabama; affidavit of William W. Whitaker and four others, Russellville, December 6, 1819; and affidavit of W. F. Whitaker and fifteen others, Courtland, Alabama, January 22, 1833, all in Memorials and Petitions, file John Bird; Comptrollers Military Service Records, file Henry Bird. See also *Journals of the House of Representatives of the Republic of Texas, First Congress-First Session* . . . (Houston: Printed at the Telegraph Office, 1838), 219-20.

29. *Journals of the House of Representatives of the Seventh Congress of the Republic of Texas, Convened at Washington, on the 14th Nov. 1842.* . . (Washington: Thomas Johnson, Public Printer, 1843), 45, 63, 73, 80, 198; *Journals of the Senate of the Seventh Congress of the Republic of Texas, Convened at Washington on the 14th Nov. 1842* . . . (Washington: Thomas Johnson, Public Printer, 1843), 29, 33, 84; draft of bill in Congressional Papers. 7th Cong., No. 2706; abstract of act in Gammel (comp.), *Laws*, II, 875. For lands acquired from Texas by Aaron, Abner, Mrs. D., David, Luke, Mary, Moses, and William Ashworth, Henry and John Bird, and Aaron Nelson, see original manuscripts in General Land Office, Austin: Bexar County files 2049 and 2394, Houston 1st Class 271, Houston 3rd Class 924, Jefferson 1st Class 27 and 85, Jefferson Bounty 11 and 25, Liberty 1st Class 6, Milam 1st Class 302, 331, 710, 808, 855, 856, 867, 1350, 1426, and 1522, Milam Bounty 118, 930, and 1446, Red River 1st Class 395, and Travis Bounty 712. See also *Abstract of All Original Texas Land Titles Comprising Grants and Locations to August 31, 1941* . . . (no facts of publication), I, 94, 354, 483, 735, 737, 887, 963; II, 254, 549; III, 20, 177, 178, 197, 548, 946; IV, 945; V, 49.

30. U. S. Census, 1850, Schedule 1, Jefferson County, dwelling and family No. 119.

31. *Ibid.,* No. 3.

32. *Ibid.,* No. 107.

33. *Ibid.*, No. 36.

34. *Ibid.*, No. 37.

35. *Ibid.*, No. 166.

36. *Ibid.*, No. 38.

37. *Ibid.*, No. 110.

38. *Ibid.*, No. 145.

39. *Ibid.*, No. 122.

40. *Ibid.*, No. 121.

41. *Ibid.*, No. 127.

42. *Ibid.*, No. 126.

43. John M. Joice, 23, laborer, a native of Alabama, with real estate valued at $150, and Gertrude Joice, 17, a native of Kentucky. There is no certainty that these were free blacks, for the census taker made the letters W (for white) and M (for mulatto) so similarly, that at times they are indistinguishable. In the footing of the page on which these two names appear all of the persons listed are counted as white. *Ibid.*, 1860, Schedule 1, Jefferson County, dwelling and family No. 409.

44. *Ibid.*, 1860, Schedule 1, Orange County, dwelling and family No. 144.

45. *Ibid.*, No. 145.

46. *Ibid.*, No. 186.

47. *Ibid.*, No. 157.

48. *Ibid*, No. 214.

49. The conveyances, in which Aaron, Aaron, Jr., Abner, David, Delaide, Henderson, Jesse, Joshua, Luke, Mary, Rozella, Sublett, and William Ashworth were either grantors or grantees, in Deed Records of Jefferson and Orange Counties (MSS. in County Clerks' Offices, Beaumont and Orange, respec-

tively), are too numerous to cite. In 1846, Aaron owned 4578 acres, Abner 320, David 50, Henderson 1 town lot, Jesse 392, Joshua 50, Luke, 64, and William 7957. Tax Rolls (MSS. in Office of Comptroller of Public Accounts, Austin), 1846, Jefferson County.

50. U.S. Census, 1850, Schedule 4, Productions of Agriculture, Jefferson County.

51. William Ashworth to Richard Balew, August 8, 1839, in Deed Records of Jefferson County, D, 143-44.

52. John A. Williams to William Ashworth, September 30, 1839, *ibid.*, 462–63.

53. William Ashworth to David Burrell, May 13, 1842, *ibid.*, 464–65.

54. Nathan Bonner to Abner Ashworth, January 17, 1846, *ibid.*, E, 360.

55. Mary Ashworth's will, December 3, 1863, in Will Books of Orange County (MSS. in County Clerk's Office, Orange), A, 7–8.

56. Frederick Law Olmsted, *A Journey Through Texas; or, A Saddle-Trip on the Southwestern Frontier; With a Statistical Appendix* (New York: Dix, Edwards & Co., 1857), 386. I am indebted to Mr. Floyd Seyward Lear, professor of history at The Rice Institute, for calling this source to my attention.

57. U. S. Census, 1850, Schedule 2, Slaves, Jefferson County, 2–3.

58. *Ibid.*, 1860, Schedule 2, Orange County, 3–4.

59. Miss Lucinda Perkins to Luke Ashworth, married October 9, 1844; Miss Margarette Ashworth to Sillasta Gallier, January 14, 1845; Miss Syvena Gibson to Aaron Ashworth, Jr., January 8, 1846; Miss Catherine Ashworth to Elijah B. Thomas, July 9, 1846; Miss Elizabeth Nelson to Drury Ashworth, December 31, 1846; Miss Missina Willis to Jackson G. Ashworth, August 5, 1857; Miss Easther Gowins to Mr. Larkin Ashworth, October 5, 1852; Miss Sidney Jane Ashworth to Mr. S. A. Ashworth, March 5, 1861; and Miss Lydia Ann Ashworth to Luke Ashworth, Jr., September 12, 1861. Marriage Records of Jefferson County (MSS. in County Clerk's Office, Beaumont), A, 53, 55,

60, 62; B, 2, 9; Marriage Records of Orange County (MSS. in County Clerk's Office, Orange), A, 4, 94, 110, respectively.

60. Abner, Luke, Mary, Serena, and William Ashworth; Eliza Bunch; William and Moses Nelson. Deed Records of Jefferson County, C, 333-35; A, 386–88; J, 288–90; U. S. Census, 1850, Schedule 1, Jefferson County, dwellings and families Nos. 3, 107, 110, 122, 126.

61. Christian Hillebrant v. Abner Ainsworth [*sic*] and others, 18 Tex. 307–12 (1857).

62. Minutes of the Orange County District Court (MSS. in District Clerk's Office, Orange), A, 100, 124.

63. *Ibid.,* 43, 58–59.

64. *Ibid.,* 6, 421.

65. *Ibid.,* 60, 98.

66. *Ibid.,* 147, 155, 393, 422.

67. Minutes of the Jefferson County District Court (MSS. in District Clerk's Office, Beaumont), A, 76, 97, 98, 130, 146; Minutes of the Orange County District Court, A, 100, 125.

68. Ashworth's attorney, J. B. Jones, claimed that the district court had erred in not giving the charge that Ashworth and Letitia were married. Henderson Ashworth v. The State, 9 Tex. 490–91 (1853).

69. U. S. Census, 1950, Schedule 1, Jefferson County, dwelling and family No. 166.

70. 9 Tex. 490–91.

71. Minutes of the Jefferson County District Court, A, 98, 130, 146.

72. *Ibid.,* A, 74, 96, 98, 99, 100, 163; Minutes of the Orange County District Court, A, 100, 124.

73. Minutes of the Orange County District Court, A, 17, 36, 100, 125.

74. *Ibid.*, 17, 38, 100, 124.

75. *Ibid.*, 23, 39.

76. *Ibid.*, 23, 38.

77. Ibid., 100, 124.

78. The will listed Josephine, Sarah, and Vorilla Burwick, and Absilla, Laura, and Delphin Pender. Will Books of Orange County, A, 7–8.

79. Marriage Records of Orange County, A, 24.

80. Minutes of the Orange County District Court, A, 100, 124.

81. Marriage Records of Jefferson County, A, 55.

82. Minutes of the Jefferson County District Court, A, 20, 23, 40, 63, 95.

83. Minutes of the Orange County District Court, A, 371–72, 377, 414.

84. The best account of the disturbance is a letter signed V., and dated Madison, which appeared in Galveston *Weekly News*, July 15, 1856, 2bc, abstracted in Houston *Weekly Telegraph*, July 23, 1856, 1f. Less adequate accounts may be found in Galveston *Civilian*, copied in Dallas *Herald*, July 12, 1856, 1f, in Galveston *Weekly News*, June 24, 1856, 3c, and in Olmsted, *A Journey Through Texas*, 386–88.

85. Letter of Cracero, Madison, July 1, 1856, in Houston *Weekly Telegraph*, July 16, 1856, 3c.

86. Abner Ashworth to Charlton Midkiff, August 11, 1856, in Deed Records of Orange County, B, 187–90.

87. Letter in Liberty *Gazette*, quoted in Galveston *Weekly News*, September 23, 1856, ld.

88. As late as November 28, 1864, a case against him on a charge of larceny was still continued. Minutes of the Orange County District Court, A, 421.

89. Houston *Weekly Telegraph*, October 22, 1856, 2b.

90. Letters of Hal, Beaumont, November 5 and 25, 1856, *Ibid.*, December 2, 1856, le, and December 9, 1856, 3c.

10

FREE BLACKS IN GALVESTON COUNTY, TEXAS

Andrew Forest Muir

When a student of American history uses the term free black, he means simply a black in the United States, especially in a slaveholding area before the end of the Civil War, who was not a slave. The term is not identical with freed black, for while a freed black was one who had once been a slave and had been emancipated, a free black might have either been born free or been emancipated.

Free blacks were never numerous in Texas, but there is no way of determining the precise number at any time. Only two federal censuses had been taken in Texas before the outbreak of the Civil War. That of 1850 showed a total of 397 free blacks,[1] and that of 1860 a total of 355 blacks.[2] Unfortunately, these figures can be easily proved inaccurate. In some counties, every person enumerated as a free black turns out to have been a Mexican.[3] Greenbury Logan, a free black who had been wounded while serving in the Texan Revolution, was listed as a free black in one of the two censuses and as a white in the other.[4] And there is no reason for assuming that many free blacks were not listed as slaves.

The laws of the Republic of Texas and the State of Texas, both in the United States and in the Confederate States, were rather severe in reference to free blacks. It would require a Philadelphia lawyer at this late date to determine precisely what was and was not the law on the subject. In general, though, no free black was supposed to remain in Texas after September, 1836, without specific approval of the legislature of either the Republic or the State, and such approval was given in only a few instances. Also, beginning in 1840, no free black was supposed to immigrate to Texas. But law does not enforce itself, and both of these laws were widely disregarded.[5]

I do not propose to speak at this time on the general subject of the free black in Texas. Instead I shall speak on the free black in a particular area, Galveston. After its founding in 1838, the city of Galveston rapidly became the largest city and the largest port in Texas. Because it was a seaport and a commercial mart, its population was not representative of Texas cities. It was less Anglo-Saxon than most places in Texas, less English-speaking, and less Evangelical Christian. From the beginning it had a population drawn from many areas. There were numerous natives of France who spoke French and were Roman Catholics. There were also many natives of the numerous German states who spoke German, some of whom were Jews.

As Galveston Island is no more than a sandbar, there was no agriculture except truck farming in the immediate neighborhood. There was then, no vast body of agricultural laborers. There were, however, black slaves in Galveston. Some of these were employed as domestics, while others were employed as draymen and the like in the bustling port of Galveston. There were also a few free blacks, how many, no one knows. According to the 1850 census there were thirty in Galveston County, all in the city of Galveston.[6] Ten years later there were only two enumerated in the census.[7] What happened to the other twenty-eight? I wish I knew. As a matter of fact, while these figures do not lie, there is good reason to believe that in this instance liars surely did figure. Many of the free blacks listed in Galveston in 1850 and not listed in 1860 were probably still there in 1860 and living precisely as they had been living ten years before, but, as a result of the growing racial as well as sectional tension that was soon to lead to the Civil War, some of them did not proclaim their free status from the housetops. Thomas Low Nichols, who visited Galveston about this time, described the phenomenon in his book, *Forty Years of American Life, 1821–1861*:

> Though largely colonised from the Northern and Eastern States, Texas at the period of my visit was a thoroughly slave State. No free negro could lawfully reside within its boundaries. A short time before my visit to Galveston a law had been passed, banishing every free negro or person having a perceptible show of negro blood from the State, under penalty of being reduced to slavery. I inquired particularly the effect of this enactment, and found that few negroes had left the State in consequence. They have strong local attachments. What they did was to choose their masters, selecting persons in whom they had confidence, and becoming nominally, and in fact legally, their property. They were as free as ever, only that they paid over to these masters a small sum out of their wages, and the masters became responsible for their good behavior, care in sickness, and support in old age. It was a kind of character and life assurance. Two negroes in Galveston were excepted by common consent from the operation of this law. One was the most fashionable barber in the place, and the other a musician and dancing-master, who had taught them all to dance, and played the fiddle at every social party.[8]

There are, of record, in the Deed Records of Galveston County, two earlier cases of free blacks indenturing themselves. In March, 1841, Francis Marshall, *alias* Francis Hamilton, a free person of color, then resident in Galveston, bound himself for five years to John H. Walton, a prominent citizen and sometimes mayor.[9] In December of the same year, Peter Williams, who had fallen into the debt of Henry N. Potter, a prominent lawyer, bound himself to Potter. According to the contract, Potter's death was to release Williams. Potter committed himself to furnishing Williams with good and decent apparel and a sufficiency of wholesome food at all times and medicines and medical attention when he was ill.[10]

Two free blacks in Galveston were specifically granted permission to remain in Texas by the legislature. In 1840 the Congress of the Republic of Texas authorized Cary, a free man of color, lately the slave of Thomas Freeman McKinney, to remain, provided that Cary made bond that he would "demean himself in a peaceable and orderly manner" and that he would "never become a charge to said Republic or County."[11] Almost twelve years later, the Legislature of the State of Texas authorized Mary Madison, "a free woman of color, in consequence of her age and the length of time that she has resided in the State, during which time she has demeaned herself with becoming propriety and a strict observance of the laws, and also in consequence of the services she has rendered as a nurse to the city," to remain in Galveston.[12]

The first of these two people was the best known free black in Galveston. During the course of the year 1835, when Thomas Freeman McKinney was in partnership with Samuel May Williams in Brazoria, Cary performed some service for which McKinney rewarded him by permitting him to hire his own time and to utilize his earnings to purchase his own, his wife's, and his daughter's freedom.[13] During the Texan Revolution, Cary was, as McKinney wrote, "of much service in carrying expresses."[14] When Captain and Mrs. Houstoun, a Scotch couple, twice visited Texas during the 1840s, Cary was the proprietor of a livery stable. In her two books, *Texas and the Gulf of Mexico* and *Hesperos: or, Travels in the West,* Mrs. Houstoun referred to Cary as a drunken rascal, who had a "countenance of singular rascality and cunning."[15] The drink must have soon killed him, for in 1850, his wife but not he was listed in the census.[16]

The Deed Records of Galveston County show five instruments in which slave owners emancipated their slaves in Galveston. Three of the slave owners were from out of the State of Texas, and doubtlessly they had taken their slaves to Galveston for no other purpose than to emancipate them. In 1841, William S. Winn, of Georgia, "for and in consideration of the faithfulness, honesty, integrity, and obedience which has characterized the conduct of my . . . Slave [Louisa] towards me and my business entrusted to or committed to her charge," absolutely emancipated her.[17] Two years later, Mary C. Palmer, of New Orleans, emancipated her "dutiful and most faithful servant," Emeline and her three-year-old daughter, Calesta.[18] In 1851, E. Bates, a local man, "from motives of benevolence and humanity," manumitted a woman, Morning, and her child, Henry Bennett, by conveying the two of them in trust to another man, who had agreed to serve as their guardian and to permit them to "enjoy all the benefits of their labor."[19] Two years later, Alfred Millard, of Jefferson Parish, Louisiana, sold to Philip Evans his own freedom, as well as that of his wife and his four-year-old daughter.[20] In 1856, John L. Sleight, a local man, set free a woman Katey, whom he had purchased but sixteen days before.[21]

The will records of Galveston County record four wills in which testators emancipated slaves. In 1847, Alphonse Aulanier executed a will in French in which he emancipated his slave, Julia, and gave her $300.[22] Two years later, William M. Beal, executed a will in which he emancipated one slave and left his entire estate for the purpose of purchasing and emancipating eight others that he had once owned. "No man," he wrote, "was ever more attached to negroes than I was to those, and I should die the most unhappy man in the world did I not hope that the Emancipation of the said negroes would speedily follow my death."[23] In 1856, David Webster executed a will in which he emancipated his woman, Betsey, and gave her his entire estate,[24] and in 1861, Alley Rodgers executed a will in which he or she emancipated a slave named Violet.[25]

Perhaps the most interesting free black connected with Galveston was Henry Sigler, a native of Virginia and a barber, who was shown in the 1850 census as aged thirty-five.[26] In 1856 this gentleman, then in Houston, advertised that he would provide a "few tunes of good violin music" with each haircut.[27] Two years earlier he had obtained from the United States Patent Office a patent on an improvement in fishhooks, whereby he had rendered sockdologer fish-hooks simpler in their construction, perfect and sure in their operation, and less dangerous to handle while baiting.[28] In 1858 he sold the patent for $625 to two New Orleans men.[29]

It would be an error, though, to think that Galveston was a haven for free blacks. On the contrary, the evidence shows that a number of them found the city to be an unfortunate place. The British consul there was constantly on the alert to prevent British citizens from being sold into slavery in Galveston. Many ships that called at the port had aboard black seamen from the British West Indies. As early as 1838, the consul was involved in a protracted and intricate correspondence with the Secretary of State of the Republic of Texas on the subject of a number of British black seamen who had allegedly been enslaved.[30] In 1854 Consul Lynn rescued two sailors who "were about to be sold into slavery." Three years later, he served his Queen and his conscience by kidnapping a British black sailor, Charles H. Thomas, who had, obviously under duress, signed a contract indenturing himself to a Galvestonian for a period of sixty years. The consul smuggled the lad aboard a Yankee ship, and he no doubt got safely to Boston.[31]

Four black sailors from Boston failed to fare so well. Their sad story is graphically told in the sentence pronounced upon one of their number by the judge of the district court that met in Galveston in January, 1852:

> ANTONY HAYS: You, a free person of color, have been tried by a jury of your own choice, and found guilty of the charge of having aided, assisted, concealed and secreted, on board of the brig "Billow," bound hence for the port of Boston, a runaway slave

named Frank, the property of George H. Delesdernier, with the intent to prevent the return of said slave to his owner.

The charge of which you have been convicted is the highest offense that can be committed against the institution of slavery as it exists by the laws of Texas.

You, a free person of color, resident in the city of Boston, incapable of becoming a citizen of the State and prohibited by the laws of Texas from placing your foot upon her soil, have had the hardihood to come in our midst and attempt to rob one of our citizens of his property with a full knowledge of the consequences if detected, and as the evidence shows—and this too, in furtherance of the views and wishes, if not instructions, of your abolition Friend of Boston, who seems to have been similarly engaged on former occasions.

It is to be regretted that your principal does not occupy your position on the present occasion. The moral effects of this judicial proceeding would he much more potent if such were the case.

Your color, which placed you below the white man ordinarily, on this occasion has secured you not only a fair and impartial trial, in which you were defended by able counsel,[32] but a much more lenient penalty than would have been imposed on a white man guilty of the same offense.

It is true that you love your liberty; but, if not colored, death would be the penalty of the law.

The sentence of the law is that you pay a fine of $850 and the cost of prosecution within five days, in default of which you are to be sold as a slave for life to the highest bidder, by the sheriff, after giving ten days' notice of the time and place of sale.[33]

On January 26, the four were sold into slavery,[34] but it is probable that all four were subsequently purchased by agents of their abolitionist friends and returned to Massachusetts and freedom.

The study of the free black is a frustrating one, for, with notable exceptions, like that of the free black barber in Natchez, Mississippi, whose diary was recently published, the free black was historically inarticulate. He left few records of a revealing personal nature. In Texas, at least, we always see him from the outside, mostly in formal, legal situations. The historian, however, must deal with what he can find, and his work, no matter how irksome and exacting, is its own reward.

NOTES

1. J. D. B. DeBow, *Statistical View of the United States* (Washington: Beverly Tucker, Senate Printer, 1854), 314.

2. Joseph C. G. Kennedy, *Population: The United States in 1860* (Washington: Government Printing Office, 1864), 476–479.

3. Andrew Forest Muir, "The Free Negro in Harris County, Texas," *Southwestern Historical Quarterly* 46 (January 1943), 216, n. 13.

4. United States Census (MSS. in The National Archives, Washington, D. C.). 1850, Texas, Schedule 1, Fort Bend County, dwelling and family 119; ibid., 1860, Schedule 1, Fort Bend County, dwelling 47, family 51.

5. See Muir, "The Free Negro in Harris County, Texas," passim.

6. DeBow, *Statistical View of the United States*, 308, 314.

7. Kennedy, *Population of the United States in 1860*, 476–479.

8. *Forty Years of American Life, 1821–1861* (New York: Stackpole Sons Publishers, c.1937), 143.

9. Deed Records of Galveston County, Texas (MSS. in County Clerk's office, Galveston), B-1, 202–203.

10. Ibid., B-2, 111–112.

11. Harriet Smither (ed.), *Journals of the Fourth Congress of the Republic of Texas, 1839-1840* (Austin: Texas State Library and Historical Commission, 1930), I, 198–199, 212, 228–229, 285, 288, 310; II, 235, 254, 259, 305; III, 238.

12. H. P. N. Gammel (comp.), *The Laws of Texas, 1822–1897* (Austin: Gammel Book Company, 1898), III, 1042.

13. Deed Records of Galveston County, C.97.

14. Certificate of Thomas F. McKinney, Galveston, Nov. 11, 1839, in Samuel May Williams Papers (MSS. in Rosenberg Library, Galveston).

15. (Matilda Charlotte) Houstoun, *Texas and the Gulf of Mexico; or, Yachting in the New World* (Philadelphia: G. B. Zieber and Co., 1845), 140; *Hesperos: or, Travels in the West* (London: John W. Parker, 1850), II, 100.

16. United States Census, Texas, 1850, Schedule 1, Galveston County, dwelling 308, family 319.

17. Deed Records of Galveston County, B.1, 421.

18. Ibid., C, 130.

19. Ibid., J, 675.

20. Ibid., K, 275.

21. Ibid., L 458.

22. Wills, Galveston County, Texas (MSS. in County Clerk's office, Galveston), I, 26–27; II, 15–16.

23. Ibid., II, 35–36.

24. Ibid., II, 88–89.

25. Ibid., II, 195–196. For contingent emancipations, see will of Richard Morris, March 10, 1842, ibid., I, 19–20; II, 12, and of Eli Manadere Justice, October 2, 1857, ibid., II, 102–103.

26. United States Census, 1850, Texas, Schedule 1, Galveston County, dwelling 106, family 114.

27. Writers Program, Works Projects Administration (comp.), *Houston, a History and Guide* (Houston: The Anson Jones Press, 1942), 195.

28. *Report of the Commissioner of Patents for the Year 1854* (Washington: Beverley Tucker, Printer, 1855), I, 96, 164, 319; II, 187.

29. Deed Records of Galveston County, N, 382–383. I am indebted to Miss Lorene Pouncey, of Houston, for finding the citation to this Instrument in the index to the Deed Records.

30. Earl W. Fornell, "The Abduction of Free Negroes and Slaves in Texas," *Southwestern Historical Quarterly*, LX (January, 1957), 370. See also George P. Garrison, *Diplomatic Correspondence of the Republic of Texas* (Washington: Government Printing Office, 1911), III, 900-905, 911–914.

31. Fornell, "The Abduction of Free Negroes and Slaves in Texas," *passim*.

32. The defendants were represented by very able counsel appointed by the court: Lorenzo Sherwood, Samuel Yerger, Fenton M. Gibson, and Gustavus A. Jones.

33. *Texas State Gazette* (Austin), III (February 21, 1852), 211, col. 3, quoting *Galveston News*. See also Houston *Weekly Telegraph*, January 30, 1852, p. 2, col. 4.

34. *Texas State Gazette*, III (February 7, 1852), 198, col. 1. For other materials on the cases of Antony Hays, Levan Smith, William Brown, and Jacob Thompson, see Minutes of Galveston County District Court (MSS. in District Clark's office, Galveston), II, 438, 444–446, 471–473, 511–512, and *Texas State Gazette*, III, 202 (February 14, 1852), col. 2.

A Bibliography of Secondary Sources

Free Blacks in Antebellum Texas

Bruce A. Glasrud and Milton S. Jordan

Abernethy, Francis E. "The Elusive Emily D. West, Folksong's Fabled 'Yellow Rose of Texas'." In *A Texas Folklore Odyssey*. Edited by Francis E. Abernethy. Denton: University of North Texas Press, 2001. Pp. 319–329.

"Andrew Forest Muir." *The Handbook of Texas Online* (http://www.tshaonline.org/handbook/online/articles).

Ashworth, Vanda V. *The Ashworth Family*. Lufkin, TX: privately printed, 1987.

Barr, Alwyn. "Explorers and Settlers." In *Black Texans: A History of African Americans in Texas, 1528–1995*. 2nd ed. Norman: University of Oklahoma Press, 1996. Pp. 1–12.

Barriffe, Eugene Jr. "Some Aspects of Slavery and Anti-Slavery Movements in Texas, 1730–1660." Master's thesis, University of Southwestern Louisiana, 1968.

Berlin, Ira. *Slaves without Masters: The Free Negro in the Antebellum South*. New York: New Press, 1974.

Biesele, Rudolph L. "The Texas State Convention in 1854." *Southwestern Historical Quarterly* 33 (April 1930): 247–61.

Blyth, Lance R. "Fugitives from Servitude: American Deserters and Runaway Slaves in Spanish Nacogdoches, 1803–1808." *East Texas Historical Journal* 38.2 (2000): 3–14.

Boswell, Angela. "Black Women during Slavery to 1865." In *Black Women in Texas History*. Edited by Bruce A. Glasrud and Merline Pitre. College Station: Texas A&M University Press, 2008. Pp. 13–37.

———. "Traveling the Wrong Way Down Freedom's Trail: Black Women and the Texas Revolution." In *Women and the Texas Revolution*. Edited by Mary L. Scheer. Denton: University of North Texas Press, 2014. Pp. 97–122.

Bunkley, Anita. *Emily: The Yellow Rose—A Texas Legend*. Houston: Rinard Publishing, 1989.

Campbell, Randolph B. *An Empire for Slavery: The Peculiar Institution in Texas*. Baton Rouge: Louisiana State University Press, 1989.

Campbell, Randolph B., ed. *The Laws of Slavery in Texas*. Austin: University of Texas Press, 2010.

———. "Rachel Hamilton Hornsby," *Handbook of Texas Online* (http://www.tshaonline.org/handbook).

———. "George Ruble Woolfolk." *The Handbook of Texas Online*. http://www.tshaonline.org/handbook/online.

Carroll, Mark M. *Homesteads Ungovernable: Families, Sex, Race and the Law in Frontier Texas, 1823–1860*. Austin: University of Texas Press, 2001.

Claridy, Christy. "Britton Johnson." *Texas Ranger Dispatch Magazine* 33 (2011): 4–7.

Clegg, Patricia. "The Free Negro in the Republic of Texas: The Experiences of the Ashworth Family of Southeast Texas and Others." *Texas Gulf Historical and Biographic Record* 41 (2005): 35–54.

Collins, Michael L. "The Callahan Expedition." *Texas Devils: Rangers and Regulars on the Lower Rio Grande, 1846–1861*. Norman: University of Oklahoma Press, 2008. Pp. 79–88, 271–72.

Cornell, Sarah E. "Citizens of Nowhere: Fugitive Slaves and Free African Americans in Mexico, 1833–1857." *Journal of American History* 100 (September 2013): 351–374.

Cravens, John N. "Felix 'Zero' Ervin: Louisiana Slave and East Texas Freeman." *East Texas Historical Journal* 10.2 (1972): 125–30.

Davidson, Mark. "Emeline's Story." *The Houston Lawyer* (January/February 2005) http://www.thehoustonlawyer.com/aa_jan05/page2 8.htm).

———. "Gess v. Lubbock: One Woman's Fight for Freedom." *The Houston Lawyer* (January/February 2008): 10–15.

De la Teja, Jesus F. "Blacks in Colonial Spanish Texas." *The Handbook of Texas Online*. http://www.tshaonline.org/handbook/online.

Devereaux, Linda. "William Goyens: Black Leader in Early Texas." *East Texas Historical Journal* 45.1 (2007): 52–57.

Dillon, Merton L. "Benjamin Lundy in Texas." *Southwestern Historical Quarterly* 63 (July 1959): 46–62.

Dunn, Jeffrey D. "'To the *Devil* with your Glorious History!' Women and the Battle of San Jacinto." In *Women and the Texas Revolution*. Edited by Mary L. Scheer. Denton: University of North Texas Press, 2014. Pp. 179–208.

———. "One More Piece of the Puzzle: Emily West in Special Collections." *The Compass Rose* 19 (Spring 2005), http://libraries.uta.edu/speccoll/croseo5/Compass.Rose_Spring 2005....pdf.

———. "Emily West de Zavala and Emily D. West: Two Women or One?" *The Compass Rose* 20 (Spring 2006), http://www.tamu/ccbn/dewitt/images/texforum/drose06.pdf.

Fields, Barbara Jeanne. *Slavery and Freedom on the Middle Ground: Maryland during the Nineteenth Century*. New Haven: Yale University Press, 1985.

Fisher, John E. "The Legal Status of Free Blacks in Texas, 1836–1861." *Texas Southern Law Review* (1973): 342–362.

Fornell, Earl W. "The Abduction of Free Negroes and Slaves in Texas." *Southwestern Historical Quarterly* 60 (1957): 369–380.

Galan, Francis X. "Between Esteban and Joshua Houston: Women, Children, and Slavery in the Texas Borderlands." *Journal of South Texas* 27 (Fall 2014): 22–36.

Glasrud, Bruce A. "Jim Crow's Emergence in Texas." *American Studies* 15 (1974): 47–60.

Glasrud, Bruce A., and Paul H. Carlson. "Black Americans in West Texas." In *Slavery to Integration: Black Americans in West Texas.* Abilene, TX: State House Press, 2007. Pp. 13–26.

Glasrud, Bruce A., and James M. Smallwood, eds. *African Americans in Texas History.* Lubbock: Texas Tech University Press, 2007.

Hales, Douglas. "Free Blacks." *The Handbook of Texas Online.* http://www.tshaonline.org/handbook/online.

Harris, Trudier. "The Yellow Rose of Texas: A Different Cultural View." *Juneteenth Texas: Essays in African-American Folklore.* Edited by Francis E. Abernethy, Patrick B. Mullen, and Alan B. Govenar. Denton: University of North Texas Press, 1996. Pp. 315–332.

Hawkins, Marjorie Brown. "Runaway Slaves in Texas." Master's thesis, Prairie View Agricultural and Mechanical College, 1952.

Henson, Margaret Swett. "West, Emily D." *The Handbook of Texas Online.* http://www.tshaonline.org/handbook/online.

Henson, Margaret S. "She's the Real Thing." *Texas Highways* 33 (April 1986): 60–61.

Hunter, J. Marvin. "Runaway Slaves in Texas." *Frontier Times* 26 (1948): 40–43.

John, Elizabeth A. H. "A View from the Spanish Borderlands." *Proceedings of the American Antiquarian Society* 101 (1991): 86–87.

Katz, William Loren. "William Goings and Greenbury Logan—Patriots of the Lone Star Republic." In *Black People Who Made the Old West.* Trenton, NJ: Africa World Press, 1992. Pp. 45–48.

Kubiak, Daniel James. *Monument to a Black Man (William Goyens).* San Antonio: Naylor, 1972.

Lutzweiler, James. "Emily D. West and the Yellow Prose of Texas." In *A Texas Folklore Odyssey.* Edited by Francis E. Abernethy. Denton: University of North Texas Press, 2001. Pp. 294–316.

Marks, John Garrison. "Community Bonds in the Bayou City: Free Blacks and Local Reputation in Early Houston." *Southwestern Historical Quarterly* 117.3 (January 2014): 267–282.

McClellan, Michael E. "Britton Johnson." *The Handbook of Texas Online.* http://www.tshaonline.org/handbook/online.

Meacham, Tina L. "The Population of Spanish and Mexican Texas, 1716–1836." Ph.D. dissertation, University of Texas at Austin, 2000.

Moorer, Virginia C. "The Free Negro in Texas, 1845–1860." Master's thesis, Lamar State College of Technology, 1969.

Muir, Andrew Forest. "The Free Negro in Fort Bend County, Texas." *Journal of Negro History* 33.1 (January 1948): 79–86.

———. "The Free Negro in Galveston County, Texas." *Negro History Bulletin* 22 (1958): 68–70.

———. "The Free Negro in Harris County, Texas." *Southwestern Historical Quarterly* 46.3 (1943): 214–238.

———. "The Free Negro in Jefferson and Orange Counties, Texas." *Journal of Negro History* 33 (1950): 183–206.

———. "The Mystery of San Jacinto." *Southwest Review* 36 (Spring 1951): 77–84.

———. *William Marsh Rice and His Institute.* Edited by Sylvia Stallings Morris. Houston: William Marsh Rice University, 1972.

———. *Thomas Jefferson Ewing: Ward Politician.* Houston: privately published, 1952.

———, ed., *Texas in 1837: An Anonymous Contemporary Narrative.* Austin: University of Texas Press, 1958.

Nash, A. E. Keir. "Texas Justice in the Age of Slavery: Appeals Concerning Blacks and the Antebellum State Supreme Court." *Houston Law Review* 8 (January 1971): 438–456.

———. "The Texas Supreme Court and Trials Rights of Blacks, 1845–1860." *Journal of American History* 48.3 (December 1971): 622–642.

Pratt, Alexander T. M. "Free Negroes in Texas to 1860." Master's thesis, Prairie View Agricultural and Mechanical College, 1963.

Prince, Diane Elizabeth. "William Goyens, Free Negro on the Texas Frontier." Master's thesis, Stephen F. Austin State University, 1963.

———. "William Goyens, Free Black on the Texas Frontier." In *The Bicentennial Commemorative History of Nacogdoches.* Nacogdoches, TX: Nacogdoches Jaycees, 1976. Pp. 73–76.

Randel, Jonathan. "San Antonio Zeitung." *The Handbook of Texas Online.* http://www.tshaonline.org/handbook/online.

Reynolds, Donald E. "Anthony Bewley." *The Handbook of Texas Online.* http://www.tshaonline.org/handbook/online.

———. "Reluctant Martyr: Anthony Bewley and the Texas Slave Insurrection Panic of 1860." *Southwestern Historical Quarterly* 96 (1993): 344–61.

Richmond, Douglas W. "Africa's Initial Encounter with Texas: The Significance of Afro-Tejanos in Colonial Texas, 1528–1821." *Bulletin of Latin American Research* 26. 2 (2007): 200–221.

Schoen, Harold. "The Free Negro in the Republic of Texas: Origin of the Free Negro in the Republic of Texas." *Southwestern Historical Quarterly* 39 (April 1936): 292–308.

———. "The Free Negro in the Republic of Texas: The Free Negro and the Texas Revolution." *Southwestern Historical Quarterly* 40 (July 1937): 26–34.

———. "The Free Negro in the Republic of Texas: Manumissions." *Southwestern Historical Quarterly* 40 (October 1936): 85–113.

———. "The Free Negro in the Republic of Texas: Legal Status." *Southwestern Historical Quarterly* 40 (January 1937): 169–199.

———. "The Free Negro in the Republic of Texas: The Law in Practice." *Southwestern Historical Quarterly* 40 (April 1937): 267–289.

———. "The Free Negro in the Republic of Texas: The Extent of Discrimination and Its Effects." *Southwestern Historical Quarterly* 41 (July 1937): 83–108.

Schoen, Harold R., Walter Woodul, L. W. Kemp, and Pat Neff. *Monuments Erected by the State of Texas to Commemorate the Centenary of Texas Independence.* Austin, TX: The Steck Company, 1939.

Schwartz, Rosalie. "Runaway Negroes: Mexico as an Alternative for United States Blacks, 1825–1860." Master's thesis, San Diego State University, 1974.

———. *Across the Rio to Freedom: United States Negroes in Mexico.* El Paso: Texas Western Press, 1975.

Schweninger, Loren. *Black Property Owners in the South, 1790–1915.* Urbana: University of Illinois Press, 1984.

Shearer, Ernest C. "The Callahan Expedition, 1855." *Southwestern Historical Quarterly* 54 (October 1951): 430–451.

Shively, Charles. "An Option for Freedom in Texas, 1840–1844." *Journal of Negro History* 50 (1965): 77–96.

Thompson, Nolan. "Aaron Ashworth." *The Handbook of Texas Online.* http://www.tshaonline.org/handbook/online.

———. "Ashworth Act." *The Handbook of Texas Online.* http://www.tshaonline.org/handbook/online.

———. "William Ashworth." *The Handbook of Texas Online.* http://www.tshaonline.org/handbook/online.

Tjarks, Alicia V. "Comparative Demographic Analysis of Texas, 1777–1793," *Southwestern Historical Quarterly* 77 (January 1974): 291–338.

Treat, Victor H. "William Goyens: Free Negro Entrepreneur." In *Black Leaders: Texans for Their Times.* Edited by Alwyn Barr and Robert A. Calvert. Austin: Texas State Historical Association, 1981. Pp. 19–47.

Turner, Martha Anne. *The Yellow Rose of Texas: Her Saga and Her Song.* Austin: Shoal Creek Publishers, 1976.

———. "Emily Morgan: Yellow Rose of Texas." In *Legendary Ladies of Texas.* Edited by Francis Edward Abernethy. Denton: University of North Texas Press, 1994. Pp. 21–30.

Tyler, Ronnie C. "Slave Owners and Runaway Slaves in Texas." Master's thesis, Texas Christian University, 1966.

———. "Fugitive Slaves in Mexico." *Journal of Negro History* 57 (1972): 1–12.

———. "The Callahan Expedition of 1855: Indians or Negroes?" *Southwestern Historical Quarterly* 70 (1967): 574–585.

Vasquez, Irene. "The *Longe Duree* of Africans in Mexico: The Historiography of Racialization, Acculturation, and Afro-Mexican Subjectivity." *Journal of African American History* (2010): 183–201.

Williams, David A. "Spanish Colonial Period to Statehood." In *Bricks Without Straw: A Comprehensive History of African Americans in Texas*. Edited by David A. Williams. Austin: Eakin Press, 1997. Pp. 1–33.

Winegarten, Ruthe. "Free Women of Color." In *Black Texas Women: A Sourcebook*. Austin: University of Texas Press, 1996. Pp. 1–13.

———. "Free Women of Color." In *Black Texas Women: 150 Years of Trial and Triumph*. Austin: University of Texas Press, 1995. Pp. 1–13.

Woolfolk, George Ruble. *The Free Negro in Texas, 1800–1860: A Study in Cultural Compromise*. Ann Arbor, MI: University Microfilms International, 1976.

———. *Prairie View: A Study in Public Conscience*. New York: Pageant Press, 1962.

———. "Cotton Capitalism and Slave Labor in Texas." *Southwestern Social Science Quarterly* 37 (1956): 43–52.

———. "The Free Negro and Texas, 1836–1860." *Journal of Mexican-American History* 3 (1973): 49–75.

———. "Sources of the History of the Negro in Texas, With Special Reference to Their Implications for Research in Slavery." *Journal of Negro History* 42 (1957): 38–47.

———. "Taxes and Slavery in the Antebellum South." *Journal of Southern History* 26.2 (May 1960): 180–200.

———. "Turner's Safety Valve and Free Negro Migration." *Pacific Northwest Quarterly* 56 (July 1965): 125–130.

Wortham, Sue Clark. "The Role of the Negro on the Texas Frontier, 1821–1836." Master's thesis, Southwest Texas State University, 1970.

INDEX

Flint, James T., 210
Forbes, Henry, 175
Fontaine, Henry W., 207
Foote, Henry, 128, 172
Fornell, Earl W., 12, 20, 273
Forster, Thomas Gales, 116
Fort Bend County, 7–8, 17, 56, 78,
     84, 227–228, 231–235, 271
Franklin, Benjamin C., 184, 207, 220
fugitive slaves, 12, 20

Gallier, Sillasta, 249, 259
Galveston, Texas, 90
Galveston County, 7–8, 17,
     263–265, 267, 271–273
Garner, David, 178
General Council, 87–88, 95–97,
     121–122, 186, 198, 200, 239
General Land Office, 87, 150, 241,
     257
German, 11, 264
Gladden, William, 105, 147, 156
Glover, E.C., 251
Goliad, 46, 50–51, 95–96
Gonzales, 28, 85, 142
Gowns, David, 42
Gowns, Sophia, 30, 138, 155
Goyens, William, 4, 10, 15, 18–19,
     137–138, 148–150, 156, 162–166,
     168, 171, 173, 176–177, 184,
     188–189
grand jury, 94, 108–109, 111–114,
     125, 202, 206, 248
Granger, Gordon, 2, 217
Gray, Peter, 209–211, 255–256
Green, Richard, 206
Greer, John A., 77, 116–117, 129
Grigsby, Joseph, 55, 133, 178, 191,
     256
Grubbs, Chance (Charles), 145, 147
Guizar, Pedro, 3

Hales, Douglas, 9, 18
Hamblet, Violet, 170
Hamilton, Andrew Jackson, 12
Hamilton, Joseph, 176–177,
     190–191
Hardin, Emanuel J., 30, 162
Hardin, Samuel H, 3, 32, 42, 135,
     148, 162, 164
Harrisburg, 90, 108, 125, 186–187,
     220
Harris County, 7, 17–18, 168,
     186–187, 195, 197–199, 204, 206,
     214, 219–224, 233, 271
Harris, DeWitt Clinton, 201
Harris, Jane, 170, 222
Harrison, Ann C., 82
Harrison, G.H., 82
Hawkins, Marjorie Brown, 11, 19
Hays, Antony, 273
Hayti, 29, 40
Headright(s), 104, 151, 253
Hemphill, John, 145, 181
Hicks, Edward, 176, 178
Hidalgo, Miguel, 58
Hillebrant, Christian, 248, 260
Hockley, George, 128, 172, 220
Holmes, F.M., 73
Houston (city of), 4–5, 9, 16–18,
     27, 32, 49–50, 54, 73, 90, 97,
     100–101, 103, 106, 108, 110,
     113–114, 117, 125, 137, 139–140,
     144, 146–147, 154, 160, 172, 175,
     186–187, 197–201, 203, 206, 209,
     211, 214–216, 218, 220–225, 228,
     238, 255–257, 261, 268, 272–273
Houston, Sam, 4, 54, 140, 146–147
Houstoun, Matilda, 79, 91, 188, 266,
     272
Hunt, Memucan, 103, 147, 161, 220
Husk, Zelia, 32, 139, 144

CPSIA information can be obtained at www.ICGtesting.com
Printed in the USA
LVOW07*2108040915

452890LV00010BA/41/P